ST. CHARLES COUNTY COMMUNITY COLLEGE

C0-AVO-338

THE LEGACY
OF REAGANOMICS

A Conference Sponsored by
the Changing Domestic Priorities Project
of The Urban Institute

THE LEGACY OF REAGANOMICS

Prospects for Long-term Growth

Edited by
Charles R. Hulten and Isabel V. Sawhill

ST. CHARLES COUNTY
COMMUNITY COLLEGE LIBRARY
WITHDRAWN
102-L COMPASS POINT DRIVE
ST. CHARLES, MO 63301

The Changing Domestic Priorities Series
John L. Palmer and Isabel V. Sawhill, Editors

 THE URBAN INSTITUTE PRESS · WASHINGTON, D.C.

Copyright © 1984
THE URBAN INSTITUTE
2100 M Street, N.W.
Washington, D.C. 20037

Library of Congress Cataloging in Publication Data
Main entry under title:

The Legacy of Reaganomics.

(The Changing domestic priorities series)
Papers presented at a conference held Sept. 22, 1983, under the auspices of the Urban Institute Changing Domestic Priorities project.
Includes bibliographical references.
1. United States—economic policy—1981—Congresses.   2. United States—Economic conditions—1981-   —Congresses.   3. Supply-side economics—United States—Congresses.   I. Hulten, Charles R.   II. Sawhill, Isabel V.   III. Urban Institute.   IV. Series.
HC106.8.L44   1984   338.973   84-20901
ISBN 0-87766-368-8 (cloth)
ISBN 0-87766-345-9 (pbk.)

Printed in the United States of America.

BOARD OF TRUSTEES

Carla A. Hills
  Chairman
Katharine Graham
  Vice Chairman
William Gorham
  President
Warren E. Buffett
John J. Byrne
Joseph A. Califano, Jr.
William T. Coleman, Jr.
John M. Deutch
Anthony Downs
Joel L. Fleishman
Philip M. Hawley
Aileen C. Hernandez
Ray L. Hunt
Robert S. McNamara
David O. Maxwell
Lois D. Rice
Elliot L. Richardson
George H. Weyerhaeuser
Mortimer B. Zuckerman

LIFE TRUSTEES

John H. Filer
Eugene G. Fubini
Vernon E. Jordan, Jr.
Edward H. Levi
Bayless A. Manning
Stanley Marcus
Arjay Miller
J. Irwin Miller
Franklin D. Murphy
Herbert E. Scarf
Charles L. Schultze
William W. Scranton
Cyrus R. Vance
James Vorenberg

 THE URBAN INSTITUTE is a nonprofit policy research and educational organization established in Washington, D.C., in 1968. Its staff investigates the social and economic problems confronting the nation and government policies and programs designed to alleviate such problems. The Institute disseminates significant findings of its research through the publications program of its Press. The Institute has two goals for work in each of its research areas: to help shape thinking about societal problems and efforts to solve them, and to improve government decisions and performance by providing better information and analytic tools.

Through work that ranges from broad conceptual studies to administrative and technical assistance, Institute researchers contribute to the stock of knowledge available to public officials and to private individuals and groups concerned with formulating and implementing more efficient and effective government policy.

Conclusions or opinions expressed in Institute publications are those of the authors and do not necessarily reflect the views of other staff members, officers or trustees of the Institute, advisory groups, or any organizations which provide financial support to the Institute.

THE CHANGING DOMESTIC PRIORITIES SERIES

Listed below are the titles available, or soon to be available, in the Changing
Domestic Priorities Series

Books

THE REAGAN EXPERIMENT
> *An Examination of Economic and Social Policies under the Reagan
> Administration* (1982), John L. Palmer and Isabel V. Sawhill, editors

HOUSING ASSISTANCE FOR OLDER AMERICANS
> *The Reagan Prescription* (1982), James P. Zais, Raymond J. Struyk, and
> Thomas Thibodeau

MEDICAID IN THE REAGAN ERA
> *Federal Policy and State Choices* (1982), Randall R. Bovbjerg and John
> Holahan

WAGE INFLATION
> *Prospects for Deceleration* (1983), Wayne Vroman

OLDER AMERICANS IN THE REAGAN ERA
> *Impacts of Federal Policy Changes* (1983), James R. Storey

FEDERAL HOUSING POLICY AT PRESIDENT REAGAN'S MIDTERM
> (1983), Raymond J. Struyk, Neil Mayer, and John A. Tuccillo

STATE AND LOCAL FISCAL RELATIONS IN THE EARLY 1980s
> (1983), Steven D. Gold

THE DEFICIT DILEMMA
> *Budget Policy in the Reagan Era* (1983), Gregory B. Mills and John
> L. Palmer

HOUSING FINANCE
> *A Changing System in the Reagan Era* (1983), John A. Tuccillo with John L.
> Goodman, Jr.

PUBLIC OPINION DURING THE REAGAN ADMINISTRATION
> *National Issues, Private Concerns* (1983), John L. Goodman, Jr.

RELIEF OR REFORM?
> *Reagan's Regulatory Dilemma* (1984), George C. Eads and Michael Fix

THE REAGAN RECORD
> *An Assessment of America's Changing Domestic Priorities* (1984), John L.
> Palmer and Isabel V. Sawhill, editors (Ballinger Publishing Co.)

THE SOCIAL CONTRACT REVISITED
  Aims and Outcomes of President Reagan's Social Welfare Policy (1984), edited
  by D. Lee Bawden
NATURAL RESOURCES AND THE ENVIRONMENT
  The Reagan Approach (1984), edited by Paul R. Portney
FEDERAL BUDGET POLICY IN THE 1980s (1984), edited by
  Gregory B. Mills and John L. Palmer
THE REAGAN REGULATORY STRATEGY
  An Assessment (1984), edited by George C. Eads and Michael Fix
THE LEGACY OF REAGANOMICS
  Prospects for Long-term Growth (1984), edited by Charles R. Hulten and Isabel
  V. Sawhill
THE REAGAN PRESIDENCY AND THE GOVERNING OF AMERICA
  (1984), edited by Lester M. Salamon and Michael S. Lund

Advisory Board of the
Changing Domestic Priorities Project

Martin Anderson, Hoover Institution
John Brademas, President, New York University
Hale Champion, Executive Dean, John F. Kennedy School of
    Government, Harvard University
Nathan Glazer, Professor of Education and Sociology,
    Harvard University
Aileen C. Hernandez, Partner, Aileen C. Hernandez Associates
Carla A. Hills, Partner, Latham, Watkins & Hills (Chairman)
Juanita M. Kreps, Economist and former Secretary of Commerce
Thomas G. Moore, Hoover Institution
Richard F. Muth, Professor of Economics, Stanford University
Eleanor Holmes Norton, Professor of Law, Georgetown University
Paul H. O'Neill, Senior Vice President—Planning and Finance,
    International Paper Company
Peter G. Peterson, Chairman, Peterson, Jacobs and Company
Henry B. Schacht, Chairman, Cummins Engine Co., Inc.
Robert M. Solow, Professor of Economics, Massachusetts Institute of
    Technology
Herbert Stein, Professor of Economics, University of Virginia; Senior
    Fellow, American Enterprise Institute
Arnold Weber, President, University of Colorado
Daniel Yankelovich, Chairman, Yankelovich, Skelly and
    White, Inc.

CONTENTS

FOREWORD

In late 1981 The Urban Institute initiated a three-year project—Changing Domestic Priorities—to examine the shifts in domestic policy occurring under the Reagan administration and the consequences of those shifts. This volume, a product of the Changing Domestic Priorities project, is one of six collections of analyses by leading scholars on the impacts of current federal policies in a number of areas. The other five volumes are focused upon budget policy, social welfare policy, governance, regulatory policy, and natural resources and the environment.

The volume is based on a set of papers presented at a conference held in the fall of 1983. Its focus is the impact of the Reagan economic program on economic growth. The authors are concerned less with the effects of the Reagan program to date and more with providing the best possible estimates of its long-term effects. These estimates are necessarily uncertain and somewhat speculative, and not all of the authors would agree with one another about the nature or magnitude of some of the impacts. Nevertheless, there is a degree of consensus among the experts not found among policymakers or the public at large, and we offer their scholarly verdicts as a healthy antidote to less informed discussions of the ultimate promise of supply-side economics.

The papers cover a range of issues from the impact of recent shifts in federal tax and spending policies on economic growth to the implications of deficits and the rising political power of interest groups for the long-term health of the economy. (One paper—focusing on the impact of taxes and transfers on labor supply—was commissioned after the conference.) Each paper was criticized by several discussants as indicated on the conference agenda (reprinted at the back of this book) and was subsequently revised. William Nordhaus provided an interpretive overview and his remarks are also included in the volume along with a summary by the volume's editors, Charles Hulten and Isabel Sawhill. We are grateful to all of the authors, discussants, and other participants for their contributions to this effort. We would also like to thank the Ford Foundation and the John D. and Catherine T. MacArthur Foundation for their generous support of this effort.

John L. Palmer
Isabel V. Sawhill
Editors
Changing Domestic Priorities Series

THE LEGACY OF REAGANOMICS: AN OVERVIEW

Charles R. Hulten and Isabel V. Sawhill

Soon after taking office, President Ronald Reagan sent to Congress his Program for Economic Recovery. This program was based on four central elements: reduction in the rate of growth in federal spending; broad reduction in personal and business income taxes; relief from the burden of government regulations; and commitment to a policy of stable money growth. The objective of this program, in the words of Ronald Reagan, was to "put the Nation on a fundamentally different course—a course leading to less inflation, more growth, and a brighter future for all of our citizens."

Two basic presumptions underlie President Reagan's economic policies. First, improved economic welfare can be achieved by a reduction in the scope and power of the federal government. This presumption is, of course, the sine qua non of conservative economic thought, and it defines the "fundamentally different course" to which President Reagan referred. The old liberal "course," in effect over much of the preceding fifty years, was based on the opposite view that government intervention in the private market system improves, rather than reduces, overall economic welfare.

The second basic presumption of Reaganomics was that all the program's goals could be achieved simultaneously, and, according to some members of the administration, immediately. No trade-off between policy objectives was seen to exist: inflation could be controlled without recession, and could thus be reduced without jeopardizing near-term economic growth; increased economic growth would generate enough additional revenue that the deep cut in tax rates would not lead to larger budget deficits; and economic growth in

1

the private sector would more than compensate those people who lost benefits from cutbacks in social welfare programs.

It is now clear that important policy trade-offs did in fact exist, and that the main goals of Reaganomics could not be achieved either simultaneously or immediately. The inflation objective was successfully met, but only by sacrificing near-term growth. Federal spending proved far harder to cut than taxes, and the resulting budget deficits are widely viewed as a drag on future economic growth. Unemployment soared to the highest rates since the 1930s.

This collision of objectives has led some people to pronounce Reaganomics a failure. This judgment may be premature. The economy has now recovered from the deep recession of 1981-1982, a recession that many economists believe was needed to curb a decade of accelerating inflation. A more complete evaluation of Reaganomics must, therefore, involve an assessment of the prospects for a high and sustained rate of economic growth in the 1980s and beyond. Such an evaluation was the subject of a conference held September 22, 1983, under the auspices of The Urban Institute's Changing Domestic Priorities project, a multiyear research effort aimed at evaluating the consequences of the Reagan revolution.[1]

Seven papers by leading scholars were presented at the conference, and an overview of the conference proceedings was provided by William Nordhaus. The papers ranged over a number of growth-related policy areas: taxation, trade policy, the composition of the federal budget, and the impact of the recession and large budget deficits on future economic growth.

This chapter briefly describes each of these papers, as well as one additional paper that was solicited after the conference. We then provide some concluding comments based on our own reading of the evidence.

The Sources of Economic Growth: Framework and Forecasts

The factors influencing the growth in real gross national product (GNP) may be grouped into three categories: those influencing the growth in labor input; those influencing the growth in capital input; and those influencing the growth of the productive efficiency with which capital and labor are employed ("total factor productivity"). The various factors influencing economic growth

---

1. Other parts of the project have examined such areas as regulatory relief, federal budget deficits, the impact of the Reagan program on state and local governments, and the consequences of Reaganomics for the distribution of income. A series of monographs and discussion papers is available on these and other topics from The Urban Institute. A summary volume has also been published, *The Reagan Record* (Cambridge, Mass.: Ballinger Publishing Co., 1984).

may also be distinguished by the time horizon over which they operate. In the short run, variation in the rate of economic growth depends mainly on the demand for, or the use of, existing capital and labor. Over the intermediate run, the supply of capital and labor determines the growth in output. In the long term, economic growth is driven by population growth and the rate of change of total factor productivity.

The first paper presented to the conference, by John W. Kendrick, discusses the quantitative importance of the factors influencing economic growth. Output in the U.S. private domestic business economy increased at a rate of 3.7 percent per year from 1948 through 1973; during the subsequent eight years, 1973 through 1981, the growth rate of output fell to 2.2 percent per year. The corresponding drop in labor productivity (output per unit of labor input) was even larger: it plummeted from 3.0 percent per year during the earlier period to 0.8 percent in the later one.

The sharp decline in growth after 1973 is, of course, the widely publicized "productivity slowdown." It was this slowdown that gave impetus to the "supply-side" movement underlying many of the administration's policies. In the supply-side view, the productivity slowdown was due in large part to inadequate capital formation, and this inadequacy was attributed to high marginal rates of taxation on capital income, exacerbated by high rates of inflation in the 1970s. Interestingly, Kendrick reports that inadequate capital formation was *not* a major cause of the productivity slowdown. Rather, the collapse of total factor productivity was primarily responsible for the decline.

In considering the future, Kendrick is optimistic. Output growth for the 1980s is projected to average 4.0 percent per year, a figure that exceeds the 3.7 percent growth rate of the 1948–1973 period. This projection assumes a strong and sustained recovery, a return of total factor productivity to approximately the growth rate before 1973, and a small, but nevertheless significant, increase in capital formation.

Kendrick gives some, but not all, of the credit for this relatively optimistic scenario to the Reagan administration. He notes that much of the groundwork was laid before Reagan was elected as a result of the Revenue Act of 1978, the earlier deregulation of several key industries, and the shift in Federal Reserve policy in 1979. To these factors must be added the effects of the business and personal tax cuts enacted since 1981, including a tax credit for research and development (R&D), the leveling off of the trend toward more social regulation, and the improved climate for investment that has accompanied disinflation. He concludes by observing that the present period may be the beginning of an upward phase in a long (fifteen to twenty years) Kuznets growth cycle, just as the prosperity of the 1960s and early 1970s followed a slowing of growth in the 1950s.

Tax Policy

Of the four policy objectives enunciated in the Program for Economic Recovery, the administration viewed the reduction in income tax rates as the most important for increasing economic growth. The cuts in individual and corporation income taxes were designed to increase the rate of capital formation by increasing the rate of saving, shifting relative tax incentives in favor of capital formation in the corporate sector, and increasing the supply of labor to the business sector. The tax-induced increase in capital and labor, when weighted by their respective contributions to output, translate directly into an increased growth rate of real output.

The impact of the 1981 and 1982 tax acts on capital and labor are the subject of the two chapters that follow Kendrick's. Don Fullerton and Yolanda Henderson examine the impact of these acts on the overall effective tax rate on capital income originating in various sectors of the economy. This paper, which was presented at the conference, is followed by a paper that treats the effects of tax policy on labor supply contributed by Robert Haveman after the conference. No separate paper on saving behavior was commissioned, but the subject is touched on in the paper by Lawrence Summers.

The Taxation of Capital Income

The paper by Fullerton and Henderson examines the impacts of the tax legislation of 1981 and 1982 on the taxation of income from capital. These impacts are estimated using a cost-of-capital model, which is used to show that the combined effect of the two acts was to lower the effective tax rate on all types of capital income from 28.8 to 26.4 percent. The reduction in corporate tax burdens is significantly greater, with effective tax rates falling from 34.5 to 30 percent.

We may thus conclude that the administration, in conjunction with Congress, achieved two major goals in its tax reduction efforts: (1) reduction in the overall level of effective tax rates, and (2) less discrimination against business investment in plant and equipment. The reduction in tax rates is consistent with the objective of stimulating the demand for capital. Although Fullerton and Henderson do not forecast the impact of the tax reduction on *actual* capital formation, their results can be shown, under plausible assumptions about the values of certain key parameters, to imply an approximate 10 percent increase in the demand for structures and equipment by corporations. If this increased demand is matched by an increased supply of funds rather than being choked off by high interest rates, a significant increase in the stock of corporate capital should occur.

Supply-side economists stress the importance of improving the allocation of capital in addition to encouraging growth in the capital stock. Historically, capital income has been subject to vastly different effective tax rates, depending on the source of the income (owner-occupied housing was particularly favored). Fullerton and Henderson confirm this bias: capital income originating in the corporate sector was taxed at 34.5 percent under pre-1981 law, while income attributed to owner-occupied housing was taxed at a rate of 18.6 percent. Fullerton and Henderson also argue, however, that this differential "was less dramatic than some architects of the Economic Recovery Tax Act (ERTA) might have believed." They thus cast doubt on the urgent necessity for the so-called Feldstein twist—i.e., the policy of running a tight monetary policy and loose fiscal policy—which was designed to ameliorate this tax distortion by reallocating investment from the housing sector to the corporate business sector.[2] The Fullerton-Henderson analysis does, however, suggest that to the extent this policy twist was needed to reduce the distortion between the corporate and housing sectors, some benefits were achieved.

Fullerton and Henderson also address another theme of supply-side economics—the adverse impact of inflation on the tax system. Inflation will tend to increase tax burdens on corporate income because depreciation allowances are not indexed for inflation and because many firms use first-in-first-out (FIFO) inventory accounting. But the deductibility of nominal interest payments reduces tax burdens as inflation increases. On balance, Fullerton and Henderson find that overall effective tax rates do not vary with inflation.[3]

Tax Policy and Labor Supply

The chapter by Robert Haveman addresses the following question: to what extent have changes in human resource programs and personal income taxation under Reagan caused changes in the desired work effort of various population groups? This question is answered by estimating how the work effort of the 1980 population would have changed if the Reagan program had been in effect in that year. Haveman's analysis starts with a detailed exam-

---

2. The high interest rates resulting from the tight monetary policy were designed to reduce the overall demand for credit, while the easy fiscal policy—i.e., the tax cuts—were targeted to increase spending on corporate plant and equipment.

3. They do note, however, that the variation in effective tax rates across assets does increase somewhat with inflation, although the mean remains constant, implying a potential decline in efficiency as inflation increases.

ination of the cuts in human resource programs (for example, Unemployment Insurance, Food Stamps, AFDC, Social Security, retirement, employment and training programs). Haveman then presents upper and lower bounds on the change in labor supply due to the programmatic cuts and estimates that overall labor supply will increase by 0.1 percent to 0.9 percent (that is, by 140,000 to 950,000 full-time workers) as the result of these changes. He shows the distribution of this impact to be far from even across demographic groups. The bulk of the increase stems from the elimination of many disabled persons less than sixty-two years old from the disability roles and the entry of prime-age women into the work force.

Haveman also provides upper- and lower-bound estimates of the impact of the individual income tax cuts. Overall labor supply is found to increase by 1.2 percent to 2.9 percent of the labor force (by 1.3 million to 3.1 million workers). But, as with the programmatic cuts, the effect of the tax cuts is distributed unevenly across population groups. Prime-age women (twenty-five to sixty-one years of age) and both men and women over sixty-two years of age experience the largest percentage increase in desired labor supply. Prime-age men experience some increase, but it is relatively small.

The overall effect of the tax and human resource policies is thus to increase the desired labor supply. Not all the increase is attributable to the policies of the Reagan administration, however, because a second Carter administration would probably have enacted a cut in individual income taxes. But, even when this factor is taken into account, Haveman finds that overall work effort is increased by 0.8 to 2.5 percent. This increase is due mainly to the individual tax cuts and to increases in the labor supply of groups other than prime-age men.

A 2.5 percent increase in the work force phased in over, say, three years could produce a strong surge in output growth. When weighted by labor's relative contribution to output, the policy-induced change in labor supply could add an additional 0.5 percent to the annual growth rate of output over those three years. This is a sizable effect in view of the common baseline assumptions of 3 to 4 percent real annual output growth in the 1980s. However, an increased desire to work will only translate into more employment and higher output if the demand for labor is strong and jobs are available.

Trade and Industrial Policies

Two significant trends in U.S. foreign trade relations emerged during the 1970s: the share of exports in GNP increased dramatically, and the technological superiority of U.S. industry eroded relative to that of our major trading partners. The burden of these events has fallen with disproportionate severity on certain industries and products (autos, steel, television sets, cameras, etc.), and pockets of high unemployment have developed in some of these industries and the regions where these industries are located. This pattern of industrial decline evokes an image of industry after industry succumbing to international competition, with devastating consequences for the long-term vitality of the U.S. economy.

The paper by Paul Krugman throws cold water on this scenario. It is true, Krugman argues, that the technological superiority of the United States has eroded over the years, but this erosion is a natural consequence of the "catching up" of our trade competitors. The economies of these nations were severely damaged by World War II, and the U.S. technological lead could not be expected to persist as our trading partners recovered. In this view, it is not the 1970s that were unusually bad, but the 1950s and 1960s that were unusually good.

The catching-up process has important implications for the industrial structure of the U.S. economy. Krugman argues that foreign competition will not challenge U.S. industry across the board, but will push the United States up the technology scale; that is, it will cause the United States to increasingly specialize in producing the highest-technology goods. The weight of foreign competition will thus fall most heavily on those industries located at the lower end of the technology scale, exerting a strong downward pressure on the growth of wages in those industries. Classical trade theory suggests, however, that a country cannot have a comparative disadvantage in all goods, even though its absolute advantage has eroded. Competition from countries with relatively lower wage rates will not drive the United States off the technology scale altogether, but will force this country to specialize in high-technology products for which high wages are appropriate. It may also force workers in "down-scale" industries to accept lower wages. As this process unfolds, other countries will move up the technology scale and may catch up to the United States in living standards and technological sophistication, but they will find it hard to surpass the United States and maintain the lead.

The main conclusion, then, is that there is little substance to the fear that foreign competition is threatening long-term U.S. economic growth. On the contrary, evidence for the 1970s suggests that increased foreign competition did not lead to a reduction in the U.S. share of industrial employment among the Organization for Economic Cooperation and Development trading nations, nor did it lead to a decline in the U.S. share of manufactured exports. The main impact of foreign competition is on the industrial structure of the economy and on relative wages rather than on the growth rate of GNP.

As for the role of government policy, Krugman concludes that the Reagan administration's commitment to free trade (albeit with occasional lapses) is the best strategy. He considers the argument that an industrial policy aimed at helping key industries would improve U.S. competitiveness, and rejects it on the grounds (1) that the notion of "key industries" is operationally meaningless and (2) that an explicit industrial policy could not have prevented our trading partners from closing the postwar technology gap.

Federal Spending Priorities

An avowed purpose for the Program for Economic Recovery was to shrink the growth rate of government spending while shifting resources from domestic programs to the defense budget. Although not all the administration's budget objectives have been met to its satisfaction, a major shift in spending priorities has taken place. The paper by Donald Nichols examines the implications of this shift for long-term economic growth.

Nichols identifies three areas in which the change in budget priorities is likely to have an impact on economic growth: government R&D spending, direct public investment in infrastructure and human capital, and changes in federal programs, such as Social Security, that may affect private savings.

Nichols shows that federal R&D outlays as a percentage of GNP peaked in 1964. Since Reagan took office, the share has remained constant, but defense-related R&D spending has increased significantly (from 0.6 percent of GNP in 1980 to an estimated 0.8 percent in 1983), while nondefense R&D has declined sharply (from 0.6 percent of GNP in 1980 to 0.4 percent in 1983.) The implications of this shift are hard to assess, according to Nichols, because of the inherent difficulties in measuring the economic impact of different kinds of government-financed R&D spending. He believes that the shift away from nondefense spending probably has not increased growth and may have decreased it. In any event, the shift was not motivated by any conscious effort on the part of the administration to stimulate productivity growth in the private sector.

Nichols tells a similar story about direct investment by the federal government. Direct investment includes such diverse items as highway and water projects, military hardware expenditures, and investments in human capital through education and training programs. Here, again, a shift toward defense spending is documented. With the exception of highways, every major category of civilian investment is scheduled to decline between 1982 and 1984. It is once more argued that the impact of the change in priorities on growth is hard to determine, since the rate of return on public investment varies from project to project and is hard to measure for any single project. If projects with low rates of return are trimmed from the budget, the implicit shift in resources to the private sector may increase growth. Conversely, termination of projects with a high rate of return will have the opposite effect. Given the state of the art, analysts can disagree over which projects are which, and the net effect of reduced public investment is uncertain.

As part of his discussion of Nichols's paper, Charles Schultze presented some arguments with supporting tables that provide still more grist for this particular mill. Because of the interest they elicited, we have included them as an addendum following the Nichols paper. Schultze's overall conclusion is similar to Nichols's, but Schultze shows that even after excluding outlays which, in his view, contribute nothing directly to measured GNP or which have relatively low rates of return, real investment spending still declined between 1981 and 1984, although not as much in percentage terms as did all expenditures nominally classified as investment in the budget.

Nichols's last spending category deals with reduction in Social Security and federal loan programs (student loans, farm loans, etc.). He reviews the debate over the possible reduction (or increase) in private saving due to the substitution of federal for private funds for such purposes. For example, does the pay-as-you-go funding of the Social Security system cause a reduction in private saving? Nichols believes the issue is so ambiguous, and the changes made by the administration so small, that one cannot assume there will be much change in overall saving.

Two general conclusions emerge from Nichols's analysis: First, the shifts in spending priorities under this administration were not motivated by a desire to stimulate growth, but reflect the desire to change the scope and character of the federal government. Second, despite substantial measurement diffi- culities, the prospects for growth have probably been hurt by the reduction in federal outlays for investment-type activities.

The Legacy of Current Macroeconomic Policies

Increasing the long-term rate of economic growth was not the only policy objective of the Reagan program. The fight against double-digit inflation was at least equally important to the administration. Disinflation has been achieved, but only at the cost of a severe recession, and the tax cuts have contributed to the largest budget deficits in U.S. history. The permanency of the decline in inflation and the consequences of the recession, the deficits, and the tax cuts for long-term growth are discussed in the paper by Lawrence Summers.[4]

A lower rate of inflation is, according to Summers, a major achievement of the Reagan administration and one of the most important legacies of current macroeconomic policy. The durability of this progress depends on the relative importance for inflation of the level versus the rate of change in the amount of excess capacity in the economy. Summers reads the rather weak evidence on this critical issue as lying somewhere beween these two extremes, and barring any new supply shocks, believes that much, though not all, of the progress made against inflation is permanent.

These gains on the inflation front have been purchased at the price of a deep recession, with an attendant loss of capital formation—both physical and human. Summers discusses both as well as the related issues of the long-term effects of the recession on the supply of labor and on productivity. He concludes that the process of disinflation is "likely to have few lingering effects on real economic performance."

Large structural deficits are an inadvertent legacy of the Reagan economic program, caused by the tax actions of 1981 and 1982 and the interest on the federal debt accumulated as the result of these actions. According to Summers, the most important effect of these deficits is on the composition rather than the level of output. He estimates that each dollar of deficit is likely to increase private savings by about thirty cents, state and local surpluses about five cents, and net foreign investment by about twenty-five cents. This leaves forty cents that must be financed by a reduction in domestic investment, split about evenly between business fixed investment on the one hand and housing and inventory investment on the other. Summers notes that this reduction in investment would, under certain standard assumptions, reduce the growth of potential GNP by between .1 and .2 percent per year. He raises the question of whether deficits have any benefits that offset these costs and concludes that they may discipline future increases in federal spending—a discipline that some may welcome—but that their overall economic effects are harmful.

Turning to the administration's supply-side policies, Summers observes that they failed to produce the promised short-run results, but that they are likely to have a more positive effect once the economy is operating closer to full employment and households and firms have had time to adjust their behavior in response to new incentives to work, save, and invest.

---

4. Summers notes in passing that another major element of the Reagan program—the regulatory relief initiative—has been of no macroeconomic, and of little microeconomic, significance.

The Message of the Large-Scale Macroeconomic Models

The 1970s saw an increase in the use of large-scale macroeconomic models to analyze the impacts of alternative policies. These models are inherently oriented to short-term stabilization policies, and thus are relatively unsuitable for analysis of long-term growth. Moreover, they have come under increasing criticism from academics for failing to capture the effects of a change in policy on the behavioral relationships assumed by the models—the so-called Lucas critique. They do, however, permit one to analyze within a consistent framework the complex effects of a shift in various policies. Such an analysis is the subject of the paper by Alan Blinder.

Blinder uses three of the leading macroeconomic models—the Data Resources Incorporated (DRI) quarterly macro model, the Wharton annual model (WEFA), and the MIT-Penn-SSRC model (MPS)—to forecast the effects of Reaganomics relative to the outcomes that might have occurred in the absence of the Reagan program (the "no-Reagan" scenario). The no-Reagan scenario adopted by Blinder has the following general elements: personal income tax rates are initially cut by 4 percent and tax brackets rates are indexed; there is no business tax cut; real defense spending is increased by 3.1 percent a year between 1981 and 1989, in contrast to the assumed rate of 5.1 percent under Reagan; nondefense purchases and transfer payments experience somewhat more growth than under the Reagan program. The rate of growth of the money supply (M-2) is assumed to be the same in both Reagan and no-Reagan policy simulations, because Blinder's goal is to simulate the effects of the Reagan fiscal policy, not monetary policy.

A variety of interesting results are obtained from these simulations. Inflation, as measured by the GNP deflator, is found to be essentially the same under both scenarios in the WEFA and DRI models, and significantly higher under Reagan in the MPS model. The unemployment rate is lower under Reagan in the WEFA and DRI models, but higher under Reagan in the last year of the MPS simulation. Reaganomics thus looks considerably better under the WEFA and DRI models than under the MPS model. All three models agree that Reaganomics adds to the deficit, but the estimates of the amount range from $37 billion to $211 billion for 1987.

How much extra growth in real GNP does the Reagan program produce? By 1989, the last year considered in the analysis, the DRI model forecasts that real GNP under the Reagan program would be 2.2 percent higher than under the no-Reagan counterfactual, and the WEFA model puts this figure at 1.8 percent. Because of the cyclical nature of the MPS model, real GNP in 1987 (the last MPS year) is actually 4.8 percent lower under Reagan. Thus, the assessment of Reaganomics depends largely on which model one believes. Furthermore, as Blinder notes, none of the models is designed to incorporate changes in total factor productivity—the single most important factor determining long-run economic growth. However, he believes that one overall conclusion is warranted: the Reagan program simply does not produce significantly more growth than would have occurred under the alternative policies assumed in the analysis.

Blinder also assesses whether the Lucas critique of the models has any empirical validity in this context. He does this by analyzing the residuals (errors) in the equations that predict labor supply, consumption, investment, and wage inflation. He also examines the term structure of interest rates to see if large expected deficits are driving up long-term rates. Overall, he finds little evidence that changes in policy have altered people's behavior by influencing their expectations about the future. Thus he concludes that econometric models, though imperfect, are still a useful tool for analyzing policies.

Ideology and Economic Growth

In his recent book, *The Rise and Decline of Nations*, Mancur Olson advances the hypothesis that the rate of long-term economic growth depends on the power of special interest groups within society. Policies that maximize long-run economic growth and overall welfare—free trade, a neutral tax system—are not necessarily advantageous to specific interest groups, and such groups seek to gain special concessions that net the group more in direct benefits than it loses from a concomitant decrease in overall economic efficiency. Restrictions on foreign trade, for example, may increase wages and profits in a given industry. The full benefit of this increase goes to the workers, managers, and owners in the industry, but the price increases are experienced throughout the economy, and not simply by the groups in question. Thus, the gains to these groups greatly exceed the cost that they bear personally. As a result, such groups have strong incentives to increase their own welfare at the expense of overall economic growth or efficiency.

Olson argues that this process explains the U.S. productivity slowdown. In his view, collective action groups gain strength during periods of peace and economic prosperity. As they gain influence, growth begins to slow and is restored only by a cataclysmic event such as war. The rapid growth of the U.S. economy after World War II and the subsequent slowdown are consistent with the Olson hypothesis, as are the rapid recoveries of the war-devastated economies of Japan and West Germany.

The implications of this analysis are both strong and pessimistic. The factors causing the slowdown will not be easily undone: the same collective action groups that are responsible for the problem also exert a tremendous influence on the very policies designed to be part of the solution. A prediction of Olson's theory is, therefore, that traditional policies will tend to be ineffective and subject to frequent reversals as different political parties and ideologies win and lose favor with the electorate. Tax policy, federal spending priorities, trade, and regulatory policies are thus portrayed as ineffectual: they are the creation of the special interest group in power at a particular time. In examining the first three years of the Reagan administration, Olson finds little evidence to alter his general diagnosis. In sum, Olson concludes that the Reagan administration's policies will not significantly increase efficiency and may well reduce it. A similar comment would apply to a Democratic administration that is responsive to the special interest groups traditionally allied with that party. What is needed, says Olson, is a reassessment of *how* policies are made, rather than an assessment of the Reagan policies themselves.

Reaganomics and Economic Growth: A Summing Up

In his summary comments, William Nordhaus notes that much of the discussion at the conference fell into the trap of equating improvements in economic welfare with increases in measured GNP. He then evaluates the short- and long-run effects of Reaganomics. In the short run a given path for potential GNP is assumed. His long-run evaluation focuses on whether the path itself has shifted.

Over the short run, according to the macro models investigated by Blinder, real output increased while inflation rose only slightly. This could be interpreted as an indication that there was a favorable shift in the Phillips curve— i.e, the trade off between inflation and unemployment—as a result of Reagan policies. Nordhaus suggests that these effects are due to the particular way in which the DRI and WEFA models handle productivity and the cost of capital, and he cites a number of other studies that suggest that the Phillips curve has not shifted. In short, the costs of disinflation are as high as they have ever been.

Turning to the long run, Nordhaus examines the impact of Reagan policies on the growth of private capital, public capital, R&D, and regulation, and quantifies each of the various effects in terms of "basis points" (or contributions to annual output growth in hundredths of a percentage point).

Adding up all effects, Nordhaus finds the Reagan program has contributed an amount that ranges between minus 0.23 percentage point and plus

0.06 percentage point to the annual growth rate of potential GNP (see his table 1). In other words, taking the most optimistic end of the range and ignoring the short-run (cyclical) effects of the recovery, at best the Reagan program may raise real GNP by 0.6 percentage points by 1990. Using a more pessimistic set of assumptions, it could reduce real GNP by 2.3 percentage points. (Nordhaus had not had the opportunity of seeing the analysis of labor supply effects in Robert Haveman's paper at the time he prepared his own summary.)

Nordhaus ends his overview by observing that the Reagan program was designed to reverse the pattern of dependency associated with the growth of the welfare state and that traditional economic analysis may miss the significance of this broader transformation. However, he sees no evidence that convinces him of its practical importance, and concludes that "the Reagan administration's dismantling of the welfare state is a shot in the dark whose only casualties so far are the economy and the poor."

Concluding Remarks

The conference produced an informed, often provocative, discussion of each paper. Although we are not able to reproduce all the discussion here, some highlights can be briefly noted.

Not everyone agreed with Kendrick's assumption that the rate of productivity growth in the 1980s would be substantially different from the rate in the 1970s. However, Dale Jorgenson, among others, expressed the view that the macro models examined in the Blinder paper fail to capture the impact of policy on total factor productivity, leaving Kendrick's growth-accounting framework as a better way to approach the issue.

Summers's contention that a dollar of deficit crowds out only twenty cents of business fixed investment was challenged, especially by Ben Friedman, who presented a much more pessimistic view of the impact of deficits on growth. Nor were participants able to agree on the merits of the Feldstein twist. Some suggested that encouraging business investment at the expense of housing was appropriate on the grounds that the latter has received preferential treatment in the past, whereas others believed that the preference was either small or desirable and that we should not therefore be deliberately encouraging business fixed investment at the expense of housing.

No one favored an industrial policy that involved picking winners and losers, but not everyone was as sanguine as Krugman about a laissez-faire regime. Richard Cooper, for example, felt that more emphasis on human capital, research and development, and a more favorable macroeconomic environment would produce more innovation and help to keep the U.S. economy competitive.

There was extensive debate about the effectiveness of the R&D tax credit in encouraging higher R&D outlays in the private sector, about the payoffs from government-financed R&D (especially in the defense area), and about rates of return to public investment. The paper by Olson sparked considerable interest, but not everyone agreed with his thesis that collective action retards growth; such action may frequently improve economic welfare, by forcing governments to take actions that compensate for the failure of private markets.

Much greater consensus existed on at least two points: First, the administration should never have expected an immediate response to its supply-side program; whatever the effects, they will take time to emerge. Second, most policy actions have small, temporary effects on the rate of growth of output, a fact that is generally understood by economists, but not by politicians or the general public.

We believe that two additional general conclusions are warranted by the evidence presented in these papers and elsewhere: First, unless drastic action is taken soon, deficits will be the primary factor shaping the growth rate of the capital stock for the rest of the decade. The tax cuts put in place in 1981, and modified in 1982, do increase the demand for capital, but this beneficial effect could be overwhelmed by the crowding out of private investment by government borrowing. We arrived at this conclusion in the following way: the 1981–1982 business tax cuts are estimated to increase the demand for business capital by approximately 10 percent (a conclusion based on the Fullerton-Henderson and Kendrick papers in this volume). Furthermore, the Bureau of Labor Statistics estimates that the 1982 stock of business fixed investment was approximately $2.3 trillion (in 1982 dollars). Together, these estimates imply that the tax cuts result in a once-and-for-all increase of $230 billion in the desired stock of capital under certain plausible assumptions.

As for the budget deficits, the Congressional Budget Office has estimated that the deficit will add $1.7 trillion to the national debt over the remainder of the 1980s. Expressed in 1982 dollars, for comparison with the tax cuts, this amount is $1.4 trillion. Applying Summers's 20 percent crowding-out effect to this estimate yields a reduction in business fixed investment of $280 billion. The impact of the budget deficit thus more than offsets the beneficial investment effects of the tax cut, even under highly optimistic assumptions: a highly elastic demand for capital, a low degree of crowding out over the remainder of the 1980s, and no crowding out thereafter.

Our second general conclusion is that the prospect for improved long-term growth depends crucially on the behavior of total factor productivity. The decline in the growth rate of this variable accounts for most of the post-

1973 slowdown of output per hour in the private business sector, and any significant increase in overall growth will almost certainly have to come from this source. Attempts to forecast future trends in this key variable are, unfortunately, confounded by the fact that the sources of total factor productivity growth have never been well understood, and its recent slowdown has been characterized by one leading productivity analyst, Edward F. Denison, as largely a mystery.

Although the sources of total productivity growth are uncertain, a number of factors are generally viewed as contributing to this growth: in particular, advances in knowledge, improvements in the allocation of resources from less to more productive uses, and improvements in the quality of labor due to education and experience.

Technological change through advances in knowledge is widely viewed as the most important of these factors. Advances in knowledge occur for many reasons, but R&D spending is usually viewed as one important policy lever on technical progress. Total federal outlays for R&D have increased slightly since 1980, but all the increases have come in the defense area. As Nichols points out, current nondefense R&D expenditures are lower than they have been in any recent administration. The net impact of this shift depends on whether there are large spillovers from defense research to the civilian sector, a point of some dispute. The R&D tax credit enacted as part of the 1981 tax act was intended to encourage private-sector outlays for R&D, but a consensus is yet to emerge on the effectiveness of the tax credit.

The 1981 and 1982 tax cuts also affect total factor productivity growth through the efficiency with which resources are allocated among sectors. The cut in business taxes reduces the tax distortion between the corporate sector and tax-favored investments such as municipal bonds and owner-occupied housing. Furthermore, the reduction in the top bracket rate from 70 percent to 50 percent reduces the value of tax shelters to high-income investors, and further reduces the tax advantages of investments in real estate and municipal bonds. At the same time, the structure of the business tax cuts introduces additional distortions among the various types of business capital and is relatively unfavorable to high-technology assets and industries.[5]

On balance, it is hard to credit the 1981 and 1982 tax acts with significantly improving the allocation of resources. The same is true of the administration's policies on government regulation. Because of its faith in private markets, the Reagan administration has given little or no emphasis to government intervention to correct widely perceived breakdowns in the market

---

5. Charles R. Hulten and James W. Robertson, "The Taxation of High Technology Industries," *The National Tax Journal*, September 1984.

mechanism. It has set out, for example, to *undo* rather than merely to *reform* social and environmental regulations. Where regulations are burdensome and distortionary, this strategy of regulatory relief will tend to improve economic efficiency. But where private markets undervalue the benefits of a cleaner environment or safer work places, deregulation will produce the opposite effect on economic efficiency, broadly defined.

As for education and training, Congress has reduced outlays by 37 percent below prior levels since 1981 as the result of administration efforts to curtail the growth of domestic spending. As Nichols notes, some past expenditures for these programs have produced a rate of return that exceeds the return on private investments (for example, the Job Corps). Others clearly have not. Although Congress has cut the least effective programs more deeply than the more effective ones, the administration's general lack of interest in, and support for, these kinds of activities is difficult to reconcile with its pro-growth orientation.

Finally, like Nordhaus, we wonder whether the administration's ideology may yet have implications for long-term growth. This change in ideological climate does not yet seem to have had a discernible impact on wage- and price-setting practices or, for that matter, on other kinds of economic behavior, according to the evidence in Alan Blinder's paper. Yet, public opinion surveys suggest the president has struck a responsive chord with the public, and one suspects that lectures from the Rose Garden about the importance of entre-preneurship and individual initiative may yet influence the way managers and workers behave and perhaps improve the economy's efficiency and produc-tivity. The inability of economists to adequately explain the rise and fall of national economies may rest on just such intangibles.

We are thus led to the conclusion that the policy factors shaping the growth rate of total factor productivity are complex, only partially understood, and operate in different directions. The benefits of the Reagan administration policies for productivity growth are thus hard to assess. The same cannot be said, however, of the deficit problem—deficits clearly have a negative impact on future economic growth. In view of this problem, it is hard to give the administration high marks for stimulating long-term growth.

THE IMPLICATIONS OF GROWTH ACCOUNTING MODELS

John W. Kendrick

Growth accounting models, pioneered by Edward F. Denison, provide useful statistical explanations of changes in growth rates, and of international differences in such rates.[1] Growth accounting models for recent periods also provide the background for projections of future growth trends. Properly specified, the growth rate of real product is the sum of the contributions of all tangible inputs and all of the significant components of total factor productivity (defined as the efficiency with which inputs are transformed into output). The projection of future growth thus becomes the sum of the estimated contributions of each separate factor.

While estimates derived from the growth accounting framework are judgements, this framework ensures a systematic and comprehensive treatment of the significant variables. It is also important to recognize that the components of growth are proximate determinants, behind which lie other important causal variables that must also be analyzed. Of course, the effects of all variables are modified by the underlying values and institutions of a society. These usually change slowly, but when the change is significant, as with new laws or regulations affecting real costs or outputs, they must also

---

1. See Edward F. Denison, *Accounting for United States Economic Growth, 1948–1969*; *Why Growth Rates Differ*; and *Accounting for Slower Economic Growth: The United States in the 1970s* (Washington: The Brookings Institution, 1974, 1967, and 1979, respectively). See also John W. Kendrick, "Productivity Trends and the Recent Slowdown: Historical Perspective, Causal Factors, and Policy Options," and "International Comparisons of Recent Productivity Trends," *Contemporary Economic Problems*, William Fellner, ed., (Washington: The American Enterprise Institute, 1979 and 1981–82 editions).

be taken into account either directly or in terms of their effects on the proximate determinants of growth.

In this discussion, I use a modified growth accounting framework to describe patterns in U.S. growth from World War II to the present and to project growth rates to the end of the decade. I begin by providing the baseline long-term U.S. growth trend for this century. In section 2, I focus on the period since 1948, describing both aggregate growth rates and sources of growth. In section 3, I discuss my projections for future growth. I argue that the U.S. economy is in the upward phase of a long swing, and describe my assessment of the variables that leads me to this conclusion.

Long-term Trends

Table 1 provides the base-line long-term U.S. growth rate since 1800. Real gross product has grown at about 4 percent throughout the period. However, total factor productivity accelerated from less than .5 percent over much of the nineteenth century to about 2 percent just before World War I, and hovered there until 1973. Rates of change in real product per unit of labor showed greater subperiod variation depending on the growth of real capital stocks and services, and their rates of substitution for labor. From 1973 through 1981, the most recent business cycle peak, there was virtually no growth in total factor productivity, and the average rate of increase in labor productivity fell below 1 percent a year.

TABLE 1

REAL GROSS PRODUCT, FACTOR INPUTS, AND TOTAL FACTOR PRODUCTIVITY
(U.S. domestic economy, average percentage rates of change)

	1800–1855	1855–1890	1899–1919	1919–1948	1948–1973	1973–1981
Real gross product	4.2	4.0	3.9	3.0	3.7	2.2
Total factor input	3.9	3.6	2.2	0.8	1.7	2.0
Labor	3.7	2.8	1.8	0.6	0.7	1.4
Capital	4.3	4.6	3.1	1.2	3.6	3.2
Real product per unit of labor	1.1	1.6	2.1	1.8	2.2	1.4
Total factor productivity	0.3	0.3	1.7	2.2	2.0	0.1
Labor	0.5	1.1	2.0	2.4	3.0	0.8
Capital	−0.1	−0.6	0.7	1.6	0.1	−1.0

SOURCE: 1800–1948: John W. Kendrick, "Productivity Trends and the Recent Slowdown: Historical Perspective, Causal Factors, and Policy Options" in *Contemporary Economic Problems*, 1979; 1948–1981: Bureau of Labor Statistics.

The slowdown in growth of real product and of productivity in the period 1973–1981 must be interpreted within the context of the "long swings" as identified and analyzed by Kuznets, Abramovitz, and others.[2] The term refers to the alternating periods of faster and slower growth exhibited by the U.S. economy in the past. Kuznets found that the long swings were associated with fluctuations in natural rates of population growth and immigration, in building, and in the rate of growth of the money supply.

Figure 1 summarizes the effects of these swings on real gross product, total factor input, and total factor productivity since the end of the last century. The long swings from 1891 to 1982 range from thirteen to twenty-one years and have an average length of seventeen and one-half years from one episode of low growth to the next. The swings consist of four short cycles. The up-phases have averaged about seven and one-half years while the average down-phase lasted almost ten years.

Since World War II, the low productivity growth cycle of 1946–1949 (relative to 1938–1946) was immediately followed by the high of 1949–1954. The low of 1958–1961 was followed by the high of 1961–70. It appears that the 1980–1982 cycle average marked the latest low over the prior cycle (1975–1980). My subsequent analysis suggests a marked increase in the growth rates of real product and of productivity for at least the rest of the decade.

Before explaining why I think the economy is now in the upward phase of a long swing, I shall analyze the sources of growth since 1948, with particular reference to the slowdown after 1973.

Growth Rates Since 1948

The growth accounting model shown in tables 2 and 4 and discussed below concentrates on the periods 1948–73 and 1973–1981. I will use the statistical explanations of growth in the first period and of slowdown in the

2. Simon Kuznets, *Capital in the American Economy, Its Formation and Financing* (Princeton: Princeton University Press for the National Bureau of Economic Research, 1961, especially Chapters 7 and 8). See also Moses Abramovitz, *Evidences of Long Swings in Aggregate Construction Since the Civil War* (New York: National Bureau of Economic Research, 1964). For a brief discussion and tables of long swings in productivity since 1888, see John W. Kendrick, *Postwar Productivity Trends in the United States, 1948–1969* (New York: National Bureau of Economic Research, 1974), pp. 51–59; and "Concepts and Measures of Economic Growth," in *Inflation, Growth and Employment*, a research study prepared for the Commission on Money and Credit (Englewood Cliffs, New Jersey: Prentice-Hall, Inc., 1964), pp. 231–288.

FIGURE 1

OUTPUT, INPUT, AND TOTAL FACTOR PRODUCTIVITY

(Average annual percentage rates of change from previous to current business cycle average)

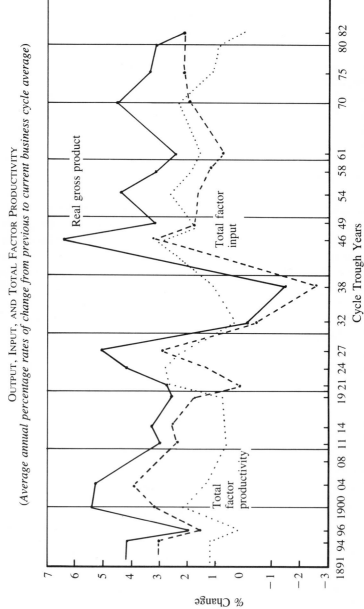

SOURCE: 1889–1949 cycle averages from John W. Kendrick, *Postwar Productivity Trends in the United States, 1948–1969, 1973.* 1949–1982 averages based on Bureau of Labor Statistics, *Multifactor Productivity Measures,* USDL 83440, 1983

second as the basis for a prediction of how recent developments and policies will affect the growth outlook for the rest of the decade.[3]

Outputs, Inputs, and Total Factor Productivity

The rates of changes in real gross product, factor inputs, and total factor productivity shown in table 2 cover the U.S. private domestic business economy, which comprises about 80 percent of total GNP as estimated by the Commerce Department.[4]

Between 1948 and 1973, the 3.7 percent average annual increase in real gross product was close to the long-run trend. The low 0.7 percent average annual rate of increase in labor hours meant that real product per labor hour (sometimes referred to as labor productivity) grew at a 3.0 percent rate, higher than in any earlier period. But because of a higher rate of growth in real capital stocks and inputs than at any time since 1890—3.6 percent a year, which translates into a 1.0 percent rate of substitution of capital for labor— total factor productivity grew at a 2 percent annual rate, more or less in line with the trend since World War I.

TABLE 2

U.S. DOMESTIC ECONOMY: AVERAGE ANNUAL GROWTH RATES *(Percentage)*

	1948–1973	*1973–1981*
Real gross product	3.7	2.2
Total factor input	1.7	2.0
Labor	0.7	1.4
Capital	3.6	3.2
Real product per unit of labor	3.0	0.8
Capital/Labor substitution	1.0	0.6
Total factor productivity	2.0	0.1

SOURCE: Bureau of Labor Statistics, 1983.

---

3. The accounting framework shown in tables 2 and 4 differs from that used by Edward Denison. In particular, I do not adjust labor input (hours of all persons engaged in production) for changes in the quality of labor, but rather count such changes as part of the explanation of changes in tangible factor productivity. Also, some of the other items, including the residual, and some of the estimates for common items, differ from Denison's. I explained the differences in the discussion.

4. The BLS estimates are close to those published in my 1980 volume (with Elliot Grossman) *Productivity in the United States: Trends and Cycles*, which have been maintained on a current quarterly basis by Dr. Grossman for the American Productivity Center. See American Productivity Center, *Multiple Input Productivity Indexes*, vol. 4, no. 1, July 1983, and earlier issues. To avoid confusion, the present analysis is based on the BLS estimates.

The deceleration of the economic growth rate to 2.2 percent a year in the period 1973–1981 was accompanied by a doubling in the growth rate of labor input. The latter reflected the accelerated growth in the labor force beginning in the mid-1960s, only partially offset by creeping unemployment through 1981. The slowing in labor productivity growth between the two periods thus came to 2.2 percentage points. About 15 percent of this is attributable to a lower rate of capital/labor substitution. Growth in total factor productivity slowed to only 0.1 percent a year, on average, between 1973 and 1981.

Observers have ascribed the 0.4 percentage point slowing of growth of real capital stocks and their services to several major forces that all had adverse reactions on before- and after-tax rates of return on investment. First, because inflation was accelerating, most corporate managers did not or could not adopt pricing policies to reflect fully the increases in cost, particularly the replacement cost of fixed capital and inventories. Second, macroeconomic policies designed to restrain inflation did so at the expense of profit margins, as in 1973–1974 and 1979–1980. As Hulten and Robertson have shown, in those years, the expectations of rising inflation reduced the present value of depreciation allowances and increased effective tax rates on profits.[5] Third, the huge increases in energy prices in 1973–1974 and again in 1979 rendered some existing energy-intensive equipment obsolete. And environmental and safety legislation caused an increase in the proportion of capital outlays devoted to nonproductive purposes, thus lowering capital productivity. Finally, the deceleration in technological advance, discussed below, tended to reduce expected returns and the volume of new capital expenditures.

What accounts for the difference in growth rates between these two periods? Table 3 compares the Denison and BLS estimates for the various components of the growth accounting model for these two periods.

Denison's estimates show a significantly greater slowdown in both output and productivity growth between the two periods than do those of BLS. In part, this is because Denison uses real national income as the output measure. Since capital consumption allowances rose faster than national income, especially after 1973, Denison's estimates rose less rapidly than those of BLS.

For the labor input comparison, I have included only Denison's estimates of employment and average hours. After this adjustment, Denison's labor hours show much the same rates of increase, but a bit more acceleration than the BLS estimates, although his estimates are, in principle, confined to hours

5. Charles R. Hulten and James W. Robertson, "Corporate Tax Policy and Economic Growth: An Analysis of the 1981 and 1982 Tax Act," Working Paper (Washington, D.C.: The Urban Institute, 1982).

TABLE 3

Sources of Differences in Economic Growth Between 1948–1973 and
1973–1981
(Comparison of Denison and BLS estimates in percentage points)

	Dennison	Bureau of Labor Statistics
Real gross product	− 1.8	− 1.5
Total factor input	0.6	0.3
Labor	0.7	0.5
Capital	− 0.1	− 0.2
Real product per unit of labor	− 2.5	− 2.2
Capital/labor substitution	− 0.2	− 0.4
Total factor productivity	− 2.3	− 1.9

NOTE: Dennison's estimates from The Economic Journal (March 1983, table 2) are rearranged according to the framework shown in table 2.

at the work place, while about 90 percent of the BLS hours estimates are on a paid-for basis.

Denison's capital estimates show smaller rates of increase and less deceleration than BLS. In part, this is due to Denison's convention of holding land input constant, whereas BLS follows the Goldsmith convention of rationing site land to the real structure estimates. Denison excludes owner-occupied as well as rental real estate, whereas BLS includes the latter. To approximate capital services (input) Denison averages real gross and net fixed capital stocks (with 3 to 1 weights), and weights by income net of depreciation. BLS uses an age/efficiency (capital deterioration) function to describe the declining pattern of services that capital goods supply as they age—slowly and gradually at first, then more quickly as the capital goods approach the end of their economic lives. BLS weights by gross rental values (including depreciation as well as interest and profit) for forty-seven types of assets; Denison uses only four types. Both Denison and BLS use the Tornquist weighting procedure whereby rates of change in the various types of capital are weighted by average rental values in successive pairs of years.[6] The heavier capital weights used by BLS mean that the deceleration of capital growth

---

6. The Tornquist weighting scheme has attractive features. In the past, I have used successive pairs of annual weights five or ten years apart to catch changes in industry structure and relative prices. However, I suspect that the difference in movements of aggregates based on the alternative weighting patterns is minor. This was the conclusion of G. S. Maddala, ''A Note on the Form of the Production Function and Productivity,'' in *Measurement and Interpretation of Productivity* (Washington: National Academy of Sciences, 1979).

caused total factor input to contribute 0.2 point more to the slowdown than in Denison's estimates. After rounding, the slowdown indicated by the BLS estimates of total factor productivity is 1.9 percentage points, substantially less than the 2.3 points estimated by Denison. Later in the discussion, I will explain why the Denison and BLS estimates differ.

The BLS procedure of using gross national product in the productivity relation accords symmetrical treatment to labor and property compensation, since human capital consumption is not deducted from the former in estimating national income and net national product. Including gross capital formation in the output estimate makes it more clear-cut from a production standpoint compared with the deduction of capital consumption estimates, which have an arbitrary element. National income is more appropriate for welfare comparisons.

Sources of Growth in Total Factor Productivity

To use a growth model for future predictions, we must have estimates of the contributions of individual factors to the aggregate growth rate (see table 4). Some of the estimates are taken from Denison's work, supplemented and adjusted as discussed below.

Technological Advance

Denison found that advances in technological knowledge as applied in production (plus miscellaneous forces he judged to have little effect) accounted for 1.4 percentage points, or more than two-thirds of the increase in total factor productivity between 1948 and 1973. Students of the production function have generally assumed that cost-reducing innovations in the ways and means of production shift outward the frontiers of the production function. But Denison and other growth analysts pointed out that technological advance is accompanied by human investments as well as by R&D and fixed investments, and by changes in the scale and structure of production. Thus, if one measures the effects of the other significant factors, the residual is what is contributed by advances in technological knowledge.

By the late 1970s, it became apparent that we needed independent indicators of the rate of advance in knowledge. Denison's residual method was

TABLE 4

SOURCES OF PRODUCTIVITY GROWTH: 1948–1981
(Percentage point contributions to growth)

	1948–1973	1973–1981
Total factor productivity	− 2.3	− 1.9
Advances in knowledge	1.4	0.7
Stock changes	1.2	0.7
Vintage effect	0.2	0
Changes in labor quality	0.5	0.6
Education and Training	0.6	0.7
Health and Safety	0.1	0.1
Age-sex composition	− 0.2	− 0.2
Changes in quality of land	0	− 0.2
Resource reallocations	0.4	0.1
Volume changes	0.3	− 0.3
Economies of scale	0.4	0.2
Capacity utilization	− 0.1	− 0.5
Government regulations	0	− 0.2
Actual/potential efficiency & n.e.c.	− 0.6	− 0.6

SOURCE: John W. Kendrick, based in part on estimates by Edward F. Denison (see text).
n.e.c. = not elsewhere classified.

showing negative changes, which did not make sense.[7] My first step was to estimate the effect of changes in the rates at which new technology was diffused due to changes in average age of capital goods. During the 1948–1973 period, this added an average 0.2 percentage point to growth, but it contributed nothing in 1973–1981 because reduced capital outlays did not lower average ages further. To a large extent, the remaining advances result from formal R&D programs. To approximate the rate of increase from this source, I have cumulated real R&D outlays with due allowances for the time that elapses between laboratory work and completed projects, and between the latter and commercial application.[8]

There is some question about the proper way to treat government R&D. Expenditures on civilian projects undoubtedly have some spillover effects on civilian technology, but there is probably not much spillover from purely military projects. On the other hand, recent work indicates that conducting

7. Denison, *Accounting for Slower Economic Growth*, op. cit., and "Accounting for Slower Economic Growth: An Update," in *International Comparisons of Productivity and Causes of the Slowdown* (Cambridge, Massachusetts: Ballinger Publishing Co. for the American Enterprise Institute, 1984).

8. See John W. Kendrick, *The Formation and Stocks of Total Capital* (New York: National Bureau of Economic Research, 1976), pp. 9–11, 54, and Appendix B-3.

R&D on government contract stimulates the market-oriented R&D of companies.[9] I have handled this problem by excluding from the cumulative real stocks that R&D performed by government laboratories, but including the publicly-financed R&D performed by business.

The growth of real R&D slowed in the 1960s and leveled off in the early 1970s; its ratio to GNP declined from 3.0 percent in the mid-1960s to 2.2 percent a decade later. As a result, the growth of the R&D stock slowed markedly in the 1973–1981 period relative to the earlier twenty-five years. The estimated contribution of the associated advances in technological knowledge dropped from 1.2 percentage points to 0.7 point. This estimate assumes that the many small technological improvements made in shops and offices tend to follow the major developments produced by formal R&D programs.

Labor Quality

The quality of the labor force is improved mainly by investments in education and training. My estimates, based on applying a rate of return to the real stock of education embodied in the labor force, gives the same result as that obtained by Denison based on the earnings differentials of workers with differing levels of educational attainment. These estimates show an increase in the contribution of education from 0.5 to 0.6 percentage point between the two periods. To this I added 0.1 for the effects of training (not estimated by Denison), based on the real stocks cumulated by outlays for that purpose. Unfortunately, it is not feasible to adjust the estimates for the apparent decline in quality of education suggested by the decline in SAT scores for two decades after the early 1960s.

My estimates of the real stocks resulting from investments in health care and safety[10] (also not covered by Denison) indicate that the returns to these investments contributed about 0.1 percentage point in both periods. The contribution comes from less time lost from illness and accidents, longer working lives, and (hopefully) greater vitality.

The estimates of the effects of changes in the age-sex composition of the labor force come from Denison. He bases them on the earnings differentials

---

9. See Nestor Terleckyj and David Levy, "Effects of Government R&D on Private R&D Investment and Productivity: A Macroeconomic Analysis," paper presented at the annual meetings of the Southern Economic Association in Atlanta, November 11, 1982 (available from the National Planning Association); and Edwin Mansfield and Lorne Switzer, "Effects of Federal Support on Company-Financed R&D: The Case of Energy," paper presented at the same SEA meetings.

10. Kendrick, Total Capital . . . , op. cit., pp. 14–16 and Appendix B-4b.

of the various age-sex groups, which reflect differences in work experience. The contributions of these shifts round to −0.2 in both periods. The shifts were much more important in explaining the earlier 1966–1973 slowdown, and their negative influence was declining during the 1973–1981 period.

Quality of Land

A negative aspect of economic growth, which can partially offset economies of scale, is the tendency towards diminishing returns in extractive industries. Until 1970, productivity in mining and in farming increased at above-average rates. Since then, mining productivity has fallen. Stricter safety and environmental regulations account for about half of the change; the other half may be attributed to declining quality of natural resources, reflected in data showing poorer ores and less accessible reserves. This factor, not covered by Denison, contributed −0.2 percentage point to productivity during 1973–1981, whereas earlier deterioration averaged less than −0.05 a year.

Resource Reallocation

As estimated by Denison, the effects of resource reallocations represent the gain in economic efficiency due to relative shifts of resources out of activities—chiefly agriculture and self-employment—in which rates of compensation are sub-standard. The effects of resource reallocations dropped from 0.4 to 0.1 between the two periods.

Volume Factors

On economies of scale, I have followed Denison in estimating the 1948–1973 contribution at 0.4, but I have adjusted the 1973–1981 contribution down to 0.2 to parallel the decline in the growth rate of production. When growth is slower, there is less benefit from spreading overhead functions over more units of output, as well as fewer opportunities for greater specialization of personnel, equipment, and plant.

The contribution of economies of scale is also affected by the cyclical position of the economy with respect to rates of capacity utilization in the boundary years between which growth rates are calculated. A lower ratio of actual to potential real gross product reduces the ratio of real product to real fixed capital about proportionately, and reduces the output/labor ratio by about one-quarter. This figure is the approximate proportion of nonproduction, overhead-type workers who are generally not laid off in cyclical downturns. Given the relative weights of labor and capital, a given reduction in capacity utilization means that total factor productivity is reduced by about one-half as much proportionately. The proportionate change is reduced to average annual rates between the boundary years. Unused capacity was much higher in 1981 relative to 1973 than it was in 1973 relative to 1948. This is reflected in the 0.4 increase in the negative effect of this factor.

My treatment of this cyclical factor is simpler than that used by Denison to estimate the effects of changes in "intensity of demand." He uses a multiple regression technique to capture the typical cyclical movement of productivity. This cyclical movement involves more than the direct effect of changing utilization rates that my procedure attempts to quantify.[11] Other aspects of productivity fluctuations, such as the tendency for labor efficiency to decline before cycle peaks and rise before troughs, would show up in my residual category. Be that as it may, Denison's estimate of the contribution of reduced intensity of demand shows a change of only − .04 between the two periods, much less than the −0.4 change in capacity utilization effects as I measure it.

Government Regulations

I have followed Denison in estimating a 0.2 percentage point increase in the negative contribution of governmental regulations. The increases in real unit factor costs came chiefly in pollution abatement and to a lesser extent in health and safety, without corresponding increases in real product as measured.

Residual

The last category, which is mine, chiefly reflects changes in the ratio of actual to potential efficiency with given technology (apart from the direct effects of changing utilization rates discussed earlier) since I judge the net effect of forces not elsewhere classified (n.e.c.) to be minor. It is not surprising that the residual is negative in both periods. Time paid for but not worked by employees has increased at an average annual rate of around 0.1 percent since 1948, but the BLS measure is primarily based on hours paid for while output is more closely related to hours at the work place. Moreover, University of Michigan surveys reveal that unproductive time at work (for personal business, coffee breaks and the like) has increased by about 0.2 percent a

---

11. Cf. Denison, *Accounting for Slower Economic Growth* . . . , Appendix I, pp. 176–189.

year since the mid-1960s.[12] Beyond this, there has been considerable speculation about a general deterioration in the American work ethic, and a resulting decline in labor efficiency, particularly since the late 1960s. Although there are many instances of restrictive work rules and practices in American industry, there is no evidence that their negative effect was growing in the 1973–1981 period.

The residual also reflects changes in other aspects of the legal, institutional, and social environment that affect unit real costs of business other than through the proximate determinants already identified. One example is the honesty of people, which affects costs through security outlays and losses from crimes. Denison estimates that the contribution of this factor fell from −.01 to −.03 between the two periods. Further research may eventually produce measures of the effects of more residual variables. The table indicates that their net effect did not change much between the two periods shown, although this may reflect offsetting errors in the other estimates.

I now return to explain the difference in the Denison and BLS estimates of the slowdown in aggregate/productivity growth between 1948–1973 and 1973–1981. Denison's estimate was −2.3 percent, and the BLS estimate was −1.9 percent.

Use of the BLS output and input estimates would narrow Denison's residual to −1.3%. If we use my estimate of −0.7 for the slowdown in technological knowledge, his residual is reduced to −0.6. This is explained in my scheme by a −0.4 greater effect of reduced volume, and a −0.2 change in the quality of natural resources. Remaining small differences are largely a matter of rounding.[13]

This exercise suggests the validity of Edward Wolff's observation that most analysts come up with much the same list of causes for the productivity slowdown, but the weights that each assigns to the several factors differ rather substantially.[14] Wolff himself (in company with Nordhaus and Thurow) at-

---

12. Frank Stafford and Greg Duncan, "The Use of Time and Technology by Households in the United States" (Ann Arbor: University of Michigan, Department of Economics, July 1977).

13. The main reason for my more complete explanation of the slowdown is the much heavier weight I attach to the negative effect on productivity of the greater unused capacity and labor in 1981 than in 1973. In a recent conference paper, Angus Maddison also stresses the importance of "conjunctural factors" in explaining the 1973–1981 slowdown in the United States, as well as in most other industrial nations whose recoveries were aborted by anti-inflationary policies. See Angus Maddison, "Comparative Analysis of the Productivity Situation in the Advanced Capitalist Countries," in *International Comparison of Productivity . . . ,* op. cit.

14. Edward N. Wolff, "Comments" on Denison's paper in *International Comparisons of Productivity*, op. cit., table 2.

tributes a much higher proportion of the slowdown to resource reallocations than Denison does. But he is concerned with the relative shifts into industries with below-average rates of productivity growth rather than the shifts out of activities with lower levels of factor remuneration, which was Denison's focus. More investigation of the Wolff effect is called for in as much industrial detail as possible.

To conclude this section, it is useful to indicate the sources of growth that are not subject to policy manipulation. These include changes in composition of the work force, changes in output (resulting in resource reallocations), and changes in quality of land and other natural resources. Together these factors contributed 0.5, or almost one-quarter, to the 1.9 percentage point slowdown in total factor productivity 1948–1973 to 1973–1981.

Looking ahead to 1990, I do not expect these non-policy variables to subtract from growth. In fact, I expect the positive effects of changes in the age-sex mix of the work force to more than offset the continued negative effects of changes in resource allocations and in quality of natural resources. This will, of course, make it easier for policy to stimulate strong growth in the years ahead.

The Outlook for Long-term Growth

Within the framework of the foregoing type of analysis, the policies chosen by the Reagan administration to reverse the much-publicized productivity slowdown are not surprising. They feature disinflation and tax measures to increase saving and investment, expanded government financing of R&D and tax incentives to stimulate technological advance, and regulatory reforms to reduce costs of compliance. Undoubtedly, the administration also hoped that emphasizing its ultimate goal of stronger and steadier growth of productivity and real product without accelerating inflation would create favorable expectations that would help to achieve that goal.

The groundwork was being laid for the Reagan revolution well before Mr. Reagan was elected President. By 1978 it was becoming clear that productivity growth was slowing again, accentuating inflation. The unanimous 1979 report of the Joint Economic Committee of Congress called for " . . . the adoption of longer-run policies aimed at expanding the nation's productive potential in a manner that raises dramatically the growth of American productivity."[15] Already in 1978, capital gains taxes—raised in 1969, thus dras-

---

15. U.S. Congress, Joint Economic Committee, midyear report and staff study, *Outlook 1980s* (August 1979), p. 6.

tically reducing the flow of venture capital—were reduced at the initiative of Congressman Steiger. The Revenue Act of 1978, which took effect in 1979, contained a number of provisions designed to increase saving, investment, and productivity. The corporate income tax was permanently cut from 48 to 46 percent on income above $100,000, increasing total after-tax net income by about $5 billion in 1979. Reductions in individual income tax rates were the major element in a $12.8 billion reduction in personal income taxes. The 10 percent investment tax credit was liberalized and made permanent.

Although President Carter and Congress let the National Center for Productivity and Quality of Working Life expire in 1978, the president did announce or recommend a series of productivity initiatives, although most of these had little effect before the end of his administration. Headway was made on deregulation in a few industries, and some paperwork and other regulatory burdens were reduced. It was also in the fall of 1979 that the Federal Reserve Board shifted its major target to controlling the growth of the money supply at rates that significantly reduced inflation by 1982. We must consider these earlier developments along with the Economic Recovery Tax Act of 1981 (ERTA), the Tax Equity and Fiscal Responsibility Act of 1982 (TEFRA), and other policy acts of the Reagan administration when we assess the outlook for longer-term growth.

Projected Outputs, Inputs, and Total Factor Productivity

Table 5 shows my projections of real product, factor inputs, and total factor productivity for the period 1981–1990. The BLS figures for 1973– 1981 are repeated from table 2 for reference.

The projections assume continuity in economic relationships, as well as the absence of a major war or other serious disruption of the economy such

TABLE 5

AVERAGE ANNUAL PERCENTAGE GROWTH RATES: PROJECTED

	1973–1981	1981–1990
Real gross product	2.2	4.0
Total factor input	2.0	2.2
Labor	1.4	1.3
Capital	3.2	4.0
Real product per unit of labor	0.8	2.7
Capital/Labor substitution	0.6	0.9
Total factor productivity	0.1	1.8

as the OPEC actions of the 1970s. They also assume that the fiscal legislation of the present administration will be kept in place, including indexing of tax brackets and exemptions, and the contingency tax or similar measures to reduce the structural deficits in the federal budget over the rest of the decade.

Labor

My point of departure for the labor input projections was the labor force projections of BLS,[16] adjusted to the most recent Census Bureau population projections.[17] The projections indicate that between 1981 and 1990, the labor force will grow at an average annual rate of 1.4 percent, with a deceleration from over 1.5 percent 1981–1985 to 1.2 percent 1985–1990. The BLS approach of projecting labor force participation ratios by age-sex groups and applying them to the population projections for those groups seems a bit mechanical. Economic factors may be more influential than appear to have been allowed for. The Social Security reforms and modifications of some private pension plans reduce the incentive for early retirement, and raising the permissible mandatory retirement age from 65 to 70 should keep more persons over 55 in the labor force than projected by BLS. Also, reducing marginal personal income tax rates may increase work incentives for some women and self-employed persons. Based on these considerations, I project 1981–1990 labor force growth at 1.5 percent a year.

Since I am assuming a 6 percent unemployment rate in 1990 compared with 7.5 percent in 1981, employment would rise by 1.6 percent a year, on average. But average hours worked per week are likely to continue their downward trend, due chiefly to more part-time work. An allowance of -0.3 for this trend, only a little less than that of the past fifty years, means that labor input (hours) would rise at a 1.3 percent annual rate. This is slightly less than the 1973–1981 growth rate.

Capital Stocks and Input

I predict that the economic climate for business investment in the 1980s will remain more favorable than in the 1970s. Higher profit margins, cash flow, and expected rates of return on investment will raise nonresidential business investment by about 1 percentage point over the 1973–1981 average.

---

16. U.S. Department of Labor, BLS printout dated May 22, 1980.
17. U.S. Department of Commerce, Bureau of the Census, ''Projections of the Population of the United States: 1982 to 2050,'' Series P-25, No. 922 (Washington: Government Printing Office, October 1982).

This would raise the annual average growth rate of capital input by 0.8 percentage point to a total of 4.0 percent—close to the projected increase in real gross product.

Important contributors to the cyclical recovery of corporate profits so far in 1983 have been the substantial increase in productivity over the past year and the deceleration in wage rate increases. Together, these factors have markedly slowed increases in unit labor costs. Indeed, since the last quarter of 1982, unit labor costs have risen by less than the general price level. This has permitted a strong increase in real product consistent with the increases in nominal GNP allowed by Federal Reserve Board monetary policy together with a widening of profit margins.

The cost-price relation should continue to be favorable for most of the 1980s. My projection of growth in output per unit of labor is 2.7 percent, up from less than 1 percent in the prior period. Unless expansion is stronger than generally expected, unemployment will remain above 6 percent of the labor force. This should keep increases in average hourly earnings more moderate than in the 1970s—probably back to the 5.5 percent or so of the 1948–1966 period. This would mean an increase in unit labor costs of about 3 percent a year for the rest of the 1980s. If Federal Reserve Board policy permits increases of 7 to 8 percent in nominal GNP, this would accommodate the real gross product growth we project consistent with moderate inflation (see figure 2).

The disinflation already experienced and the prospect of only moderate inflation ahead will help to stimulate private investment. So will a continued recovery of profits. In the third quarter of 1983, corporate profits with inventory and capital consumption adjustments rose to 7.3 percent of a rising GNP, up from 5.4 percent in 1982. The normal course of expansion should raise the percentage well above the 7.7 percent average of the 1973–1981 period. In my view, the favorable cost-price prospects for the rest of the 1980s will mean an average ratio of adjusted corporate profits of at least 9 percent. This is below the 10.2 percent of the 1960–1969 period, but together with the decline in the effective corporate income tax rate, it should be sufficient to increase the business investment share of GNP by at least 1 percent.

Hulten and Robertson have estimated the effects of the ERTA business tax cuts (as modified by TEFRA) as a 15.8 percent effective marginal corporate tax rate on plant and equipment compared with a 32.8 percent average for the years 1973–1981.[18] This should increase the investment share of GNP as did the deep

---

18. See Charles R. Hulten and James W. Robertson, "Corporate Tax Policy and Economic Growth: An Analysis of the 1981 and 1982 Tax Acts," Working Paper (Washington, D.C.: The Urban Institute, 1982).

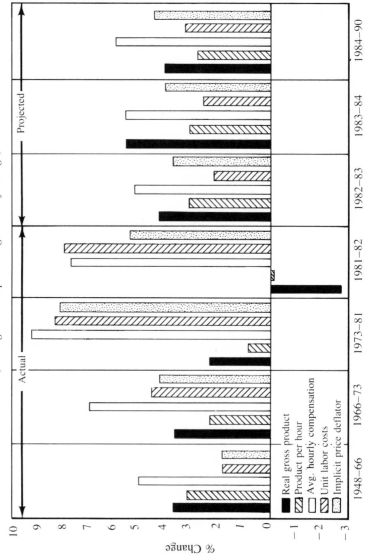

FIGURE 2

PRODUCTIVITY, LABOR COSTS, AND PRICES
(*Average annual percentage rates of change*)

■ Real gross product
▨ Product per hour
☐ Avg. hourly compensation
▨ Unit labor costs
░ Implicit price deflator

SOURCE: Bureau of Labor Statistics.

Kennedy-Johnson tax cuts of the 1962–1964 period, assuming no further major take-backs.

The substantial increases in net income after tax, corporate saving, depreciation allowances, and thus total cash flow as a source of financing should make business investment less vulnerable if nominal and real interest rates remain high. Actually, because high interest rates have a greater depressing influence on residential construction, they would tend to shift saving more to nonresidential investments. But if my projection of costs and prices is near the mark, it would be surprising if long-term interest rates did not moderate further, thus strengthening business investment.

A somewhat different approach was followed by Jane Gravelle of the Congressional Research Service.[19] She estimates that ERTA would have expanded the long-run equilibrium fixed capital stock by 12.2 percent, but after TEFRA the expansion is reduced to 7.3 percent. If this expansion were accomplished by 1990, it would mean about the same rate of growth of real capital that we show in the table.

The marginal efficiency of investment should be further strengthened by the accelerated pace of technological advance discussed in the next section. In addition, the fixed capital stock has aged over the past several years, and there is a growing backlog of replacement demand. Moreover, as capacity utilization increases, the prospects for growth in the 1980s should begin to induce substantial investments to expand capacity.

In the 1981–1982 contraction, plant and equipment spending fell less than in 1973–1975 and 1957–1958, and recovery has been stronger, although it has exhibited the usual lag. But the surveys of business plant and equipment spending plans indicate strong advances for the rest of 1983 and 1984.[20] In the third quarter of 1983, the ratio of nonresidential structures and equipment outlays to GNP was 10.4, compared with an average 11.4 over the period 1973–1981. I would expect the ratio to rise well above that average before this expansion is over. Given the favorable developments reviewed in this section, an average ratio of 12.5 for the 1981–1990 period is not unreasonable.

---

19. Jane G. Gravelle, "Long-Run Growth and Efficiency Effects of the 1981 and 1982 Depreciation Changes" (Washington: The Library of Congress Congressional Research Service, January 21, 1983).

20. See "Capital Spending Stokes the Recovery," *Business Week*, November 14, 1983, pp. 44–45. The subsequent Commerce Department survey indicates plans to raise real fixed investment by 12 percent in 1984.

Sources of Productivity Growth

Table 6 summarizes my projections for the contributions of each variable to the total factor productivity growth rate during the period 1981–1990. The estimates for 1973–1981 are repeated from table 4 for reference.

Technological Advance

The outlook for advances in applied technological knowledge in the United States is very bright. After sagging between 1968 and 1975, real R&D outlays started up in 1976, although as a ratio to GNP the low point came in 1977–1978 at 2.2 percent. But the average annual rate of increase in real R&D outlays between 1975 and 1983 has been 4.4 percent, well above the average rate of growth in real GNP. As a consequence, the R&D/GNP ratio recovered to 2.5 percent in 1982. A better than 4 percent increase in real R&D outlays in 1983 and 7 percent projected for 1984 will raise the ratio to 2.7 percent, according to recent National Science Foundation estimates.[21]

TABLE 6

SOURCES OF PRODUCTIVITY GROWTH: PROJECTED *(Percentage)*

	1973–1981	1981–1990
Total factor productivity	0.1	1.8
Advances in knowledge	0.7	1.2
Stock changes	0.7	1.0
Vintage effect	0	0.2
Changes in labor quality	0.6	0.9
Education and training	0.7	0.7
Health and safety	0.1	0.1
Age-sex composition	−0.2	0.1
Changes in quality of land	−0.2	−0.3
Resource reallocations	0.1	0
Volume changes	−0.3	0.6
Economies of scale	0.2	0.4
Capacity utilization	−0.5	0.2
Government regulations	−0.2	0
Actual/potential efficiency & n.e.c.	−0.6	−0.6

NOTE: The analysis of future growth trends is, at best, a difficult and problematic endeavor. Informed judgments are nevertheless needed in order to provide a context for policy analysis. The growth accounting model pioneered by Edward Denison provides a systematic and comprehensive treatment of the significant variables.
n.e.c. = not elsewhere classified.

---

21. "Defense and Economy Major Factors in 7% Real Growth in National R&D Expenditures in 1984" (Washington: National Science Foundation, Division of Science Resources Studies, July 22, 1983); also *National Patterns of Science and Technology Resources, 1983* (Washington: Government Printing Office, in press).

Federal and non-federal funding have been rising more or less proportionately over the past several years, and NSF projects a 7 percent increase
for each in 1984. The projected increases in national security outlays for some
years ahead suggest continued increases in federal R&D funding. The current
economic expansion, plus the special incentive of the 25 percent incremental
R&D tax credit enacted as part of ERTA in 1981, will undergird continued
increases in industrial R&D, which comprises more than half the total. More
fundamentally, the strong growth trends of science and technology-based
industries require continued increases in R&D to defend profit margins as
well as to pioneer new products and processes.

My projection assumes that the growth in real R&D spending will gradually slow from 7 percent in 1984 to 4 percent in 1990. With a growth trend
in real GNP of 4 percent a year 1984–1990, the R&D/GNP ratio would
gradually rise from 2.7 in 1984 to 3.0 percent in 1990. These projections
imply a significant acceleration in the growth of the real R&D stock and an
increase in its contribution to productivity advance. In addition, the accelerated
pace of real fixed investment discussed above will reduce the average age of
the fixed capital stock, contributing to a more rapid diffusion of new technology. Also significant is the greatly increased flow of venture capital caused
by the reduction of the capital gains tax in 1978 from 49 percent to 28 percent,
the relaxation of pension trust fund investment rules in 1979, and the further
reduction in the capital gains tax for individuals from 28 to 20 percent in
1981. New private venture capital committed rose from less than $60 million
a year on average between 1970 and 1977 to about $1.8 billion in 1982.
Initial public stock offerings increased almost tenfold from 1977 to 1982,
with further large gains in 1983. Since many of the new firms are technology
based, their burgeoning will help accelerate technological progress. It should
also be noted that this administration has sought, with some success, to
encourage joint R&D ventures among existing firms.

Labor Quality

Age-sex Composition. The most important factor in increasing the
average quality of the work force is hardly amenable to policy manipulation.
During the 1980s, changes in the composition of the labor force are favorable
as the post-World War II baby boom generation moves into prime working
ages. The proportion of females will continue to rise, but at a slower pace
than in the 1970s. The average work experience of women in the labor force
will be increasing, and wage differentials with men will tend to narrow. Even
using 1981 wage-differentials among eight age-sex groups, the changes in

labor force composition projected by BLS for 1990 results in a 0.1 percent contribution to productivity growth.

Human Investments. Investments in education, training, health and safety continue to rise relative to population, but I expect the real stock of human capital per worker to grow at about the same rate as in the 1973–1981 period with approximately the same effect on growth. As increasing proportions of youth receive higher education, it might be expected that the growth of educational capital would slow down. Opposing this tendency is the rapid pace of technological advance, which continues to increase the demand for professional and highly trained personnel, as well as for periodic retraining and adult education. Similarly, the success of the health care industry, reflected in rising life expectancy, results in increasing proportions of older people in the population who, along with rising per capita incomes, continue to increase the demand for health care.

In the past several years, it appears that SAT scores may be turning around. Just halting the decline in the average quality of education would help, and increasing its quality would augment the contribution of education to technological advance. As for the reciprocal influence, new educational technologies such as computer-assisted instruction in the schools, home computers, new audio-visual devices, and the like have a good potential for raising educational efficacy.

Quality of Land

The declining average quality of natural resources as production expands is almost certain to have a larger negative effect on productivity in the 1980s than in the 1970s. The mineral content of ores continues to decline, and oil and gas extraction comes increasingly from deeper wells and higher-cost sites. Some analysts expect a more substantial effect on future growth than I project, but they overlook the possibilities of domestic substitution, imports, and the relatively small weight of extractive industries in GNP.[22]

Resource Reallocation

I expect that the influence of resource reallocation will be neutral in the 1980s. Denison estimated the effect of the farm-nonfarm shift at only −0.06 1973–1981; with the further decline in the share of agriculture in GNP and

---

22. For example, see E. F. Renshaw, ''Productivity,'' in Joint Economic Committee print, U.S. Economic Growth from 1976 to 1986: Prospects, Problems and Patterns, vol. 1, *Productivity*, pp. 21–23 ff.

the narrowing of the earnings gap compared with nonfarm industries, further shifts will be minor and not significant for growth. The shift out of nonfarm self-employment already had a slightly negative effect 1973–1981, and is not expected to become significant again.

I am not convinced that resource shifts among industries with different productivity growth rates have a significant effect, and so I have made no allowance for this factor in the 1981–1990 period. My studies show that, outside of farming and services in which weak price elasticities are outweighed by strong income elasticities of demand, there is a positive correlation between relative industry changes in productivity and output.[23] The effect on resource allocation is essentially neutral.

As noted earlier, the relative shift out of agriculture is no longer significant. In addition, there is no assurance that farming will continue to register higher rates of productivity increase. One of these years, the tendency towards diminishing returns may catch up with agriculture as it has with mineral extraction. With regard to services, there are signs that productivity growth is accelerating there.[24]

Volume Factors

If the result of this growth accounting exercise is correct, the contribution of scale economies should be at least as great as estimated by Denison for the 1948–1973 period.

With regard to cyclical forces, I assume that the unemployment rate will drop from the high rates near 8 percent in 1981 and 1983 to a more normal 6 percent in 1990, although the decline may be interrupted by another recession along the way. In that case, the ratio of actual to potential GNP should be at least 4 percent higher in 1990 than in 1981. Given the rule of thumb mentioned earlier, productivity should then be at least 2 percent higher as overhead capital and labor are spread over more units, and plants are operating closer to the most efficient capacity utilization. Spread over nine years, the 2 percent boils down to around 0.2 percent a year productivity improvement.

23. John W. Kendrick, *Interindustry Differences in Productivity Growth, A Study in Contemporary Economic Problems, 1982*, William Fellner, Project Director (Washington: American Enterprise Institute, 1983).

24. "A Productivity Revolution in the Service Sector: The Spread of High Technology Will Boost U.S. Growth and Help Curb Inflation," *Business Week*, September 5, 1983, pp. 106–108.

Government Regulations

To some extent, Reagan continued efforts to deregulate formerly regulated industries, and to rationalize social regulations (primarily anti-pollution and safety) begun in the late 1970s. Figures have been cited to indicate large savings to both government and industry, although it is only the latter that would directly affect our numbers. The important thing is that the real compliance costs per unit of output have leveled off, eliminating the negative effect on productivity estimated by Denison for 1973–1981. In some cases, regulatory burdens have declined, but because of the expected acceleration of economic growth and the political appeal of environmental protection to the public, I do not expect declines to be large enough to exert a positive effect on productivity.

Labor Efficiency and N.E.C.

A recent survey shows a tremendous increase in "employee involvement" (EI) schemes designed to increase labor productivity.[25] Some, such as joint labor-management productivity teams and quality circles, do not involve financial incentives. Others, like Improshare, the Scanlon plan, employee stock ownership, and profit sharing, do. The basic idea is to get workers to participate more fully in the production process and to identify with the objectives of the firm. The survey just cited indicates that the vast majority of managements who have instituted EI plans believe that the plans have increased productivity.

If, as I have argued, the strong productivity gains of 1982–1983 presage a higher trend-rate in the 1980s, there may be less emphasis on EI. But the organizational structure is set up in many firms, and the programs may well continue to spur productivity in the future. Of course, once workers are already performing well under given technology, the main way to increase productivity is by improving technology. One function of EI programs is to elicit suggestions from employees for cost-reducing innovations. So in addition to improving efficiency with given technology, such programs can contribute to technological progress itself. But to be conservative, I have left the residual unchanged, in the absence of knowledge of changes in any other residual force that could affect productivity differently from the past.

---

25 *People and Productivity: A Challenge to Corporate America* (New York, N.Y.: Stock Exchange, Office of Economic Research, 1982).

Concluding Comments

Adding up all the components of growth for the period 1981–1990, I project total factor productivity to increase at an average annual rate of 1.8 percent, real product per labor hour at 2.7 percent, and total real gross product in the business sector at about 4 percent. Given the economic contraction through the last quarter of 1982, and a below-average year-to-year gain in 1983 (though the expansion *during* the year was healthy), it is clear that growth from 1983 to 1990 will have to be even stronger than the 1981–1990 rates shown in the table. Indeed, as I suggested at the outset of this discussion, the present period may be viewed as the beginning of an up-phase of the Kuznets long wave. Just as a slowing of growth in the latter 1950s was followed by strong growth 1961–1973, so the weakness of the period 1973–1981 appears to be leading to renewed strength.

Not that I would subscribe to a mechanistic notion of the long wave. Both economic and political forces influence growth rates. The slowdown in recent years eventually brought down rates of inflation and reduced unit costs even more, so that longer-term investments now look more attractive. Further, the population in the prime home-buying age brackets will continue to grow until the late 1980s.[26] And as we have seen, the slowdown brought political consensus that tax and other measures were needed to stimulate investment and productivity advance, and a variety of policy measures has been instituted. Thus, there is a kind of socioeconomic mechanism that helps to reverse the down-phase of a long wave, as well as short cycle contractions. The mechanism works in reverse in the latter stages of expansions and long wave up-phases, but this does not concern us here.

In any case, I believe that we have begun a period of strong economic growth that may extend into the 1990s. I hope that we are all around then to assess the forecasts presented at this conference.

---

26. See Data Resources, Inc., *U.S. Long-Term Review*, Fall 1983, pp. 11.125–137. Largely because of unfavorable demographic developments, DRI projects a slowing of economic growth in the 1990s. I adopted a similar scenario in projections to 2000 in my Presidential Address to the Southern Economic Association, "Long-Term Economic Projection," *Southern Economic Journal*, April 1984 (in press).

INCENTIVE EFFECTS OF TAXES ON INCOME FROM CAPITAL: ALTERNATIVE POLICIES IN THE 1980s

Don Fullerton and Yolanda Kodrzycki Henderson

A major goal of tax policy in recent years has been to increase saving, investment, and the productivity of American workers. To a great extent, the perceived success of President Reagan's tax program will depend upon its long run effects on total capital formation. However, many economists and an increasing number of policymakers are becoming concerned not just with the total amount of capital but with the efficiency of its use.

The amount of capital formation is influenced by the overall rate at which capital income is taxed. By driving a wedge between the gross and net returns to a capital asset, taxes lower the incentives to save and invest. Taxes thus induce an intertemporal distortion because sacrificing a given amount of current consumption provides less return in the form of future consumption than would be true if there were no taxes.

Taxes also affect the efficiency with which capital is allocated across assets and industries. If there were no taxes, investors would tend to seek the most productive investments and combine them efficiently. By contrast, the current tax system contains many features that create very high effective rates of tax on some investments and very low rates of tax or even subsidy on others. Investors are attracted to lightly taxed investments at the expense of

This paper was written in part while Don Fullerton was a National Fellow at the Hoover Institution, Stanford University. We are grateful to Dale W. Jorgenson for providing unpublished data and to Michael J. Boskin, Harvey Galper, Charles R. Hulten, Mervyn A. King, Andrew B. Lyon, and participants at the Urban Institute Conference on the Legacy of Reaganomics: Prospects for Long-term Economic Growth, Washington, D.C., September 1983, for helpful suggestions.

highly taxed investments, and the otherwise efficient use of capital is disrupted. Tax differentials tend to change the allocation of capital away from its most productive allocation. As a result, the total value of output is reduced. Moreover, these efficiency costs arise even if overall incentives increase the total stock of capital in the long run.

Some of these distortions involve the allocation of financial capital. For example, because corporations can deduct interest payments but not retained earnings or dividends, they have an artificial incentive to use debt rather than equity finance. Within equity, corporations may have an artificial incentive to retain rather than distribute their earnings because of additional personal taxes on dividends. Individuals have incentives from the tax system to invest in municipal rather than corporate bonds and to save through pensions rather than regular savings accounts. All of these misallocations entail costs, as do misallocations in terms of who saves and who bears risk.

Taxes may also distort the allocation of real capital: equipment, structures, inventories, land, and rental or owner-occupied housing. Differential tax rates on such assets arise because only equipment receives an investment tax credit, because inventories and land receive no special allowances, and because there is no taxation on the imputed return to owner-occupied housing. Effective tax rates may differ even within one of these categories, as when the same rate of investment tax credit is granted to machines with different useful service lives, or when the same depreciation schedule is assigned to assets that actually wear out at different rates. Because of different taxes in the corporate and noncorporate sectors, further distortions arise in the allocation of real capital between sectors or among the various industries.

In this paper, we concentrate on distortions in the allocation of real capital. We evaluate six tax regimes:

- Existing tax law as of 1980;

- President Reagan's tax reform initiatives as enacted in the Economic Recovery Tax Act of 1981 (ERTA) and

- The Tax Equity and Fiscal Responsibility Act of 1982 (TEFRA);

- The Auerbach-Jorgenson proposal to allow a first year recovery equivalent to economic depreciation at replacement cost;

- The proposed integration of corporate and personal taxes; and

- The possible elimination of the corporate income tax.

For each tax regime, we measure marginal effective total tax rates for capital in the corporate sector, the noncorporate sector, and the owner-occupied housing sector. These rates include the corporate income tax, the personal taxes, and property tax in order to assess the total impact on individuals' choices between present and future consumption and to estimate the distortions in the choice of investment.[1]

Our discussion is organized as follows. In the remainder of this section, we briefly summarize our results. Next, we discuss in more detail the cost of capital and effective tax rates for all assets in the corporate sector under each tax regime. Following that discussion, we provide the same information for the noncorporate sector and housing. Then, we investigate the sensitivity of our results to our modeling assumptions, and we measure the effect of inflation. Finally we present our conclusions.

Summary of Results About the Taxation of Capital

We obtain four rather surprising results regarding the taxation of capital.

(1) We find a lower effective tax rate on capital than might have been predicted on the basis of previous studies. The average effective total tax rate in the corporate sector, including all observed taxes on past investment, has been estimated at about 70 percent prior to the Reagan tax cuts.[2] Several studies have indicated that the marginal effective corporate tax rate in 1980, including only corporate taxes on equity-financed marginal investments, was about 33 percent.[3] In the current study, we add personal taxes and property taxes, and we assume that the marginal investment is financed by the average mix of equity and debt. Here, the corporate sector has an overall rate of about

---

1. This study emphasizes changes in capital cost recovery and in the investment tax credit under ERTA and TEFRA. These laws also lowered marginal personal income tax rates and affected other features of the tax law regarding saving. We do not consider these other effects in this study.

2. See Martin Feldstein, Louis Dicks-Mireaux, and James Poterba, "The Effective Tax Rate and the Pretax Rate of Return," *Journal of Public Economics*, vol. 21 (1983), pp. 120–158; and Martin Feldstein and Lawrence Summers, "Inflation and the Taxation of Capital Income in the Corporate Sector," *National Tax Journal*, vol. 32 (1979), pp. 445–470.

3. See Jane G. Gravelle, "Effects of the 1981 Depreciation Revisions on the Taxation of Income from Business Capital," *National Tax Journal*, vol. 35 (March 1982), pp. 1–20; Charles R. Hulten and James W. Robertson, "Corporate Tax Policy and Economic Growth: An Analysis of the 1981 and 1982 Tax Acts," discussion paper, The Urban Institute, 1982; Don Fullerton and Yolanda K. Henderson, "Long Run Effects of the Accelerated Cost Recovery System," NBER Working Paper 828 (revised) (Cambridge, Mass.: National Bureau of Economic Research, 1983).

35 percent in 1980,[4] but the low taxation of the large owner-occupied housing sector pulls the marginal rate for the economy down to 29 percent. Under 1982 law, these rates are 30 percent for the corporate sector and only 26 percent for all capital income in the economy.

(2) Although any given asset would be taxed more in the corporate sector than in the noncorporate sector, the mean rate in the noncorporate sector is higher than the mean rate in the corporate sector. This reversal occurs because the noncorporate sector has more assets in highly taxed categories such as land and structures.

(3) We find a tax rate on owner-occupied housing of 19 percent. This is contrary to the common perception that owner-occupied housing faces zero taxation as a result of exemption of imputed rents. Although this feature serves to lower the effective tax rate in this sector, property taxes are levied at a higher rate on housing than on industrial capital. With the lower-than-perceived tax rate on corporate capital and the higher-than-perceived tax rate on housing, our study suggests that the differential between tax rates in the two sectors was less dramatic than some architects of ERTA might have believed.

(4) Inflation adds to taxes in the corporate sector because of historical cost depreciation, taxation of nominal capital gains, and tax rules for insurance companies, but it subtracts from total taxes because the corporate rate for nominal interest deductions exceeds the personal rate at which nominal interest is taxed. Here, as in King and Fullerton, we find that taxes on corporate equipment and structures increase with inflation. When we add assets that do not receive depreciation allowances, such as corporate land and owner-occupied housing, we find that nominal interest deductions are important. Total taxes in the economy do not vary with inflation, even though disparities in the tax treatments of different assets increase with inflation. The approximate constancy of capital taxation contrasts with the findings of Feldstein and Summers, who found sharp increases in tax rates as a result of inflation.

Summary of Tax Rates in the 1980s

(1) If ERTA, the 1981 tax law, had been left in place through 1986, it would have greatly reduced the cost-of-capital in all industries except owner-

---

4. Our finding for the corporate sector is close to the 37 percent rate found by Mervyn A. King and Don Fullerton, eds., *The Taxation of Income from Capital: A Comparative Study of the U.S., U.K., Sweden, and West Germany* (Chicago: University of Chicago Press, 1984). Don Fullerton, "Which Effective Tax Rate?" *National Tax Journal*, vol. 36 (March 1984), pp. 23–41, catalogues reasons why average total tax rates may differ from marginal total tax rates.

occupied housing. This law would have substantially reduced intertemporal distortions, thus promoting expansion of the capital stock in the long run. However, capital costs for most types of equipment would have been reduced much more than costs for structures, land, or inventories. As a result, the 1981 law would have introduced major interasset distortions, which increase with the elasticity of substitution among assets.

(2) TEFRA, the 1982 law, aborted the transition to lower capital costs. Effects are similar to those of the ultimate 1981 law, but they are smaller. Nevertheless, the reductions in the cost of business capital are still significant. The overall reduction in taxation should help to spur investment in the long run, as intended by the architects of the Reagan program.[5]

We also examined the effects of some other recently suggested tax reforms.

(3) The Auerbach-Jorgenson proposal,[6] because it allows economic depreciation at replacement cost, would result in uniform capital costs across assets. Interasset distortions would be eliminated, and the efficiency gain from this reform could be expected to increase with the assumed substitution elasticity among assets. Because corporate firms would still be taxed differently from noncorporate firms, intersectoral distortions would remain dependent on the intersectoral substitution elasticity.

(4) If the corporate income tax were repealed, corporations would no longer receive investment tax credits, accelerated depreciation allowances, interest deductions, or property tax deductions. As in King and Fullerton, we find that eliminating the corporate tax would reduce taxes in the corporate sector by 2 percentage points under 1980 law, but it would *raise* effective tax rates and capital costs under 1982 law. Thus the corporate "tax" is really a marginal subsidy, but variations in capital costs remain high.

(5) Integration of the corporate tax and personal tax does not eliminate credits and deductions. All taxable corporate income would be passed through to the stockholders and would be taxed only at their personal rates. Overall capital costs would fall slightly, but the variation among capital costs would fall dramatically.

---

5. Our aim is to measure the long run consequences of tax reform. Changes in monetary policy between 1980 and 1982 might have altered observed interest rates and inflation rates, and therefore might have offset (or reinforced) the impact of the accelerated cost recovery provisions on effective tax rates. We are not concerned with such factors, however, because we do not attempt to measure tax rates in 1982 as opposed to 1980. Rather, we look at the difference between the tax laws, holding all other economic variables constant.

6. Alan J. Auerbach and Dale W. Jorgenson, "Inflation-Proof Depreciation of Assets," *Harvard Business Review*, vol. 58 (1980), pp. 113–118.

Effects of Alternative Tax Regimes on the Corporate Sector

In this section, we discuss in more detail the effects of each alternative tax regime on assets in the corporate sector. We refer to the Appendix for a discussion of the uses of cost-of-capital data in examining economic efficiency and for a derivation of the capital cost formulas for each asset in each sector.[7] These capital costs, or required pre-tax rates of return, are sometimes difficult to interpret by themselves. For this reason, when we report the results of our calculations, we always compare this pre-tax return to a fixed real after-tax return. The difference, as a fraction of the pre-tax return, is an effective tax rate measure which includes corporate taxes, personal taxes, and property taxes.

We use notation in the text to discuss the values of the parameters needed to calculate capital costs.

Summary of Cost-of-Capital Formulas

For our analysis, we consider a hypothetical firm that is trying to decide whether or not to buy a particular asset. This asset may be any one of the 38 assets listed below.

Asset	Hulten-Wykoff Depreciation Rate
Equipment	
1. Furniture and Fixtures	0.110
2. Fabricated Metal Products	0.092
3. Engines and Turbines	0.079
4. Tractors	0.163
5. Agricultural Machinery	0.097
6. Construction Machinery	0.172
7. Mining and Oil Field Machinery	0.165
8. Metalworking Machinery	0.123
9. Special Industry Machinery	0.103
10. General Industrial Equipment	0.123
11. Office and Computing Machinery	0.273
12. Service Industry Machinery	0.165
13. Electrical Machinery	0.118

---

7. We use cost-of-capital formulas like those in Robert Hall and Dale Jorgenson, "Tax Policy and Investment Behavior," *American Economic Review*, vol. 57 (June 1967), pp. 391–414.

14. Trucks, Buses, and Trailers	0.254
15. Autos	0.333
16. Aircraft	0.183
17. Ships and Boats	0.075
18. Railroad Equipment	0.066
19. Instruments	0.150
20. Other Equipment	0.150
Structures	
21. Industrial Buildings	0.036
22. Commercial Buildings	0.025
23. Religious Buildings	0.019
24. Educational Buildings	0.019
25. Hospital Buildings	0.023
26. Other Nonfarm Buildings	0.045
27. Railroads	0.018
28. Telephone and Telegraph	0.033
29. Electric Light and Power	0.030
30. Gas Facilities	0.030
31. Other Public Utilities	0.045
32. Farm Structures	0.024
33. Mining, Shafts, and Wells	0.056
34. Other Nonbuilding Facilities	0.029
35. Residential Structures	0.015
Inventories and Land	
36. Inventories	0.0
37. Business Land	0.0
38. Residential Land	0.0

These definitions are combinations of more diverse asset types, but they still provide considerable disaggregation. We treat each of these assets as individually homogeneous, in the sense that each has a single tax treatment and economic depreciation rate (δ). The first 20 assets are types of equipment, the next 15 are types of structures, and the last three are inventories and land.[8] We show values for δ for each asset. These rates of depreciation were estimated by Hulten and Wykoff,[9] and their availability provides the major

---

8. The firm may also earn income on intangible assets such as knowledge acquired through research, or goodwill acquired through advertising. Because we do not have adequate estimates for the stock of these assets in each industry, they are excluded from this study.

9. Charles R. Hulten and Frank C. Wykoff, "The Measurement of Economic Depreciation," in Charles R. Hulten, ed., *Depreciation, Inflation, and Taxation of Income from Capital* (Washington, D.C.: The Urban Institute Press, 1981).

reason for using this particular set of asset definitions.[10] The estimated depreciation rates range from a low of .015 for housing to a high of .333 for automobiles. Inventories and land do not depreciate, nor are they given depreciation allowances under any tax regime.

When our hypothetical firm purchases an asset, it receives an investment tax credit at rate k. Discussion of these values is deferred to the section for each tax regime, but we always assume that the firm has enough tax liability to make use of the credit.

Out of the return to the asset, the firm must pay a wealth tax (at rate w) on the value of the asset each year. These state and local property tax rates vary among thousands of jurisdictions, so we estimate average tax rates based on data from the Advisory Commission on Intergovernmental Relations (ACIR), as found in Harriss.[11] These data provide property taxes paid in 1972 on business realty (land and structures), business personalty (equipment and inventories), public utility structures, and household realty (rental and owner-occupied housing). We scale each of these tax amounts upward to 1977, using Commerce Department data on total property taxes in 1977 and 1972; we then divide each 1977 estimate by the corresponding 1977 capital stocks as described below. The resulting rates, applied either to the corporate or noncorporate sector, are .00768 for equipment and inventories, .01126 for business land and structures, .01550 for public utilities, and .01837 for household realty (land and structures).

On its return net of property taxes, the corporation is taxed at the statutory rate u. We use .46 for the federal statutory rate on marginal corporate income, because this top bracket rate applies to the largest firms with essentially all of the corporate capital stock. The weighted-average of the states' top-bracket rates is .0655, including zeros for states without corporate taxes, and using personal income to weight the fifty states. The total statutory rate, accounting for deductibility of state taxes at the federal level, is then .46 + .0655(1 − .46). We use this value, .495, for u.

The noncorporate firm is taxed at the statutory rate τ_{nc}. We use .365 for this parameter, obtained as the weighted average of marginal statutory tax rates on entrepreneurial income of 25,000 individual tax returns in the TAXSIM data file of the National Bureau of Economic Research (NBER).

---

10. For assets 27 through 31, the depreciation rates come from Dale W. Jorgenson and Martin A. Sullivan, "Inflation and Capital Recovery in the United States," in Charles R. Hulten, ed., *Depreciation, Inflation, and Taxation of Income from Capital* (Washington, D.C.: The Urban Institute Press, 1981). They use the Hulten-Wykoff methodology to obtain estimates for these additional assets. The rate for housing is an unpublished estimate of Hulten and Wykoff.

11. C. L. Harriss, *Property Taxation in Government Finance*, Research Publication 31 (Washington, D.C.: The Tax Foundation, 1974).

The after-tax return to this hypothetical firm is expected to grow in nominal terms at the rate of inflation (π), generally set at 7 percent. For most tax schemes, the firm also receives future depreciation allowances that are specified in nominal amounts for a fixed number of years. We calculate the present value of these depreciation allowances (z), and the present value of the nominal after-tax returns, using the nominal after-tax discount rate for the firm. These discount rates are discussed in the Appendix, but they are derived so that the real after-tax return to the average investor is a parameter s, set to 5 percent.

In considering this investment, our hypothetical firm compares the acquisition cost (net of investment tax credits) to the present discounted value of after-tax returns and tax savings from depreciation allowances. In equilibrium, the net outlay would just equal the present value of net returns from the marginal investment. We then use this equality to solve for the gross-of-tax return that the asset must earn in order to cover taxes and still yield the minimum required after-tax return. The required pre-tax return net of depreciation (ρ) is the cost-of-capital for that asset.

Because firms can make certain choices about depreciation lifetimes and schedules, actual capital costs may be affected by those choices. For example, when accelerated depreciation was first introduced, Vasquez found that firms were slow to adopt the more advantageous schedules.[12] However, because there is no procedure to predict actual choices for untried tax schemes, we compare all schemes under the assumption that firms make choices that minimize their taxes. This approach has the further advantage of allowing us to calculate comparable capital costs based only on tax provisions rather than on actual practices. We extend this assumption to firms' choices with respect to inventory accounting. Under all tax regimes, we assume that firms minimize their taxes by using only last-in-first-out (LIFO) inventory accounting. This method allows the firm to avoid taxes on purely nominal accounting profits, but it does not avoid taxes on real profits associated with investing in inventories.[13]

Our parameter s, the real return after personal taxes, is defined as a weighted-average of returns to different individuals who finance the marginal investment. In the corporate sector, the asset's purchase is financed by new share issues, retained earnings, and debt, in the proportions c_{ns}, c_{re}, and c_d

---

12. Thomas Vasquez, "The Effects of the Asset Depreciation Range System on Depreciation Practices," OTA Paper 1 (Washington, D.C.: U.S. Treasury Department, 1974).

13. An equity-financed investment in inventories must yield a return in the form of real corporate profits that is at least as high as the return that could have been earned on an alternative investment. These real corporate profits are taxed at the .495 corporate rate.

ST. CHARLES COUNTY
COMMUNITY COLLEGE LIBRARY
WITHDRAWN
102-L COMPASS POINT DRIVE
ST. CHARLES, MO 63301

respectively. King and Fullerton provide information on these three proportions for each of three different corporate industry groups. When we weight
by corporate capital stock, we obtain overall proportions of .0490 for new
shares, .6143 for retained earnings, and .3367 for debt.

Investments financed by new shares earn a return which is paid out in
dividends and taxed at rate τ_{ns}. The TAXSIM data file of the NBER provides
a tax rate of .475 for marginal dividend income, including state taxes and
averaged over 25,000 households. King and Fullerton provide additional tax
rates and weights for dividends received by tax-exempt institutions and insurance companies. When marginal tax rates for these three categories are
weighted together, we obtain .356 for τ_{ns}.

Investments that are financed by retained earnings provide owners of
equity with accrued nominal capital gains that are taxed at the effective accrued
rate τ_{re}. We again used the NBER's TAXSIM file to find the weighted-
average statutory rate on marginal capital gains of households, incorporating
the 60 percent exclusion on long-term capital gains. We further reduced this
28 percent rate to account for the deferral advantage and the increase of basis
at death. Following King and Fullerton, the final 7 percent rate for households
is averaged with zero for tax-exempt institutions and .14 for insurance companies to obtain .058 for τ_{re}.

Finally, investments financed by debt earn a return which is paid out as
interest and taxed at rate τ_d. The TAXSIM file places the average household's
marginal rate at .325, including state taxes, but King and Fullerton reduce
this rate to .284 to account for interest that is paid to banks and received by
households in the form of tax-free banking services. Insurance companies'
tax rates increase with inflation because of the complex Menge Formula, but
the net effect is summarized in the estimate $(.149 + 3.88\pi)$, where π is the
rate of inflation.[14] When households, tax-exempts, and insurance companies
are weighted together, the overall value for τ_d comes to $(.196 + .595\pi)$.
This rate changes as we vary π, but τ_d is .238 in the standard case where
inflation is 7 percent.

Of marginal investments in the noncorporate sector, a fraction n_d
is financed by debt, and n_e is financed by equity of the entrepreneur.
Little evidence is available on the complicated financing of noncorporate
business in the United States, but our rough estimates suggest that it is

---

14. The estimate of the effective tax rate on life insurance companies summarizes a
complex set of rules. For a description of this aspect of the tax code and discussion of
modeling choices, see King and Fullerton. Revisions in the tax treatment of insurance companies are under discussion in Congress at the time of this writing, but we have not included
any new proposals in this paper.

not dissimilar in aggregate to the financing of corporate business, that is, one-third debt.[15]

Finally, for owner-occupied housing, we need a fraction h_d for debt and h_e for equity. New homes are financed with a very large proportion of debt, but we are considering a permanent change in the steady state allocation of capital. The loan-to-value ratio typically falls as the house ages, and we want total mortgage debt as a fraction of total market value. Unpublished estimates from the Census Bureau suggest that this ratio is again very close to one-third.[16] As a consequence, we use the same fraction for debt financing in all three sectors.

The weighted-average marginal tax rate for these homeowners is τ_h, estimated at .26 by the TAXSIM model of NBER. Data in Fullerton and Gordon[17] suggest that 44.8 percent of property taxes are deducted, so the effective homeowners' property tax rate is $[1 - (.448)(.26)](.01837)$, which equals .01623.

The required pre-tax returns from each tax scheme are important parameters in that they summarize the cumulative effect of personal taxes, property taxes, and corporate taxes. Because they are numbers like .06 or .08, however, they are sometimes difficult to interpret by themselves. The parameter s represents the real return after all taxes, so the difference $(\rho - s)$ is due solely to taxes. This difference, expressed as a fraction of the pre-tax return, is a measure of the "marginal effective total tax rate" in the terminology of Fullerton. These numbers are presented in the tables below because they are comparable to tax-inclusive *ad valorem* tax rates such as the 46 percent statutory corporate rate. They are reduced relative to the corporate rate because of investment tax credits and accelerated depreciation allowances, but they are raised relative to the corporate rate because of property taxes and personal taxes.

Effects of Alternative Tax Regimes

Having defined the cost-of-capital formulas that we use, we now present the marginal effective total rates for each asset and for each industry, under the various tax regimes.

Tax Law as of 1980. The investment tax credit was introduced in 1962, repealed in 1969, reintroduced in 1971, and raised in 1975. As of

---

15. The ratio of noncorporate interest payments to an estimate of the share of noncorporate income attributable to capital, from the July 1982 *Survey of Current Business*, is almost identical to the ratio of corporate interest payments to corporate income from capital.

16. We are grateful to Peter Fronczek for providing these numbers.

17. Don Fullerton and Roger H. Gordon, "A Reexamination of Tax Distortions in General Equilibirum Models," in Martin Feldstein, ed., *Behavioral Simulation Methods in Tax Policy Analysis* (Chicago: University of Chicago Press, 1983).

1980, the credit stood at a 10 percent rate for all public utility structures and for equipment with tax lifetimes of at least 7 years; two-thirds of that for equipment with lifetimes of at least 5 years; and one-third for equipment with lifetimes of at least 3 years. Because we treat each asset as individually homogeneous, column 2 of table 1 assigns a 10 percent credit to all public utility structures (assets 27–31) and to any type of equipment that has a tax lifetime of at least 7 years. Tractors (asset 4) and trucks (asset 14) have 5-year lives and 6.67 percent credits, while autos (asset 15) have a 3-year life and 3.33 percent credit.

The lifetimes for each asset are shown in column 3. The 1962 Guideline lifetimes applied to many diverse assets, and these were aggregated by Jorgenson and Sullivan to the 35 depreciable asset types shown here. The Asset Depreciation Range (ADR) System, introduced in 1971 and still effective in 1980, allowed firms to use 80 to 120 percent of these Guideline lifetimes for equipment and public utility structures. Because firms minimize their taxes by assumption, they would use the shortest available lifetimes unless that choice had the effect of raising taxes by lowering the investment tax credit. We reduce the Guideline lifetime estimates accordingly. For example, computers (asset 11) may be depreciated over 5, 6, or 7 years under 1980 law. If not for the credit, firms would choose 5 years, but they choose 7 years (as shown in column 3 of table 1) in order to receive the 10 percent credit and minimize taxes.[18]

The 1980 tax scheme, like most others, has separate depreciation rules for different kinds of assets. Double declining balance (DDB) and sum-of-the-years'-digits (SYD) can be used for equipment, public utility property, single-purpose agricultural structures, and residential structures. If we define L as the asset's lifetime for tax purposes, then DDB allows depreciation equal to $2/L$ of the remaining basis each year. Because of the half-year convention, however, all assets are assumed to have been purchased on July 1. They receive half of the DDB amount, $(1/L)$, in the year of purchase and $2/L$ of the remaining basis, $(1-1/L)$, in the first full year of ownership. At this point, as shown in Fullerton and Henderson, the firm would minimize taxes by switching to SYD. If there are 3.5 years left (as for a 5-year asset), the firm takes the basis remaining at the time of the switch and divides it over the

---

18. Lifetimes for many of the 35 assets are actually averaged over more diverse asset categories. As a result, only some of the assets in one of our categories may need their lifetimes adjusted to receive higher credits. Since the aggregation to 35 assets provides considerable detail, however, it seems appropriate to treat each asset as individually homogeneous. One example of where this treatment may be less appropriate is in mining, shafts and wells. The 6.8 year life here reflects an average of intangible drilling with a zero life and other structures with a longer life.

TABLE 1

TAX PARAMETERS FOR EACH ASSET

Asset	1. Hulten-Wykoff Depreciation Rate	1980 Law		1981 and 1982 Laws	
		2. ITC Rate	3. Lifetime	4. ITC Rate	5. Lifetime
Equipment					
1. Furniture and Fixtures	0.110	0.100	8.00	0.100	5.00
2. Fabricated Metal Products	0.092	0.100	10.00	0.100	5.00
3. Engines and Turbines	0.079	0.100	12.48	0.100	5.00
4. Tractors	0.163	0.067	5.00	0.100	5.00
5. Agricultural Machinery	0.097	0.100	8.00	0.100	5.00
6. Construction Machinery	0.172	0.100	7.92	0.100	5.00
7. Mining and Oil Field Machinery	0.165	0.100	7.68	0.100	5.00
8. Metalworking Machinery	0.123	0.100	10.16	0.100	5.00
9. Special Industry Machinery	0.103	0.100	10.16	0.100	5.00
10. General Industrial Equipment	0.123	0.100	9.84	0.100	5.00
11. Office and Computing Machinery	0.273	0.100	7.00	0.100	5.00
12. Service Industry Machinery	0.165	0.100	8.24	0.100	5.00
13. Electrical Machinery	0.118	0.100	9.92	0.100	5.00
14. Trucks, Buses, and Trailers	0.254	0.067	5.00	0.100	5.00
15. Autos	0.333	0.033	3.00	0.060	3.00
16. Aircraft	0.183	0.100	7.00	0.100	5.00
17. Ships and Boats	0.075	0.100	14.40	0.100	5.00
18. Railroad Equipment	0.066	0.100	12.00	0.100	5.00
19. Instruments	0.150	0.100	8.48	0.100	5.00
20. Other Equipment	0.150	0.100	8.16	0.100	5.00

Table 1 (continued)

TAX PARAMETERS FOR EACH ASSET

Asset	1. Hulten-Wykoff Depreciation Rate	1980 Law		1981 and 1982 Laws	
		2. ITC Rate	3. Lifetime	4. ITC Rate	5. Lifetime
Structures					
21. Industrial Buildings	0.036	0.0	28.80	0.0	15.00
22. Commercial Buildings	0.025	0.0	47.60	0.0	15.00
23. Religious Buildings	0.019	0.0	48.00	0.0	15.00
24. Educational Buildings	0.019	0.0	48.00	0.0	15.00
25. Hospital Buildings	0.023	0.0	48.00	0.0	15.00
26. Other Nonfarm Buildings	0.045	0.0	30.90	0.0	15.00
27. Railroads	0.018	0.100	24.00	0.100	15.00
28. Telephone and Telegraph	0.033	0.100	21.60	0.100	15.00
29. Electric Light and Power	0.030	0.100	21.60	0.100	15.00
30. Gas Facilities	0.030	0.100	19.20	0.100	10.00
31. Other Public Utilities	0.045	0.100	17.60	0.100	10.00
32. Farm Structures	0.024	0.0	25.00	0.0	15.00
33. Mining, Shafts, and Wells	0.056	0.0	6.80	0.0	5.00
34. Other Nonbuilding Facilities	0.029	0.0	28.20	0.0	15.00
35. Residential Structures	0.015	0.0	40.00	0.0	15.00
Inventories & Land					
36. Inventories	0.0	0.0	∞	0.0	∞
37. Business Land	0.0	0.0	∞	0.0	∞
38. Residential Land	0.0	0.0	∞	0.0	∞

remaining years according to the fractions obtained by using a denominator of 8.0 and numerators of 3.5, 2.5, 1.5, and 0.5.

For other structures, firms could use 150 percent of declining balance (1.5/L of remaining basis each year), with an optimal switch to straight-line after one-third of the life of the asset. However, the firm must begin straight-line depreciation at the start of a tax year, and we assume that they make this choice to take the earliest allowable deductions (to minimize taxes). We also assume that the firm buys only new assets and holds them forever, so that we can abstract from problems with recapture taxes or scrap values.

These depreciation allowances, specified by law over a finite number of years for each asset, are discounted by the firm's nominal after-tax rate of return because allowances are based on historical cost. The present value of allowances per dollar of original basis is the parameter z in equation (A2) of the Appendix. Since the entire purchase price was depreciable in 1980, we use 1.0 for the parameter a.[19]

We have now specified enough information to calculate effective tax rates under 1980 law for each asset. Rates for the corporate sector are shown in column 1 of table 2. Note that types of equipment (assets 1–20) have rates that vary from a subsidy of 27 percent (for computers) to a tax of 22 percent (for ships and boats). Public utility structures (assets 27–31) also receive investment tax credits, but they have longer depreciation lifetimes and tax rates that are all about 33 percent. Other structures receive no credits, have longer tax lifetimes, and depreciate at only 150 percent of declining balance, so their tax rates vary from 44 to 56 percent. With inflation, these allowances are sometimes less than economic depreciation at replacement cost. Business land and inventories, which actually receive economic allowances since they do not depreciate, have total effective tax rates of 40 and 36 percent, respectively. These rates include property taxes, which differ by asset, and personal taxes, which do not. The wide disparities in effective tax rates— from -27 to $+56$ percent across all assets—indicate the potential for significant misallocation of capital.

The left-hand column of table 3 shows a marginal effective tax rate for each of eighteen industries, obtained by averaging the asset tax rates in the corporate and noncorporate sectors, and weighting by the industry's actual

---

19. Fullerton and Henderson provide more thorough descriptions of depreciation allowances and discounting. In particular, the formulas in that paper indicate that while the depreciation allowances are discrete amounts for each year, we discount them continuously over the course of the year. This procedure recognizes the fact that the basis declines annually, not continuously, and that deductions earlier in the year are worth more than those at the end of the year.

TABLE 2

MARGINAL EFFECTIVE TOTAL TAX RATES ON EACH ASSET IN THE CORPORATE SECTOR

Asset	1. 1980	2. 1981	3. 1982	4. AJ	5. Integration	6. Repeal
Equipment						
1. Furniture and Fixtures	−.064	−.578	−.051	.356	−.051	.302
2. Fabricated Metal Products	.071	−.490	−.058	.356	−.042	.302
3. Engines and Turbines	.164	−.433	−.064	.356	−.036	.302
4. Tractors	−.062	−.905	−.029	.356	−.079	.302
5. Agricultural Machinery	−.068	−.515	−.056	.356	−.045	.302
6. Construction Machinery	−.056	−.974	−.025	.356	−.083	.302
7. Mining and Oil Field Machinery	−.092	−.918	−.028	.356	−.080	.302
8. Metalworking Machinery	.121	−.644	−.046	.356	−.058	.302
9. Special Industry Machinery	.095	−.544	−.054	.356	−.048	.302
10. General Industrial Equipment	.099	−.644	−.046	.356	−.058	.302
11. Office and Computing Machinery	−.268	−2.325	.013	.356	−.140	.302
12. Service Industry Machinery	−.016	−.918	−.028	.356	−.080	.302
13. Electrical Machinery	.099	−.619	−.047	.356	−.055	.302
14. Trucks, Buses, and Trailers	−.041	−1.941	.006	.356	−.128	.302
15. Autos	.105	−1.040	−.029	.356	−.089	.302
16. Aircraft	−.215	−1.066	−.021	.356	−.089	.302
17. Ships and Boats	.220	−.418	−.066	.356	−.034	.302
18. Railroad Equipment	.120	−.382	−.069	.356	−.030	.302
19. Instruments	.004	−.812	−.034	.356	−.072	.302
20. Other Equipment	−.032	−.812	−.034	.356	−.072	.302

Structures						
21. Industrial Buildings	.518	.414	.414	.399	.332	.327
22. Commercial Buildings	.510	.363	.363	.399	.304	.327
23. Religious Buildings	.477	.332	.332	.399	.288	.327
24. Educational Buildings	.477	.332	.332	.399	.288	.327
25. Hospital Buildings	.503	.356	.356	.399	.300	.327
26. Other Nonfarm Buildings	.562	.450	.450	.399	.353	.327
27. Railroads	.312	.232	.302	.443	.249	.355
28. Telephone and Telegraph	.347	.268	.355	.443	.270	.355
29. Electric Light and Power	.337	.261	.344	.443	.266	.355
30. Gas Facilities	.315	.176	.267	.443	.214	.355
31. Other Public Utilities	.336	.189	.300	.443	.225	.355
32. Farm Structures	.441	.358	.358	.399	.301	.327
33. Mining, Shafts, and Wells	.358	.283	.283	.399	.237	.327
34. Other Nonbuilding Facilities	.483	.383	.383	.399	.314	.327
35. Residential Structures	—	—	—	—	—	—
Inventories & Land						
36. Inventories	.356	.356	.356	.356	.329	.302
37. Business Land	.399	.399	.399	.399	.362	.327
38. Residential Land	—	—	—	—	—	—

TABLE 3

MARGINAL EFFECTIVE TOTAL TAX RATES IN EACH INDUSTRY

Industry	1. 1980	2. 1981	3. 1982	4. AJ	5. Integration	6. Repeal
1. Agriculture, Forestry, and Fisheries	.338	.329	.335	.354	.337	.345
2. Mining	.356	.188	.273	.372	.220	.310
3. Crude Petroleum and Gas	.406	.309	.314	.389	.269	.324
4. Construction	.293	.241	.288	.355	.267	.301
5. Food and Tobacco	.370	.280	.319	.371	.276	.311
6. Textiles, Apparel, and Leather	.358	.266	.306	.368	.267	.310
7. Paper and Printing	.349	.212	.278	.372	.234	.312
8. Petroleum Refining	.417	.326	.350	.382	.296	.318
9. Chemicals and Rubber	.324	.178	.260	.369	.218	.309
10. Lumber, Furniture, Stone, Clay, and Glass	.357	.243	.299	.370	.255	.310
11. Metals and Machinery	.359	.269	.312	.368	.270	.309
12. Transportation Equipment	.380	.318	.340	.369	.299	.310
13. Motor Vehicles	.329	.192	.275	.367	.231	.309
14. Transportation, Communication, and Utilities	.275	.116	.248	.406	.192	.333
15. Trade	.352	.313	.330	.360	.306	.310
16. Finance and Insurance	.389	.322	.325	.368	.323	.326
17. Real Estate	.237	.225	.225	.241	.243	.276
18. Services	.297	.115	.210	.361	.183	.287

stock of each asset.[20] Column 1 of table 3 shows the 1980 law, where differences in industry tax rates generally reflect differences in their use of assets. Structure-intensive industries such as crude oil and petroleum refining are weighted towards the high effective tax rates on structures. The low rate on transportation, communications, and utilities reflects the tax credits for public utility structures as well as the low rate for aircraft.

The Economic Recovery Tax Act of 1981. While many provisions of the 1981 Tax Act were to phase in over several years, the investment tax credit changed immediately to a 6 percent rate for automobiles and 10 percent for all other equipment and public utility property. These credit rates are shown in column 4 of table 1. Because we assume no carryover problems, both sets of credit rates reflect statutory credits and do not reflect any increase in availability of the credit through the 1981 law's extended carryover and leasing provisions.

Column 5 displays lifetimes of each asset under the Accelerated Cost Recovery System (ACRS), assuming again that each asset is homogeneous. The law assigns a 3-year life to autos, light trucks, R&D equipment, certain racehorses, and personal property with an ADR midpoint of 4 years or less. Our level of aggregation shows autos with a 3-year life, but none of the other assets has an (average) ADR midpoint of 4 years or less. Thus, all other equipment gets a 5-year life. Similarly, for public utility structures, we assigned a 10-year life to any asset category with an ADR midpoint between 18 and 25 years, as provided in the law. All other structures have a 15-year life, except mining, shafts, and wells, which we reduced from a 6.8- to a 5-year life.

Although these shorter lives were effective immediately, depreciation of new equipment was scheduled to accelerate from 150 percent of declining balance to 175 percent of declining balance during a 5-year phase-in period. After 1985, new equipment was again to be depreciated by double declining balance, again with an optimal switch to sum-of-the-year's-digits.[21] We eval-

---

20. For weights, we use Dale Jorgenson's unpublished data on the 1977 stock of each asset used in each industry. See Jorgenson and Sullivan and Barbara M. Fraumeni and Dale W. Jorgenson, "The Role of Capital in U.S. Economic Growth, 1948–1976," in George von Furstenberg, ed., *Capital, Efficiency and Growth* (Cambridge, Mass.: Ballinger, 1980) for more detail. Briefly, they use Commerce Department investment series, a capital flow table, and an RAS scaling routine to estimate an investment matrix for every year. Then they use Hulten-Wykoff depreciation rates and the perpetual inventory method to obtain the capital stock matrix for 1977. For rental and owner-occupied housing, we use estimates for 1977 from the February 1981 *Survey of Current Business*.

21. An interesting difference, however, is that depreciation of the last half-year is moved up. The 5-year asset in the earlier example receives DDB for 1.5 years as before, but SYD over only 3 remaining years instead of 3.5. Thus, even where the asset's lifetime was not shortened (as for assets 5 and 14), the present value of allowances (z) is still higher under 1981 law.

uate only this final set of rules, originally scheduled to begin in 1986. All structures immediately received a 175 percent declining balance rate, replacing both the 150 percent rate for nonresidential property and the 200 percent rate for new residential property. All structures switch at the optimal time from 175 percent declining balance to straight-line, after three-sevenths of the life of the asset.[22]

The 1981 law also provides phased reductions of personal marginal tax rates. The top marginal rate fell from 70 percent to 50 percent immediately, but all other rates are reduced by 23 percent over 3 years. After 1985, personal rate brackets are scheduled to be indexed for inflation. We wish to compare 1980 with the ultimate (1986) version of ERTA, but we cannot simply reduce personal rates by 23 percent. Inflation after 1980 will erode at least some of these rate cuts by the time indexing starts in 1985. In fact, King and Fullerton find that it would take an annual inflation rate of only about 7 percent over those 6 years to completely negate the 23 percent cut. For this reason, we ignore personal tax changes specified in ERTA. We also abstract from changes related to tax-free "all-savers' certificates" for individuals, charitable deductions for nonitemizers, reductions in the marriage penalty for two-earner families, and other provisions that do not pertain primarily to business income from real capital assets.

Effective tax rates under ERTA are shown for each asset in column 2 of table 2. Rates for equipment are all negative, while rates for structures range up to 45 percent. Since land and inventories receive no credits or deductions anyway, their effective tax rates are unchanged from 1980. Because the relatively high 1980 rates for these assets remain high while the relatively low 1980 rates for equipment are reduced, it appears that the potential for capital misallocations would be greater under ERTA.

Previous estimates of the marginal effective *corporate* tax rate under ERTA have consistently been negative for all types of equipment. The implication is that credits and accelerated depreciation deductions outweigh the corporate tax and provide a net subsidy on income from marginal investments in these assets. Yet table 2 indicates that the marginal effective *total* tax rates

---

22. The optimal switch point for 175 percent of declining balance is calculated as $(1.75 - 1.0)/1.75$ as shown in Fullerton and Henderson. Rather than specify allowable schedules and let the firm choose, however, the 1981 and 1982 laws provide tables with depreciation amounts for each year. These amounts are calculated for the tables by using the rules described in the text, assuming that firms want the earliest possible deductions. We thus effectively use the tables for the new laws, and we use comparable tax-minimizing choices for the old law. The new law is less flexible, however, because it mandates the earliest possible deductions. If the firm did not expect a steady stream of positive taxable profits, as is assumed in this paper, it might prefer to delay some deductions by using a longer life or by making an early switch to straight-line.

are negative. This finding implies that the subsidy at the corporate level is so large that it completely offsets property taxes and personal taxes, even though personal taxes apply to nominal income.[23]

Since depreciation schedules were to be the same in 1986 as they were in 1980, we can also see how sensitive tax rates are to lifetimes and credits. When only the lifetime for computers (asset 11, table 1) changes from 7 to 5 years, the total effective tax rate changes from a − 27 percent to a − 233 percent (table 2). When only the credit for autos (asset 15, table 1) changes from .033 to .06, its effective tax rate changes from + 11 percent to − 104 percent (table 2).[24]

The corresponding industry tax rates are shown in column 2 of table 3. The fact that all these rates exceed zero reflects the weights on structures, inventories, and land in all industries. These averaged rates still vary more than they did in 1980.

The Tax Equity and Fiscal Responsibility Act of 1982. Because TEFRA effectively repealed the transition to double-declining balance, the scheduled increase for depreciation of equipment was never allowed to take place. TEFRA retained the investment tax credits and the shorter lives of ACRS, but it left equipment with 150 percent of declining balance and an optimal switch to straight-line. Structures had no transition in the 1981 law, so they are left at 175 percent of declining balance with a switch to straight-line. These specifications provide enough information to calculate z, the present value of allowances per dollar of basis. However, TEFRA also reduced the basis for depreciation by half of the investment tax credit. As a consequence, we set the depreciable proportion parameter (a) to .95 for equipment and public utility property with a 10 percent credit, and to .97 for autos with a 6 percent credit.

Again we abstract from other changes in TEFRA that are not related to the taxation of income from real business assets, including newly introduced excise taxes, medical and casualty loss deductions, and individual minimum tax provisions. Since our hypothetical firm always has sufficient tax liability

---

23. This marginal subsidy can be received by any corporation with sufficient taxable profits against which to take the credits and deductions. These taxable profits might include (a) the normal return to old investments upon which taxes were deferred, (b) normal returns to taxed investments like land and inventories, (c) unexpected returns, or (d) monopoly profits. The investing firm need not even have its own taxable profits if there is a mechanism for the transfer of tax benefits between firms. The safe harbor leasing provisions of the 1981 Tax Act provided such a mechanism. Still, the large subsidies found in this paper indicate great potential for the marginal investment to receive asymmetric treatment in firms with and without taxable profits.

24. These rate reductions also incorporate the fact that ERTA moves up the last half-year of depreciation.

to use all of its credits and deductions, it is unaffected by TEFRA's restrictions of safe-harbor leasing.

The resulting tax rates for equipment are mostly negative, as shown in column of table 2. Although they use the ACRS lifetimes of the 1981 law, their overall levels are closer to 1980 law. In fact, for many of the assets (e.g., tractors, some types of machinery, computers, trucks, aircraft, and electric utility property), 1982 tax rates are higher than 1980 rates (for the same expected rate of inflation). For these assets, the tax-raising effect of the basis adjustment outweighs the tax-reducing effect of shortened tax lives. The tendency for tax rates to be higher under 1982 law is stronger when the comparison is made under the assumption of low inflation rates in both periods. For example, when tax rates are computed under the assumption of 4 percent inflation, more types of equipment show higher tax rates under 1982 law than under 1980 law. Real depreciation allowances (z) are greater at low inflation rates, so the tax-increasing basis adjustment is more important at low inflation rates.

Taxation of structures is the same under the 1982 law as under the 1981 law. Column 3 of table 3 shows tax rates by industry, reflecting their asset compositions.

The Auerbach-Jorgenson Proposal. Our study also evaluates some investment incentive plans that were not adopted. The Auerbach-Jorgenson first-year capital recovery plan gives the firm one depreciation deduction at the time the asset is purchased, equal to the expected present value of economic depreciation at replacement cost. Since future economic depreciation is discounted at a constant real after-tax discount rate, this proposal effectively indexes depreciation allowances for inflation. It treats all assets symmetrically in the sense that it provides a high first-year deduction for equipment with a high δ, a low deduction for structures with a low δ, and no deduction for land and inventories, which do not depreciate.

If there is no investment tax credit, if Hulten-Wykoff depreciation rates are used to determine economic depreciation, and if the firm's real discount rate is used to calculate the first-year recovery, then estimates of the marginal effective corporate tax rate are equal to the statutory 49.5 percent rate for all assets. If this depreciation is well measured, then this plan removes all interasset distortions in the corporate sector.[25] Similar allowances in the noncorporate sector can remove interasset distortions there, but intersectoral distortions may remain if the noncorporate sector continues to be taxed at a

---

25. On the other hand, if actual depreciation differs from Hulten-Wykoff estimates or if the government does not use the firm's discount rate when it sets the first-year allowances for each asset, then effective tax rates can still vary among assets.

lower rate. Interindustry distortions remain if some industries are disproportionately incorporated, and intertemporal distortions remain if income from
capital is disproportionately taxed.[26]

Column 4 of table 2 shows the marginal effective total tax rate for each
asset under this plan. Although corporate taxes and personal taxes on these
assets are uniform, property taxes are imposed at a .8 percent rate on all kinds
of equipment, a 1.1 percent rate on nonresidential structures, and a 1.55
percent rate on public utility property. Marginal effective total tax rates vary
little, but they are ordered across these assets according to these property tax
rates. Industry effective tax rates in column 4 of table 3 vary even less.

Integration of Corporate and Personal Taxes.   Because of the potential for distortions when extra taxes are imposed on the corporate sector,
many have suggested integrating the corporate and personal tax systems. Some
have suggested partial integration plans such as allowing corporations to
deduct dividends, so that this income is taxed only at the personal level.
Here, we evaluate only a full form of integration, and we compare it to current
1982 tax law. Further discussion of many such plans and their effects is
provided by McLure.[27]

Our specification of this reform involves retaining investment tax credits
and depreciation allowances, just as these features exist in 1982 for the
noncorporate sector. We then trace all taxable corporate income through to
be taxed only at the level of the individuals who own the corporations. Interest
is still taxed at the rate τ_d, but all retained or distributed corporate profits are
taxed at τ_{ns}, the full personal rate of corporate stockholders. Intersectoral
distortions remain to the extent that these personal tax rates differ from the
personal rate of entrepreneurs, and interasset distortions may remain to the
extent that credits and depreciation allowances affect assets differently.

Column 5 of table 2 shows the marginal effective total tax rates on assets
in the corporate sector under the integrated tax regime. These rates are very
similar to those of the noncorporate sector in 1982. Rates on equipment are
reduced from 1982 corporate numbers, which vary around zero, to numbers
that are all negative. Thus, with integration, personal taxes and property taxes

---

26. E. Cary Brown, "The 'Net' Versus the 'Gross' Investment Tax Credit," in Charles
R. Hulten, ed., *Depreciation, Inflation, and the Taxation of Income from Capital* (Washington,
D.C.: The Urban Institute Press, 1981) suggests an investment credit that is proportional to the
difference between the acquisition cost of the asset and its first-year allowance. This particular
choice of asset-dependent credits and first-year write-offs results in uniform effective corporate
taxes at a rate lower than 49.5 percent. This uniform tax rate can be as high or as low as desired,
or even zero, equivalent to immediate expensing of the entire acquisition cost.

27. Charles E. McLure, Jr., *Must Corporate Income Be Taxed Twice?* (Washington, D.C.:
The Brookings Institution, 1979).

are effectively offset by credits and accelerated depreciation deductions for
these assets. Rates on structures are reduced from about 38 percent to about
30 percent.

Because industries use these assets in different proportions, industry tax
rates still vary (column 5 of table 3). Some interindustry distortions thus
remain, in contrast to previous models where all industry distortions are based
on extra corporate taxes and differential degrees of incorporation. Intertemporal distortions remain as well.

Elimination of the Corporate Income Tax. The last set of calculations
does not represent a serious or even necessarily desirable policy proposal.
Instead, we are merely trying to help evaluate the overall effect of the corporate
tax in any of the first four regimes described above. Since personal taxes and
property taxes are constant across all of those simulations, any of the first
four sets of tax rates (1980, 1981, 1982, AJ) can be compared to those from
a world with just personal and property taxes.

By this definition, eliminating the corporate tax involves concomitant elimination of the corporations' investment tax credits (k), depreciation deductions
(z), and interest deductions. The IRS undertakes no interactions with corporations,
but it continues to collect personal taxes as before on all nominal interest receipts,
dividends, capital gains, and noncorporate income. In equations of the Appendix,
these specifications merely imply that $k = u = z = 0$.

Column 6 of table 2 exhibits fairly high effective tax rates, differing
only to the extent that property taxes differ by asset. Tax rates for equipment
are higher than those for any other tax plan except the Auerbach-Jorgenson
plan.[28] These findings are consistent with previous findings that the corporate
tax system amounts to a net subsidy for equipment. However, other assets
receive no investment tax credits and less accelerated depreciation. Because
inflation may reduce the real values of allowances to less than economic
depreciation, effective total tax rates on structures under the 1980 law and
1982 law are about 50 and 38 percent, respectively. Under either law, taxes
on land and inventories are 40 and 36 percent. The elimination of the corporate
tax more than offsets the elimination of nominal interest deductions in these
cases, because these rates fall to 33 percent for structures, 33 percent for
land, and 30 percent for inventories.

---

28. While the AJ proposal effectively taxes all equity-financed investments at the 49.5
percent statutory rate of the corporation, it still allows deductions for nominal interest payments.
It also allows a first-year recovery for depreciation. Repeal of the corporate tax, on the other
hand, would allow no investment tax credits, no interest deductions, and no allowances for
depreciation—even economic depreciation. The estimated effective tax rates reflect the fact that
the personal tax applies to nominal interest receipts, since they are designed to include all taxes
as a fraction of real income from the asset.

Marginal effective total tax rates under this tax regime are shown in column 6 of table 3 for each of our 18 industries, weighted by each industry's use of assets.

A Comparison of Summary Statistics for the Corporate Sector, Noncorporate Sector, and Housing

The noncorporate entrepreneur is taxed by rules similar to those for the corporation but has a .365 personal tax rate rather than the .495 corporate rate. Therefore, effective tax rates vary in a similar manner across the 38 assets, but the overall level is different. For this reason, we do not provide noncorporate rates on all assets under each scheme. Instead, table 4 provides summary statistics for the average tax levels for equipment (assets 1–20 on table 1), business structures (assets 21–26, 32–34) public utilities structures (assets 27–31), and land and inventories (assets 36–38).

TABLE 4

SUMMARY STATISTICS

	1. 1980	2. 1981	3. 1982	4. AJ	5. Integration	6. Repeal
Corporate sector tax rates						
Equipment	.054	− .721	− .040	.356	− .064	.302
Structures	.496	.377	.377	.399	.308	.328
Public utilities	.332	.240	.326	.443	.253	.355
Inventories	.356	.356	.356	.356	.329	.302
Land	.399	.399	.399	.399	.362	.328
Overall	.345	.236	.300	.388	.252	.321
Noncorporate sector tax rates						
Equipment	− .020	− .311	− .056	.328	− .079	− .124
Structures	.388	.293	.293	.358	.304	.327
Public utilities	.245	.184	.241	.389	.256	.287
Residential structures	.395	.334	.334	.409	.350	.381
Inventories	.328	.328	.328	.329	.329	.331
Land	.358	.358	.358	.358	.363	.372
Residential land	.409	.409	.409	.409	.420	.441
Overall	.358	.321	.327	.371	.335	.351
Owner-occupied housing sector						
tax rates	.186	.186	.186	.186	.206	.242
Overall cost of capital	.070	.066	.068	.072	.068	.072
Standard deviation	.017	.020	.017	.014	.009	.019
Overall tax rate	.288	.247	.264	.305	.263	.305

Under the 1980 law, shown in column 1, we obtain the surprising result that the 35.8 percent overall tax rate in the noncorporate sector exceeds the 34.5 percent rate in the corporate sector. However, a noncorporate firm would not reduce its taxes by incorporating, because on any one activity, the corporate rate exceeds the noncorporate rate. In the corporate and noncorporate sectors respectively, equipment is taxed at rates of $+5$ and -2 percent, structures at rates of 50 and 39 percent, and land at rates of 40 and 36 percent. The overall noncorporate tax rate is higher than the corporate rate because noncorporate firms use much more of the highly taxed structures and land.

Still, the difference between the two sectors is not great. The fact that the corporate statutory rate exceeds the entrepreneur's rate implies higher taxes on some assets but higher interest deductions and subsidies on others. Additional personal taxes on corporate income are very small. The 5.8 percent capital gains rate applies to the large share of finance through retained earnings, and the 35.6 percent dividends rate applies only to the tiny share of financing through new issues.

The overall rate in the noncorporate sector includes 39 and 40 percent effective tax rates, respectively, on structures and land in rental housing. By contrast, the effective tax on structures or land in owner-occupied housing is only 18.6 percent. This rate represents only state and local property taxes, reduced to the degree that they are deducted from personal taxes. The rate is further reduced to the degree that mortgage interest is deducted at a rate higher than the rate at which interest receipts are taxed.

When averaged over the entire economy, the marginal effective total tax rate in 1980 was 28.8 percent, reflecting an after-tax return of .05 and a pre-tax return of .070. Though we have not yet measured misallocations associated with variations of this *cum*-tax cost-of-capital across assets and sectors, the weighted standard deviation of .017 indicates potential for excess burden.

The second and third columns of table 4 indicate that the Economic Recovery Tax Act would have reduced corporate taxes dramatically but that the Tax Equity and Fiscal Responsibility Act removed about half of that tax cut. Equipment in either sector would have been heavily subsidized under ERTA but is now only slightly subsidized. TEFRA almost completely removed the tax cuts for public utility structures but left the cuts for other structures untouched. Neither law changed taxes on inventories, land, or owner-occupied housing.

Because the largest tax cuts in ERTA applied to equipment, the assets with the lowest existing tax rates, the standard deviation among capital costs would have increased from .017 to .020 at the same time that the average capital cost would have fallen from .070 to .066. TEFRA removed tax cuts for equipment in particular, so the standard deviation returns to .017 while the overall pre-tax return climbs halfway back, to .068.

The Auerbach-Jorgenson plan, in column 4, would leave inventories and land unchanged, slightly raise the 1982 tax on structures, and significantly raise the 1982 tax on equipment. There remain interasset differences due to the property tax, and intersectoral differences due to the unintegrated corporate tax system and the exclusion of imputed net rents. Relative to 1982, effective tax rates rise by 9 percentage points in the corporate sector, 4 points in the noncorporate sector, and 4 points overall. The cost-of-capital rises to .072, but its weighted standard deviation falls to .014.

Integration of corporate and personal taxes, the way we have defined it, does not remove interasset distortions attributable to investment tax credits and differential allowances. However, it does remove almost all differences between the corporate and noncorporate sectors. These differences turn out to be important, because the standard deviation of capital costs falls to .009. Each individual asset would be taxed at the same rate in either of the two sectors, but the noncorporate sector includes highly taxed rental housing and therefore averages to a higher overall tax rate. [29]

As we noted earlier, repealing the corporate tax would greatly reduce differences in tax rates across assets in the corporate sector. Differences in tax rates for different assets remain in the noncorporate sector. Intersectoral differences are not reduced because elimination of corporate subsidies *raises* the corporate rate from 30 percent in 1982 to 32.1 percent. [30] It raises the cost of capital to .072, the overall tax rate to 30.5 percent, and the standard deviation to .019.

Sensitivity Analysis

In this section, we discuss the sensitivity of our results to the assumptions we made about inflation, debt finance, property taxation, and arbitrage.

---

29. Tax rates for noncorporate business and housing are slightly changed from column 3 to column 5, even though "integration" does not affect tax rules applicable to those sectors. We use the *ceteris paribus* assumption that the weighted-average after-tax return to capital is constant across tax schemes, however. The higher personal taxation of corporate income necessitates a higher interest rate to maintain that fixed after-tax return, and the higher market interest rate affects discounting in the noncorporate and housing sectors.

30. Corporations may not actually experience this subsidy because the size of their earnings puts a limit on use of deductions and credits. The asymmetric treatment of taxes and subsidies is accentuated when the tax law allows marginal subsidies as is currently true for equipment.

Inflation

The sensitivity of tax rates to inflation is among the most significant findings of our study. Under 1982 law, inflation raises tax rates on some assets and lowers it on others. The resulting interasset distortions become quite sizable at some levels of inflation. Specifically, we find that double-digit inflation is associated with sharply higher dispersion in the cost-of-capital than is inflation in the 0 to 5 percent range. Although we cannot measure the associated efficiency losses without performing general equilibrium simulations, these results indicate potential misallocations of capital at high rates of inflation.[31]

Our model captures four influences of inflation.

(1) Even though tax lives are sharply reduced under the accelerated cost recovery system, the basis for depreciation is still original cost rather than replacement cost. As a consequence, with higher rates of inflation, the present discounted value of depreciation allowances falls, and the cost-of-capital rises.

(2) Equity holders are taxed on nominal rather than real capital gains, and debt holders are taxed on nominal rather than real interest receipts. Thus, as inflation increases, a constant rate of tax on nominal income causes a rising real burden. The magnitude of this effect depends on the hypothesized increase in taxable income for each additional point of inflation. As described in the Technical Appendix, when we look at different rates of inflation, our model assumes that the real after-tax rate of return is constant. As a result, taxable income rises by more than point for point with inflation.

(3) A third reason that the cost-of-capital rises with inflation is the way in which insurance companies are taxed. The Menge Formula determines the deductibility of reserves in such a way that inflation raises the insurance company's rate of tax as well as its taxable income (see King and Fullerton, chapter 6). After accounting for the proportion of debt that is held by insurance companies, we find that each point of inflation adds about 0.6 points to τ_d, the tax rate on interest income.

(4) Offsetting the first three influences of inflation is the deductibility of nominal interest payments. In the corporate sector, firms deduct interest payments from taxable income at their 49.5 percent rate, while interest recipients include it at the rate $\tau_d = .196 + .595\pi$. As we vary inflation from

---

31. As we discuss below, there is also some uncertainty about the robustness of these results on dispersion when we vary modeling assumptions. The pattern that some tax rates rise with inflation and others fall seems to be general, however. Finally, although we do not present inflation sensitivity results for 1980 law in this paper, they are similar to those for 1982 law (under a given set of modeling assumptions).

0 to 15 percent in our sensitivity analysis, the tax rate for interest recipients rises from .196 to .285, which indicates a subsidy per dollar of interest $(u-\tau_d)$ that diminishes with inflation. Thus, as inflation increases the nominal interest which receives the subsidy $(u-\tau_d)$, it also reduces the rate of subsidy.

Because the marginal tax rate of noncorporate entrepreneurs is .365, there is also a subsidy on the use of debt in that sector. In our third sector for homeowners, marginal tax rates average 26 percent. Each dollar of interest is thus subsidized at rates of inflation below 10.8 percent (where τ_d reaches .26) and taxed at rates of inflation above 10.8 percent.

The list of influences of inflation explicitly excludes any bracket creep for individuals. Since we look at the long-run effect of current law, we assume the indexing provisions currently scheduled to begin in 1985. In the absence of this measure, inflation would have a greater tendency to push tax rates upward. We also exclude FIFO (first-in, first-out) inventory accounting when we look at only the tax-minimizing firm. If FIFO were required in some way, inflation would increase taxes for this reason as well.

We use two figures to display the net effects of the four included influences of inflation under 1982 law. Figure 1 plots selected tax rates as a function of inflation, and figure 2 plots the weighted standard deviation of capital costs across all assets and sectors as a function of inflation.

One striking fact in figure 1 is the relative constancy of aggregated marginal tax rates on capital. The economy-wide tax rate is .282 at zero inflation, reaches a low of .262 at about 10 percent inflation, then rises back to .270 at 15 percent inflation. The corporate rate is even more constant, staying between 29.5 and 30.5 percent.

However, this remarkable stability of mean tax rates masks underlying differences in the effect of inflation on the taxation of individual assets. Figure 1 provides a glimpse at this diversity, since it includes a plot of the tax rates in the corporate sector for the aggregate of the twenty types of equipment, for the nine types of structures, and for inventories. The effective tax rate on equipment rises monotonically from $-.359$ at zero inflation to $+.312$ at 15 percent inflation. In the cost of equipment, the erosion of depreciation allowances is more important than the net addition to nominal interest deductions. Inflation also reduces the real value of depreciation on structures and raises the effective tax rate on that asset. However, because of the relatively long tax lives for structures, a given inflation-induced increase in the discount rate has less effect on the present value of allowances than it does in the case of equipment. For assets that do not depreciate, such as inventories in figure 1, inflation adds to the nominal interest, which is deducted at a rate higher than the rate at which it is subsequently taxed. This subsidizing effect of further inflation eventually offsets the tax on this asset. Finally,

FIGURE 1

THE EFFECTS OF INFLATION ON THE TAXATION OF CAPITAL

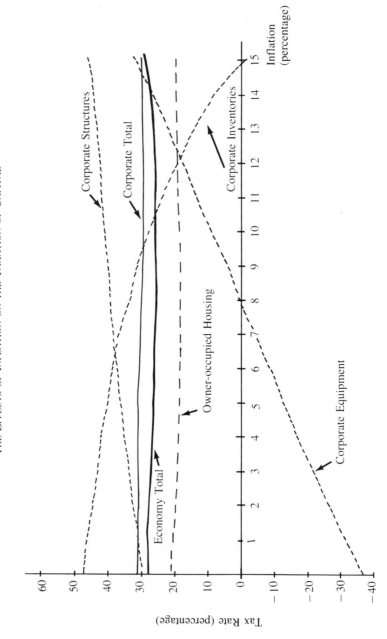

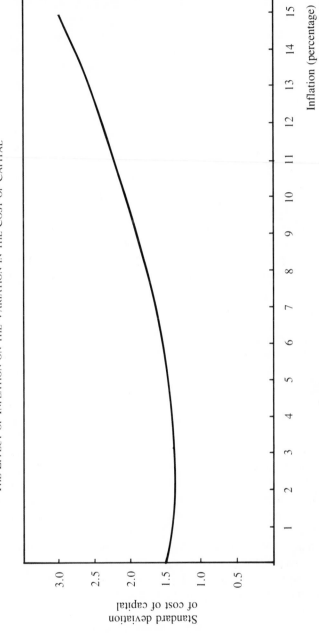

FIGURE 2

THE EFFECT OF INFLATION ON THE VARIATION IN THE COST OF CAPITAL

figure 1 indicates that the tax rate on owner-occupied housing is a U-shaped function of inflation. Initial inflation increases the nominal interest subsidy since τ_h is greater than τ_d, but subsequent inflation raises the latter rate for interest receipts above the former rate for interest deductions. Inflation then adds to the net tax in housing. Because this sector comprises a third of the total capital stock, the rate for the economy also exhibits a slight U-shaped pattern.

Figure 2 shows how inflation affects the variation in the cost of capital among assets and sectors. The standard deviation of ρ is about 1.5 percentage points when inflation is 5 percent and under. At 10 percent inflation it is one-fourth greater, and at 15 percent it is fully twice as great. Later in this section, we explore the sensitivity of these results to specifications of the model.

To summarize, high inflation seems to add more to interasset and intersectoral distortions than it adds to intertemporal distortions via overall capital costs. Because of offsetting effects from historical cost depreciation and from the taxation of interest, a rise in inflation does not affect the overall tax rate on capital. However, a rise in inflation does discourage investment in depreciable assets, thereby affecting efficiency in the use of capital.

Debt Finance

As the previous section on inflation points out, investments financed by debt are subsidized because firms that deduct interest payments are in a higher marginal tax bracket than the individuals who include interest receipts. Because the debt-to-capital ratio is about one-third in each of our three sectors, this subsidy can have a major effect on the cost of capital. This hypothesis is confirmed in our analysis of the 1982 law assuming all equity finance. These results employ the standard 7 percent inflation rate and are reported in column 2 of table 5. Without debt, the overall tax rate in the economy would rise from 26 to 38 percent. The largest increase, from 30 to 64 percent, would occur in the corporate sector, for two reasons. First, the differential between the statutory corporate rate and the personal tax rate on interest is a large 26 percentage points. Second, in the absence of debt, a larger fraction of the corporate capital stock would be taxed at the high rate for dividends. Under the assumption of no debt finance, the combination of the investment tax credit and depreciation allowances for equipment (in both the corporate and noncorporate sectors) would no longer be sufficient to offset other features of the income tax system, and these assets would face positive rates of tax.

For contrast, column 3 of table 5 presents marginal tax rates under the assumption of 100 percent debt finance at the margin. We find that the subsidies to investment in the corporate sector and in noncorporate equipment

TABLE 5

SENSITIVITY ANALYSIS FOR 1982 LAW

	1. Standard Parameters	2. No Debt	3. All Debt	4. No Property Tax	5. Alternative Model
Corporate sector tax rates					
Equipment	−.040	.483	−2.082	−.385	.169
Structures	.377	.668	−.464	.203	.424
Public utilities	.326	.640	−.561	.001	.372
Inventories	.356	.677	−.890	.238	.474
Land	.399	.694	−.665	.238	.493
Overall	.300	.640	−.847	.097	.398
Noncorporate sector tax rates					
Equipment	−.056	.107	−.528	−.249	−.042
Structures	.293	.378	.082	.169	.308
Public utilities	.241	.329	.026	.021	.257
Residential structures	.334	.408	.155	.131	.349
Inventories	.328	.418	.088	.255	.340
Land	.358	.439	.144	.255	.370
Residential land	.409	.478	.237	.255	.422
Overall	.327	.410	.116	.192	.341
Owner-occupied housing sector					
tax rates	.186	.179	.203	−.021	.231
Overall cost of capital	.068	.080	.049	.055	.075
Standard deviation	.017	.018	.017	.015	.012
Overall tax rate	.264	.376	−.025	.087	.329

are sizable, and that investment in other depreciable assets in the noncorporate sector faces very low rates of taxation.

Property Taxation

In column 4 of table 5, we show estimates of current law tax rates in the absence of the property tax. These may be useful for two purposes. First, the results highlight the importance of the property tax in measuring the cost-of-capital. This point is especially striking because many published measures of marginal tax rates on capital do not include taxes on wealth. Second, the estimates provide an alternative assessment of the tax system, under the view that property taxes are exactly offset at the margin by additional local public services. If taxpayers are sufficiently mobile and have sufficient choice among jurisdictions, then local property taxes are merely voluntary payments for local services and thus do not distort the marginal investment decision. We apply this Tiebout hypothesis to both residential and nonresidential capital.

For homeowners, whose implicit rents and capital gains go untaxed, the property tax is the only source of taxation. Without the property tax, the effective tax rate on owner-occupied housing drops from + 18.6 percent to − 2.1 percent. The remaining subsidy is due to the fact that mortgage payments are deducted by owner-occupants at a rate slightly higher than the rate at which they are included by holders of mortgage debt.

Nonresidential property taxes were estimated to be a lower fraction of the value of capital than were residential property taxes: rates ranged from 0.77 percent for equipment to 1.55 percent on public utilities, as opposed to 1.84 percent for housing. As a result, eliminating the property tax has a somewhat smaller effect in nonhousing sectors. Still, the effect is large enough to lower the overall tax rate in the economy from 26 to 9 percent. In addition, without differential property tax rates, the standard deviation in the cost-of-capital would fall from .017 to .015.

Assumptions About Arbitrage

Our standard model assumes that arbitrage takes place at the firm level: firms in all sectors compare the return to debt with the return on real capital, and they use the after-tax interest rate as the required after-tax return on all investments. The rate of return, net of personal taxes, averages .05 in the economy, but differences in the taxation of equity capital across the three sectors preclude the possibility of the same return, net of personal taxes, to all forms of investment. As described in the Appendix, an alternative model assumes arbitrage at the personal level. An investment in any sector would then earn a common return of .05, net of all taxes. In column 5 of table 5, we present the tax rates under this alternative model, using a universal net return of .05. All provisions of the tax law and all other assumptions are identical to those used in our standard estimates for 1982 law, which appear in column 1.

The most important message from this exercise is that the set of rates of return or rates of taxation varies with model assumptions. We cannot find "the" 1982 marginal tax rates. Tax rates under the alternative model are somewhat higher than under the standard model: 33 percent as opposed to 26 percent for the economy as a whole.[32] The previously reported subsidy of

---

corporate equipment becomes a tax of 17 percent. However, it is encouraging that the *ranking* of tax rates for different assets and sectors does not vary with the assumption about arbitrage. For example, equipment still faces the lowest tax rates, and corporate inventories and land the highest.

Two other differences in results deserve brief mention. First, in the alternative model, eliminating the corporate income tax causes a 2-point *cut* in the rate of taxation in the corporate sector (as opposed to a 2-point increase). Second, the variability in the overall cost-of-capital as a result of inflation is much less than in our standard model.

Assumptions About the Rate of Return

In another set of experiments, we use the standard model and vary s, the mean net-of-tax return. These results do not appear in the table. The overall tax rate falls from 36 percent at $s = .02$ to 25 percent at $s = .06$, which in part reflects the division of the tax wedge by a larger value of ρ. This result again underscores the fact that the measurement of tax rates is not unique. The sensitivity of the tax rate to the assumed after-tax rate of return appears to be especially large in the case of a subsidy: the tax rate on corporate equipment varies between -128 percent at $s = .02$ to $-.3$ percent at $s = .06$.

The study of sensitivity to s reveals a couple of pitfalls in judging relative tax rates for different assets. In a result reminiscent of the earlier inflation sensitivities, relative tax rates change as s changes. For example, while the tax rate for corporate land is 2 percentage points higher than the tax rate for corporate structures at our standard value for s, it is 45 percentage points lower when s is .02. Another case illustrates dramatically the sensitivity of the dispersion of asset tax rates to the choice of s. When s is .04, we find that all corporate equipment depreciated over 5 years is taxed at exactly the same rate, even though economic depreciation still varies among these assets. This anomalous result occurs because the corporate discount rate associated with an s of .04 happens to produce an equality between $(1-u)$ and $(1-k-uaz)$. Equations of the Appendix indicate that δ no longer enters in the determination of ρ under this condition.

Conclusions

We have examined the marginal effective total tax rates on capital as they have changed in the early 1980s, and we have analyzed how alternative reforms and alternative rates of inflation affect them. We have focused on both the magnitude of effective tax rates and the inefficiencies that these rates might induce.

In terms of rates, the tax law of 1982 results in a lower overall effective tax rate on capital than existed under 1980 law. It thus provides a larger incentive to invest in real capital. At 26 percent, this overall tax rate is also significantly lower than would be predicted by previous studies that looked at average rather than marginal tax rates or that emphasized equity finance at the margin.

In terms of efficiency, our analysis suggests that recent tax changes have not, on the whole, reduced tax differentials among different assets and industries. Our measure of the weighted deviation in the costs-of-capital across the economy remains unchanged from 1980 law. In other words, despite the reduction in overall tax rates, there has been no *apparent* improvement in the efficiency with which capital is allocated across its various uses. We also find that the corporate tax system makes significant contributions to tax rate differences, even though it makes negative contributions to the overall tax on marginal investments under our standard set of parameters. Additional inflation also contributes to tax rate disparities without adding to the overall tax burden. However, there is a lower weighted deviation for reforms such as the Auerbach-Jorgenson first-year capital recovery plan and integration of personal and corporate taxes.

APPENDIX

The first part of this appendix describes potential uses of the tax rates of this paper in examining intertemporal, intersectoral, and interasset features of tax reforms in the 1980s. The second part describes the exact computation of the tax rates presented in this paper.

The Use of Tax Rates to Measure Efficiency Gains and Losses

It is easiest to explain the applicability of our study in the context of previous efforts to measure the effects of tax distortions. In particular, we follow the tradition of Harberger who used an analytical general equilibrium model to measure the misallocation of real capital between the corporate and noncorporate sectors.[1] He found that the cost in efficiency from this distortion amounts to about one-half of 1 percent of GNP. This cost is a small fraction of a number as large as gross national product, but it amounts to between 10 and 20 percent of the revenue obtained from the additional tax on the corporate sector.

Shoven and Whalley showed how to incorporate taxes in a computational general equilibrium model with more consumer groups and production sectors,[2] and this method is used in the larger more recent general equilibrium

---

1. Arnold C. Harberger, "The Incidence of the Corporate Income Tax," *Journal of Political Economy*, vol. 70, no. 3 (June 1962), pp. 215–240; Arnold C. Harberger, "Efficiency Effects of Taxes on Income from Capital," in M. Krzyzaniak, ed., *Effects of Corporation Income Tax* (Detroit: Wayne State University Press, 1966).

2. John B. Shoven and John Whalley, "A General Equilibrium Calculation of the Effects of Differential Taxation of Income from Capital in the U.S.," *Journal of Public Economies*, vol. 8, no. 1 (August 1972). pp. 1–18.

82   THE LEGACY OF REAGANOMICS

model of Fullerton, Shoven and Whalley.[3] This model measures the misallocation of capital among eighteen industries, where tax differences arise because corporations make up a larger fraction of firms in some industries, and because corporations use different combinations of interest, dividends, and retained earnings. The model also measures the misallocation of resources over time that are due to extra taxes on saving for future consumption.

Tax rates in the FSW model are measured by the total of observed corporate taxes, property taxes, and personal taxes as a fraction of capital income in each industry. These tax rates can be revised to capture the effects of each alternative tax scheme, but rates are then held constant as the model calculates a new (counterfactual) allocation of capital among industries. For this reason, the model does not capture firms' efforts to affect their taxes by changing their mix of assets or by changing their corporate status.

Another problem is that these "average" effective tax rates, measured for existing assets, are applied to marginal uses of capital. Fullerton and Henderson amend the FSW model to measure "marginal" effective tax rates explicitly for each asset, using the cost-of-capital approach of Hall and Jorgenson. A further advantage of these marginal rates is that they can easily reflect changes in investment tax credits and depreciation allowances such as those introduced with the Accelerated Cost Recovery System (ACRS) in 1981. Yet the model in that paper assumes that each industry uses the different assets in fixed proportions. Thus, while it measures intertemporal and inter-industry distortions, it still omits interasset distortions.

Misallocations among assets are measured in papers by Hendershott and Hu[4] and Gravelle[5]. They calculate the marginal cost-of-capital in the corporate sector for each asset, and they assume Cobb-Douglas demands. By changing the cost-of-capital to reflect a new tax law, or even to remove all asset distortions, they can simulate the new economy-wide demand for each asset and measure the gain or loss in total output. The new allocation reflects

3. Don Fullerton, John B. Shoven, and John Whalley, "General Equilibrium Analysis of U.S. Taxation Policy," *1978 Compendium of Tax Research* (Washington, D.C.: Office of Tax Analysis, U.S. Treasury Department, 1978); Don Fullerton, John B. Shoven, and John Whalley, "Replacing the U.S. Income Tax with a Progressive Consumption Tax: A Sequenced General Equilibrium Approach," *Journal of Public Economics*, vol. 20, no. 1 (February 1983), pp. 2–23.

4. Patric Hendershott and Sheng-Cheng Hu, "Government-Induced Biases in the Allocation of the Stock of Fixed Capital in the United States," in George von Furstenberg, ed., *Capital, Efficiency and Growth* (Cambridge, Mass: Ballinger, 1980).

5. Jane G. Gravelle, "The Social Cost of Nonneutral Taxation: Estimates for Non-residential Capital," in Charles R. Hulten, ed., *Depreciation, Inflation, and the Taxation of Income from Capital* (Washington, D.C.: The Urban Institute Press, 1981); Gravelle, "Effects of 1981 Depreciation Revisions."

equilibrium in the market for real capital, but it is not a general equilibrium. Their models apply only to corporate capital, not total capital. They do not capture industry misallocations, and they do not capture intertemporal misallocation associated with the overall taxation of income from capital.

In this paper we compute tax rates that could be used in a more general model that incorporates all of these decisions simultaneously. When efficiency costs from all of these misallocations are combined, they can amount to substantially more than a half percent of GNP.

Such a model has four basic features. First, a marginal effective total tax rate (including corporate, personal, and property taxes) affects individual choices between present and future consumption. Saving for future consumption affects the total available supply of capital in subsequent periods. Second, in any one period, a marginal cost-of-capital formula is used to determine the demand for capital in each of the eighteen industries. Third, within each industry, separate cost-of-capital expressions are used to determine the division between corporate and noncorporate sectors. Fourth, within each sector of each industry, individual cost-of-capital calculations are used to determine demand for each of the different asset types.

In this general equilibrium model, we could simulate the change in any tax parameter such as a statutory rate, credit rate, or depreciation lifetime, and we could calculate new user costs for each asset. These user costs depend endogenously on the real after-tax rate of return determined in equilibrium. A composite of those costs applies to each sector of a given industry, and an additional composite of corporate and noncorporate costs applies to the overall use of capital for that industry. Each industry has a different mix of assets in each sector, as well as a different mix of sectors, all determined endogenously. When the total use of capital equals the total available supply, we have equilibrium in the capital market; when other markets clear as well, we have a general equilibrium.

In a generalized model, we would not be limited to a unitary elasticity of substitution among assets, as implied by the Cobb-Douglas functional form. Instead, capital in the corporate sector or in the noncorporate sector of each industry would be a different Constant of Elasticity of Substitution (CES) composite of the 38 assets. The elasticity of substitution among assets (ε) may be specified exogenously. Capital in each industry would be another CES function of composite capital stocks from each sector of that industry. The elasticity of substitution between corporate and noncorporate capital (σ) would also be pre-specified. When these elasticities are set to zero, the generalized model would reduce to the one in Fullerton and Henderson. When they are unity, the model would be very similar to that of Gravelle. This

generalization is important because the choices for ε and σ have much bearing
on the relative attractiveness of alternative proposals.

Measurement of the Cost of Capital and Effective Tax Rates

We start with a cost of capital formula like that developed by Hall and
Jorgenson. The underlying premise behind this formula is that the profit
maximizing firm will undertake a marginal investment project if it earns a
return net of tax such that the present value of cash flows is at least equal to
the initial outlay. Under competitive equilibrium conditions, the two will be
exactly equal.

Consider a marginal investment with an acquisition cost q, a rental price
c, and wealth tax rate of w per dollar of asset. The rental price is the amount
for which the asset could be rented if the owner covers maintenance, depreciation, and taxes. If the statutory marginal corporate income tax rate is u,
and if the property tax is deductible, then the rental net of property taxes and
corporate taxes is $(1-u)(c-wq)$. This return is treated as certain, and it grows
in nominal terms at the rate of inflation, π. Further assume that the quantity
of capital embodied in the investment declines at the economic depreciation
rate δ. As a consequence, the net-of-tax rental receipts from the investment
at time t will equal $(1-u)(c-wq)e^{(\pi-\delta)t}$. To derive the present value of such
a stream, these nominal cash flows would be discounted at the nominal after-
tax rate, r.

Capital cost recovery provisions affect the equilibrium rental rate in two
ways. First, an investment tax credit at rate k lowers the acquisition cost of
the asset from q to $(1-k)q$. Second, the firm receives a reduction in taxes as
a result of depreciation allowances. Let a denote the fraction of purchase
price that is eligible for depreciation allowances. The present value of this
deduction per dollar of basis will be denoted by z, so the total tax reduction
is $uazq$. The particular value for z will reflect the discount rate, the tax lifetime
for the asset, the depreciation schedule, and whether allowances are based
on historical or replacement cost. With the inclusion of all these features of
the tax code, the equilibrium condition is expressed as:

$$(1-k)q = \int_0^\infty (1-u)(c-wq)e^{(\pi-\delta)t}e^{-rt}dt + uazq \qquad (A1)$$

From this expression we can solve for the rental rate c/q as a function of the tax parameters as well as r, δ, and π. Finally, since c/q is gross of depreciation, we subtract δ to obtain the corporation's real rate of return net of depreciation:

$$\rho^c = \frac{c}{q} - \delta = \frac{r - \pi + \delta}{1 - u} (1 - k - uaz) + w - \delta \qquad (A2)$$

This crucial expression is used to find the cost to the corporate firm of employing any of the 38 assets. The discount rate, inflation rate, and corporate tax rate do not vary by asset, but parameters such as δ, k, a, z, and w are asset-specific. None of these parameters is specific to any industry.

In the noncorporate sector, we assume that the firm must earn at least its own discount rate r in nominal terms, after taxes at rate τ_{nc}, on any alternative investment. The noncorporate firm may use any of the 38 assets, and each has an equilibrium condition analogous to equation (A1) above.

$$\rho^{nc} = \frac{r - \pi + \delta}{1 - \tau_{nc}} [1 - k - \tau_{nc} az] + w - \delta \qquad (A3)$$

Corporate and noncorporate parameters are identical for depreciation rates (δ), investment tax credits (k), property taxes (w), basis adjustment (a), and depreciation schedules. Discount rates differ, however, so the present value of depreciation for any one asset (z) depends on the sector.

A final cost-of-capital formula applies to owner-occupied housing. This asset earns a rental rate c, minus property taxes, of which λ are deducted from the personal income tax at rate τ_h. The return $c - (1 - \lambda\tau_h)wq$ is not subject to income tax, but the investor receives no credits or depreciation allowances. The return grows in nominal terms at rate π, depreciates at its own rate δ, and is discounted at the individual's nominal after-tax rate r. Logic similar to that of (A1) and (A2) implies the equilibrium condition:

$$q = \int_0^\infty [c - (1 - \lambda\tau_h)wq] e^{(\pi - \delta)t} e^{-rt} dt \qquad (A4)$$

and the required rate of return:

$$\rho^h = \frac{c}{q} - \delta = r - \pi + (1 - \lambda\tau_h)w \qquad (A5)$$

The deductibility of mortgage interest is captured in the fact that these flows are discounted by an after-tax rate of return.

1. Arbitrage at the Firm Level

Next we outline two possible models for the choice of discount rates. In one model, as in Bradford and Fullerton,[6] we assume that the firm arbitrages between debt and real capital. Instead of making this investment, the firm can always use the marginal dollar of funds to retire a dollar of debt, an action which would earn the after-tax interest rate for the firm. Therefore, each alternative asset must yield the after-tax interest rate. If i is the nominal market interest rate, then the discount rate in the corporate sector is $i(l-u)$, in the noncorporate sector it is $i(l-\tau_{nc})$, and in owner-occupied housing it is $i(l-\tau_h)$. In any one sector, the discount rate does not depend upon the actual sources of finance.

A proportion c_{ns} of corporate investment is financed by new shares sold to individuals with tax rate τ_{ns}. These investments earn $i(l-u)$ after corporate taxes, and this return is paid as dividends to the owners who receive $i(l-u)(l-\tau_{ns})$ after all taxes. A proportion c_{re} is financed by retained earnings, and the return $i(l-u)$ is retained by the corporation. Individual owners are taxed at τ_{re}, the effective accrued rate on capital gains, and they receive $i(l-u)(l-\tau_{re})$ after taxes. A final proportion c_d is financed by debt sold to individuals with tax rate τ_d. The firm pays interest at rate i and the individual receives $i(l-\tau_d)$ after taxes. When these different individuals are aggregated, however, the average real net-of-tax return in the corporate sector is defined as:

$$s^c \equiv c_d\,[i(l-\tau_d)] \;+\; c_{re}\,[i(l-u)(l-\tau_{re})] \;+\; c_{ns}\,[i(l-u)(l-\tau_{ns})] \;-\; \pi \quad (A6)$$

When we compare the pre-tax return ρ^c to this average value of s^c, we implicitly assume that the marginal investment is financed by the average proportions of debt, retained earnings, and new shares.

In the noncorporate sector, a fraction n_d of investment is financed through the market for debt. The noncorporate firm pays the same interest rate i, it deducts interest at rate τ_{nc}, and the interest recipient earns $i(l-\tau_d)$ after taxes. The remaining share n_e is financed by equity of the entrepreneur, who earns $i(l-\tau_{nc})$ after taxes. The average real net return in the noncorporate sector is

$$s^{nc} \equiv n_d[i(l-\tau_d)] \;+\; n_e\,[i(l-\tau_{nc})] \;-\; \pi. \quad (A7)$$

Owner-occupants finance a fraction h_d through debt, pay the market interest rate i, and deduct interest payments at their statutory rate τ_h. The

---

6. David F. Bradford and Don Fullerton, "Pitfalls in the Construction and Use of Effective Tax Rates," in Charles R. Hulten, ed., *Depreciation, Inflation, and the Taxation of Income from Capital* (Washington, D.C.: The Urban Institute Press, 1981).

equity-financed share h_e must therefore earn $i(l - \tau_h)$, and the average real net return is

$$s^h \equiv h_d \left[i(l - \tau_d) \right] + h_e[i(l - \tau_h)] - \pi. \tag{A8}$$

The average real net return for the economy is

$$s \equiv \frac{K^c s^c + K^{nc} s^{nc} + K^h s^h}{K^c + K^{nc} + K^h}, \tag{A9}$$

where K refers to the stock of capital in each sector.

All calculations could proceed by setting the single market interest rate i. In the corporate sector, for example, the discount rate would be $i(l - u)$, the pre-tax return would be given by (A2), and the after-tax return would be given by (A6). Instead, we wish to use the *ceteris paribus* assumption that the average real net return s is constant across alternative tax regimes and different inflation rates. For this reason, we set s at .05 in each case and then calculate the interest rate compatible with above equations. We substitute (A6) – (A8) into (A9) and solve for i as a function of s, π, tax rates, finance shares, and capital stocks. Under 1982 law with 7 percent inflation, for example, i is .181. Because nominal income is subject to tax, inflation adds more than proportionately to nominal interest in order to maintain the fixed real after-tax return s. This relationship between π and i is not based on empirical observations but is a necessary consequence of the *ceteris paribus* assumption on s.

2. Arbitrage at the Individual Level

The assumption of arbitrage at the firm level precludes the possibility of arbitrage at the personal level. Individuals receive $i(l - \tau_d)$ if they purchase debt, $i(l - u)(l - \tau_{ns})$ if they purchase new shares, $i(l - \tau_{nc})$ if they invest in a noncorporate firm, or $i(l - \tau_h)$ if they invest in housing. In an alternative model, we could assume that individuals would adjust their portfolios until all these returns were equal to the real net return from holding debt, s, redefined as $i(l - \tau_d) - \pi$. The corporation's discount rate for debt is still $i(l - u)$, but a new share issue would have to earn a return after corporate taxes such that dividends could be taxed at rate τ_{ns} and still provide $i(l - \tau_d)$ to the saver. The discount rate for new shares thus equals $i(l - \tau_d)/(l - \tau_{ns})$. By a similar logic, the discount rate for retained earnings finance is $i(l - \tau_d)/(l - \tau_{re})$. A weighted-average discount rate for the corporation may be defined as:

$$c_d[i(l - u)] + c_{ns}[i\left(\frac{l - \tau_d}{l - \tau_{ns}}\right)] + c_{re} [i\left(\frac{l - \tau_d}{l - \tau_{re}}\right)] \qquad (A10)$$

We can set s at .05 calculate i as $(s + \pi)/(l - \tau_d)$, and use (A10) for corporate discounting.

By analogy, the entrepreneur's cost of deductible debt finance is $i(l - \tau_{nc})$. The equity-financed investment must earn enough that the entrepreneur as an individual can pay taxes at rate τ_{nc} and still match the return to holding debt, $i(l - \tau_d)$. The weighted discount rate in the noncorporate sector is thus:

$$n_d[i(l - \tau_{nc})] + n_e[i(l - \tau_d)] \qquad (A11)$$

By further analogy, the weighted discount rate in housing is

$$h_d[i(l - \tau_h)] + h_e[i(l - \tau_d)] \qquad (A12)$$

This second model has the advantage of a single after-tax return, but this time the assumption of arbitrage at the *personal* level precludes the possibility of arbitrage at the *firm* level. The corporation's marginal investment earns a certain return after taxes given by (A10), an amount which exceeds $i(l - u)$. The firm thus foregoes the opportunity to make pure profits by issuing one more unit of debt and undertaking one more unit of investment.

It would be possible to reconcile these alternative models by introducing a risk premium on equity and a portfolio choice model for individuals. Instead, for this perfect certainty model, we choose reconciliation through market segmentation. Firms arbitrage between debt and real capital, as in the first model, and equilibrium is established as in Miller.[7] Because some individuals hold only debt and others hold only equity, there is no arbitrage at the personal level. Thus we use the first model for primary calculations in this paper, but we test the sensitivity of these results by providing calculations based on the second model.

A final note regards the presentation of each tax law in our tables. The relevant information is embodied in various values of ρ, the gross-of-tax returns, but we sometimes find it easier to interpret effective tax rates. Since the various values of s represent the returns net of all taxes, the differences $\rho - s$ represent the combination of corporate taxes, property taxes, and personal taxes. If this difference is expressed as a fraction of ρ, we have a marginal effective total tax rate. These effective tax rates can be measured for each corporate asset by using $(\rho^c - s^c)/\rho^c$, for each noncorporate asset by

    7. Merton Miller, "Debt and Taxes," *Journal of Finance*, vol. 32, no. 2 (May 1977), pp. 261–275.

using $(\rho^{nc} - s^{nc})/\rho^{nc}$, or for owner-occupied housing by using $(\rho^h - s^h)/\rho^h$. For notational simplicity, we suppressed the index for assets $(i = 1 \ldots 38)$ in all expressions above. If we use ρ_i^c to denote ρ^c for asset i, and use K_{ij}^c to denote the stock of that asset in the corporate part of industry j, then the effective tax rate for the corporate part of industry j may be defined as:

$$t_j^c \equiv \frac{\Sigma_i K_{ij}^c(\rho_i^c - s^c)}{\Sigma_i K_{ij}^c \rho_i^c} \tag{A13}$$

We calculate similar tax rates for the noncorporate sector, replacing all c superscripts with nc superscripts. An overall rate for that industry is defined as the sum of the numerators from t_j^c and t_j^{nc} divided by the sum of the denominators. (The housing industry combines rental and owner-occupied housing instead of corporate and noncorporate sectors.) An overall rate for the economy is similarly defined as the sum of the numerators from all industry tax rates divided by the sum of the denominators.

HOW MUCH HAVE THE REAGAN ADMINISTRATION'S TAX AND SPENDING POLICIES INCREASED WORK EFFORT?

Robert H. Haveman

Changes in social policy and personal income tax rates have been the primary means used by the Reagan administration to affect the work incentives and the economic well-being of individuals and households. Until now, most analyses of these policies have focused on the flow of funds that these measures have entailed and on the distribution of the net gains and losses experienced by families of various income levels.[1] These analyses conclude that the cuts in human resources programs have cost low-income families from two to three times the losses imposed on higher-income people.[2] Conversely, higher-income families have gained substantially from tax reductions relative to lower-income families, with the lowest-income families experiencing no gain, they being largely exempt from taxation.[3]

These gain-loss comparisons are useful for assessing the equity impact of Reagan policies, but they do not take into account the fact that a primary rationale for these measures concerns the incentives for increased work which

---

Comments and suggestions on earlier drafts of the paper by Gary Burtless, Sheldon Danziger, Irwin Garfinkel, Jerry Hausman, Robert Lampman, Robert Moffitt, Isabel Sawhill, Robert Triest, and Barbara Wolfe are gratefully acknowledged.

1. U.S. Congressional Budget Office (CBO), *"Major Legislative Changes in Human Resources Programs Since January, 1981,"* Staff memorandum, August 1983; and John Palmer and Isabel Sawhill, eds., *The Reagan Experiment* (Washington, D.C.: The Urban Institute Press, 1982).

2. CBO, "Major Legislative Changes."

3. Palmer and Sawhill, *The Reagan Experiment.* In fact, the effective federal tax rate for households classified as poor has increased since 1980 as a result of increases in the payroll tax. The poor are effectively exempt from personal income tax. See Sheldon Danziger and Eugene Smolensky, "Abrupt Changes in Social Policy: The Redistributive Effects of Reagan's Budget and Tax Cuts," mimeographed, University of Wisconsin—Madison, 1983.

they embody. Less social spending, it is claimed, will induce less dependence on government, and hence more work and savings; lower tax rates and burdens will also stimulate labor supply. These supply-side effects of the policies must be measured in any assessment of the extent to which the administration's strategy is likely to achieve its economic goals.

Assessing the magnitude of the responses to changed incentives is more difficult than estimating direct distributional effects, and no studies that attempt to quantitatively evaluate this dimension of Reagan policy have been completed. What does exist is a solid body of economic theory that suggests the direction of changes in behavior which various policies will call forth, and a more or less reliable body of research that provides quantitative evidence of the extent of the changes in behavior induced by past policy measures.[4] In the following sections, we will rely on this theory and the empirical estimates—along with knowledge of the nature of the policy changes—to assess the impact of Reagan policies on work effort. Because the main impacts are judged to stem from changes in human resources programs and personal income taxes, we focus on them.

The basic question we address in this paper is: to what extent have changes in human resources programs and personal income taxation sponsored by the Reagan administration caused increases or decreases in desired work effort among various population groups and in the population as a whole?

In answering this question, we take the base-year population to be that in 1980, and ask how the *desired* labor supply for this population would have been altered if the policy changes attributable to the Reagan administration had been in effect in that year. In making this assessment, we will be forced to make several heroic assumptions, because data and empirical estimates that would permit a more reliable evaluation do not exist. We will be explicit about these assumptions, however, so that their effects on the conclusion can be determined.

The first section describes the nature of the changes in human resources and personal tax policy attributable to the Reagan administration. The second section assesses, in qualitative terms, the effect of these changes on the work

---

4. Sheldon Danziger, Robert Haveman, and Robert Plotnick, "How Income Transfer Programs Affect Work, Savings, and the Income Distribution: A Critical Review," *Journal of Economic Literature*, vol. 19 (September 1981), pp. 975–1021; and Robert Lampman, "How Has the Labor Supply Changed in Response to Recent Increases in Social Welfare Expenditures and the Taxes to Pay for Them?," mimeographed, University of Wisconsin—Madison, April 1983; and Jerry Hausman, "The Effects of Taxes on Labor Supply," in H. Aaron and J. Pechman, eds., *How Taxes Affect Economic Behavior* (Washington, D.C.: The Brookings Institution, 1981).

incentives that working-age individuals in each of six population groups face.[5] The third section provides quantitative estimates of the desired labor-supply responses of each of the groups likely to have been stimulated by the incentives incorporated in the Reagan policy changes. The last section summarizes the results of the analysis and presents cautions regarding the interpretation of these results.

The Reagan Administration's Social Program and Personal Tax Policies

Through budget cuts, program restructuring, and cuts in personal income tax rates that will ultimately total 23 percent, the Reagan administration has attempted to alter the trend of the past decade in both the size and composition of the federal government's activities. The expected changes in the size and structure of the government's budget from 1981 to 1986 relative to the pre-1980 period are shown in table 1. The relative size of defense spending is expected to grow from 30 percent of the budget to at least 35 percent by 1986. This shift is to come at the expense of domestic programs, largely those in the human resources area. Although outlays were planned to drop from 23 percent of gross national product (GNP) to 19 percent, the recession of 1982–1983 is, in fact, expected to raise the figure to 24 percent by FY 1986. The spending cuts and program restructuring were designed to reduce the role of the government in equalizing the income distribution and reducing poverty—policies that were seen as inhibiting initiative and economic growth. While a human resources program "safety net" was to be maintained for people with few other resources, the cuts were designed to wean people receiving public support from dependence on government. Similarly, the cuts in personal income tax rates were designed to reduce the burden of government and thereby encourage initiative, enterprise, and work.

Table 2 catalogues the primary legislative changes in human resources and personal tax policies that were enacted from January 1981 to August

---

5. The population groups on which we focus are these:
    1. Persons age sixty-two and older
    2. Disabled persons under age sixty-two
    3. Female family heads with children
    4. Persons ages sixteen through twenty-four not in categories (2) or (3)
    5. Women ages twenty-five through sixty-one not in categories (2) or (3)
    6. Men ages twenty-five through sixty-one not in category (2).
These groups are mutually exclusive and include the entire working-age population (i.e., all children under age 16 are excluded).

TABLE 1

THE COMPOSITION OF THE FEDERAL BUDGET, FY 1965, FY 1981, FY 1986

(Percentages)

Category	Actual Budget		Reagan's Budget Proposal for 1986 as Presented in 1981 (3)	February 1983 CBO Estimates for 1986 (4)
	1965 (1)	1981 (2)		
National defense, international affairs, and benefits and services for veterans	50.4	29.5	40.1	34.9
Transportation, community and regional development, and revenue sharing	6.5	6.0	3.7	4.6
Natural resources and environment, energy, and agriculture	5.8	4.5	2.5	2.4
Income security	21.7	34.3	32.8	31.6
Health	1.4	10.0	11.2	11.6
Education, training, employment, and social services	1.9	4.8	2.5	3.0
General government, interest, general science, space and technology, other	14.8	15.5	11.3	13.7
Offsetting receipts	−2.6	−4.6	−4.4	−1.9
TOTAL	100.0	100.0	100.0	100.0
TOTAL OUTLAYS as a percentage of GNP	18.0	23.0	19.0	24.1
TOTAL OUTLAYS (billions of current dollars)	118.4	657.2	912.0	999.0

SOURCE: Office of Management and Budget, The United States Budget in Brief, Fiscal Year 1975 (Washington, D.C.: Government Printing Office, 1975), p. 48. Council of Economic Advisers, Economic Report of the President, January 1981 (Washington, D.C.: Government Printing Office, 1981), p. 315. Congressional Budget Office, Baseline Budget Projections for Fiscal Years 1984–1988, Part II (Washington, D.C.: Government Printing Office, 1983), p. 74.

NOTE: Some slight errors may exist due to reclassification of categories between 1965 and the present.

1983 in response to the Reagan initiative (see column 3).[6] The four-year *cumulative* (FY 1982–FY 1985) reduction in federal outlays on human resources programs totals $112 billion. The aggregate reduction in personal tax liabilities over this period is $360 billion. On balance, then, individual households experience an aggregate increase in "income" (including in-kind services valued at cost) of $248 billion ($360 billion less $112 billion) over the four-year period as a result of the policy changes reported in the table.

Most of the reductions in individual program outlays from FY 1981 to FY 1983 are less than 10 percent of their January 1, 1981 levels; exceptions are Social Security Disability Insurance (SSDI), Aid to Families with Dependent Children (AFDC), Food Stamps, Child Nutrition, other health services, education programs, and employment and training programs. In dollar terms, most of the outlays for individual programs were reduced by less than $5 billion; the exceptions are SSDI, Unemployment Insurance, Food Stamps, Child Nutrition, Medicare, Guaranteed Student Loans, employment and training programs, and public service employment (PSE) programs.

The reductions in program outlays are targeted on a limited set of groups. Table 3 provides an estimate of the outlay reductions experienced by each of six mutually exclusive and comprehensive groups of working-age persons. Two columns of impacts are indicated: column 2 shows only the reductions directly targeted on a particular group, as designated in table 2; column 3 adds to these directly targeted cuts the reductions targeted on more than one of the groups, prorated among groups in proportion to population. Column 4 describes the per capita four-year reduction in outlays that each of the groups experiences.

The numbers in table 3 must be interpreted with caution. They indicate that persons age sixty-two or older, disabled persons, and female family heads have borne most of the cuts in program expenditures. Over the four-year period, FY 1982 through FY 1985, benefit losses among members of these groups are estimated to have averaged $1,000 or more—at least $250 per person per year. Within any group, however, the cuts are not distributed equally among individuals. Selected persons in each of the groups—for example, disabled persons who are actually removed from SSDI rolls, AFDC recipients with more than 150 percent of the state needs standard, families denied a guaranteed student loan, workers who lost their public service jobs—have been especially hurt.

---

6. Allocation of responsibility for policy changes to either the Reagan administration or Congress is judgmental. For example, are the changes in the Social Security retirement program appropriately attributed to the administration, or to the bipartisan Greenspan Commission appointed by the president, or to Congress? In the discussion that follows, most changes in policy enacted from 1981 to 1983 were attributed to the administration.

TABLE 2
REAGAN ADMINISTRATION CHANGES IN HUMAN RESOURCES AND PERSONAL TAX POLICIES AND THE IMPLICATIONS

Policy Area	Number Recipients, 1980 (Millions)	Nature of Policy Changes	Percentage Change from Amount Projected with 1981 Legislation	Total ($ billions)	Primary Population Group Affected	Nature of Work Incentive Effects
1. Social Security Retirement[a]	30.5	• Six-month delay in cost-of-living adjustment • Increase in employers' payroll tax (1984) • Eliminate benefits for 18–22 year olds • Taxation of higher income recipient benefits (1984)	−3	−19.1	Persons age >62	• Very small decrease in expected benefit level; no change in benefit reduction rate except for higher-income recipients
2. Social Security Disability	4.8	• See (1) above • Fourfold increase in case-load investigations and cessations, 1980–82 • Increased stringency in application of eligibility criteria	−10	−5.0	Disabled persons age <62	• Little reduction in benefits if awarded; large reduction in probability of receiving if applying, and in retaining if receiving; no change in benefit reduction rate
3. Civil Service and Railroad Retirement	2.8	• Slight modification in benefit calculations and indexing	−3	−2.5	Persons age >62	• Very small reduction in expected benefit levels; increased discouragement to early retirement

Program						
4. Veterans' Retirement and Disability Compensation and Pension	4.1	• Technical changes in benefit and COLA calculations	−1	−.6	Persons age >62 Disabled <62	• Very small reduction in expected benefit levels
5. Supplemental Security Income	4.2	• Technical changes in benefit and COLA calculations in 1982 • 6.6 benefit increase in 1983 • Increased stringency in application of eligibility criteria for blind and disabled component of program	+4.5	+1.4	Persons age >62; disabled <62	• Small increase in expected benefits; no change in benefit reduction rate; reduction in probability of receiving if applying
6. Unemployment Insurance	10.0	• Unemployment rate required to trigger extended benefits increased in 1981 • Supplemental compensation to exhaustees in 1982 and 1983 • Increased taxation of benefits for higher-income beneficiaries	−7[a]	−7.8	Men–women ages 16–61	• Benefits maintained through periodic extensions of supplemental compensation; increased taxation of benefits for higher-income recipients
7. Aid to Families with Dependent Children	10.5	• Elimination of $30 and ⅓ exclusion after 4 months • Reduced deductions for work-related expenses	−13	−4.8	Female family heads with children	• Large increase in benefit reduction rates • Benefit elimination and income loss for women with substantial work

TABLE 2 (continued)

Policy Area	Number Recipients, 1980 (Millions)	Nature of Policy Changes	Percentage Change from Amount Projected with 1981 Legislation	Total ($ billions)	Primary Population Group Affected	Nature of Work Incentive Effects
		• Elimination of benefits for post-secondary students and for persons with 150% of state needs standard • Step-parent income counted for persons with step-parent in home • Retrospective accounting and reporting • Authorization for workfare				effort; both increase and decrease in incentive implied • Reduction in expected benefits because of reduction in work-related expenses; reduced attractiveness of program relative to work
8. Food Stamps	22.0	• 1982 COLA and postponement of later adjustments • Elimination of benefits for those with incomes >130% of poverty level	−13	−7.0	Female family heads with children; persons age >62 on SSI; disabled <62 on SSI	• Benefit elimination and income loss for higher-income recipients • Reduced relative attractiveness of program because of reduced benefits
9. Child Nutrition (primarily National School Lunch Program)	25.0	• Reduction in federal subsidy rates	−25	−5.0	Men-women ages 16–61	• Reduction in expected benefit; very little change in work incentive
10. Housing Assistance	10.0	• Reduction in *new* housing assistance commitments • Increase of tenant rents from 25 to 30 percent of adjusted income	−4	−1.8	All groups	• Increased benefit reduction rate

Program				Target Group	Effects
11. Low-Income Energy Assistance	20.0	−8	−.7	All groups	• Increased discretion in administration • Constant appropriations at 1980 level • Reduction in expected benefits
12. Medicare	29.0	−5	−13.2	Persons age >62; Disabled <62	• Reduction in hospital reimbursements • Increase in copayments for radiology and pathology services • Some increase in premiums • Slight reduction in expected benefits
13. Medicaid	20.0	+4.5	−3.9	All groups, but primarily persons age >62 and female family heads with children	• Some reduction in federal grants to states • Slight reduction in expected benefits • Reduction in rolls due to AFDC changes
14. Other Health Services	NA	−22	−1.4	Men-women ages 16–61	• Reduction in appropriations • No perceptible effect on work incentive except as a result of reduction in expected benefits
15. Compensatory Education (inc. Head Start)	NA	+13	−2.6	All groups	• Reduction in appropriations • No work-incentive effects
16. Vocational Education	NA	−12	+.6	Persons ages 16–24	• Reduction in appropriations • Some reduction in net benefits of vocational rehabilitation, resulting in increased labor supply

TABLE 2 (continued)

Policy Area	Number Recipients, 1980 (Millions)	Nature of Policy Changes	Percentage Change from Amount Projected with 1981 Legislation	Total ($ billions)	Primary Population Group Affected	Nature of Work Incentive Effects
17. Guaranteed Student Loans and Other Student Assistance	3.5	• Requirement for demonstration of need for higher-income families, and increase in fees • Reduction in Pell grants for needy students	−18	−5.9	Persons ages 16–24	• Some reduction in net benefits of college attendance, resulting in increased labor supply
18. Social and Community Services Block Grants	NA	• Reduction in outlays	−25	−3.9	All groups	• No discernible work-incentive effects
19. General Employment and Training Program	NA	• Reduction in outlays	−35	−7.4	Men-women ages 16–61	• Reduction in options for training; increase in probability of labor-force participation
20. Public Service Employment	.6	• Elimination of program	−100	−16.9	Men-women ages 16–61	• Reduction of employment opportunities implies some reduction in labor-force participation
21. Job Corps	.05	• Some reduction in outlays	−6	−.1	Men-women ages 16–24	• Slight reduction in work-training opportunities and labor-force participation
22. Work-Incentive Programs	1.6	• Reduction in outlays	−33	−.6	Female family heads with children	• Some reduction in work-training-placement opportunities and labor-force participation

TOTAL OF OUTLAY CHANGES (1)–(22)

−112.0

| 23. Individual Personal Income Tax Rates | — | +26 | +360 | All groups, except bottom 15 percent of population with incomes below personal tax cut-in level | • Phased reduction in rates, from 1.25 percent in 1981 to 23 percent in 1984
• Reduction of highest tax rate on regular income from 70 to 50 percent in 1982
• Reduction of highest rate on capital gains income from 28 to 20 percent in 1982
• Expanded retirement savings incentives
• Indexing of rates in 1985 | • Reduction in marginal tax rates, targeted on higher-income tax-payers
• Higher disposable income for all tax-payers except those with zero tax liability
• Income and substitution effects work in opposite directions |

SOURCE: "Major Legislative Changes," and Joseph Minarik, "Tax Policy in the Budgetary Context of the 1980s," Urban Institute Discussion Paper, September 1983.

a. Two of the changes listed represent increases in taxation; the outlay impact is a net outlay figure.

TABLE 3

DISTRIBUTION OF CHANGED OUTLAYS RESULTING FROM REAGAN ADMINISTRATION'S CHANGES IN HUMAN RESOURCES POLICIES, FY 1982–FY 1985, BY POPULATION GROUP

Population	1980 Population (Millions) (1)	Allocable Outlay Reductions FY 1982–FY 1985 ($ billions) (2)	Allocated Plus Prorated Outlay Reductions FY 1982–FY 1985 ($ billions) (3)	Per Capita Allocated Plus Prorated Outlay Reductions FY 1982–FY 1985, (3) ÷ (1) (4)
1. Persons age 62 and older	30.5	35.4	43.6	1,430
2. Disabled persons under age 62	7.1	5.0	6.9	972
3. Female family heads with children	6.6	5.4	8.8	1,333
4. Persons ages 16–24 not in categories (2) or (3)	35.4	6.6	19.7	556
5. Women ages 25–61 not in categories (2) or (3)	43.9	—	16.3	371
6. Men ages 25–61 not in category (2)	45.7	—	16.9	370
Not targeted	—	59.8	—	—
TOTAL	169.0	112.2	112.2	664

SOURCE: Calculations by author; see table 2.

The reductions in personal income tax rates sponsored by the administration represent supply-side economics in its purest form. The personal tax changes contained in the Economic Recovery Tax Act of 1981 (ERTA) were modeled on the Kemp-Roth plan proposed a few years earlier; marginal tax rates were reduced in stages but cumulating to a 23 percent reduction in three years. The reduction amounted to 1.25 percent in calendar-year 1981, 10 percent in 1982, 19 percent in 1983, and 23 percent in 1984 and subsequent years. Moreover, beginning in calendar-year 1982 the maximum marginal tax rate was reduced to 50 percent, with accompanying reductions in capital gains taxation.

The reductions in tax rates were designed to be across-the-board cuts, not targeted at any particular population group. However, the tax cuts were substantially larger for higher-income taxpayers than for lower-income taxpayers, both in absolute amount and as a proportion of before-tax income.[7]

Work-Incentive Effects of the Reagan Administration's Policies

Human Resources Program Changes and Work Incentives

Given the targeting of program cuts on aged and disabled persons and female family heads, these groups are likely to have experienced the greatest changes in work incentives. In the following paragraphs, an impressionistic description of the changes in labor-supply incentives attributable to the program changes is presented for each of the six groups. The focus is on *desired* work effort, as opposed to actual work effort, and hence the adverse effects of the recession of 1982–83 on the demand for labor are not considered.

Persons Age Sixty-Two and Older. Of the total of $44 billion of program reductions from 1982 through 1985 targeted on the older population, $19 billion is in the Social Security retirement program and $13.2 billion in the Medicare program. While retirement benefits were reduced about 3 percent (through the COLA delay and the taxation of benefits of higher-income recipients), there was no change in benefit reduction rates for retirees (except that associated with the taxation of benefits). The Medicare cuts were largely in hospital reimbursement levels.[8] There were even smaller impacts in the

---

7. CBO, *An Analysis of President Reagan's Budget Revisions for Fiscal Year 1982* (Washington, D.C.: Government Printing Office, 1981).

8. Assignment of these reductions to persons age sixty-two or more is heroic. Perhaps hospitals absorbed these changes, or shifted them to state and local governments, private organizations, or other hospital users. Arbitrary incidence assumptions pervade our assignments.

Civil Service and Railroad Retirement programs. The small size of the shifts
in the level or slope of the budget constraint indicate that expected benefits
(as a surrogate for the guarantee) fell slightly, while the implicit marginal tax
rate rose slightly. The impact of the first of these effects on the incentive to
work is positive, if leisure is a normal good; the impact of the second would
suggest a minor reduction in work effort.

Disabled Persons under Age Sixty-Two. This group experienced little
change in benefit levels or benefit reduction rates. However, because of a
significant increase in caseload investigations and stricter application of eligibility criteria, the probability of a recipient's retaining benefits or of an
applicant's receiving them was reduced. This increase in administrative dis-
cretion can be translated into work-incentive terms—for workers with health
problems, denial of access to benefits requires increased reliance on other
sources of income, such as work, if possible, or welfare.[9]

Female Family Heads with Children. The program changes for this
population group are concentrated primarily in the AFDC program. The restructuring of AFDC has both income and substitution effects that make
judgments about work incentives ambiguous. For example, the elimination
of benefits for working AFDC recipients with incomes in excess of 150 percent
of the state needs standard may cause some higher-income recipients to work
less so as to retain benefits, whereas others may work more to offset the
benefit loss. The increase in benefit reduction rates to 100 percent for recipients who are on the AFDC rolls for more than four months (and working)
will undoubtedly reduce the incentive for these people to work at the margin.
However, accepting the guarantee may be worse than working enough to
leave the rolls. And, mandatory workfare in some jurisdictions may offset
any reduction in desired work hours. The response will also vary according
to the fixed or variable nature of work-related expenses, the recipient's expected wage rate, her tastes for income versus leisure, and the interaction of
AFDC with Food Stamps and, especially, Medicaid.[10]

Persons Ages Sixteen through Twenty-Four. The work-incentive effects of the Reagan changes on young people derive primarily from changes
in two programs: the reduction in student aid and the reduction in support for

---

9. See Robert Haveman, Jennifer Warlick, and Barbara Wolfe, "Disability Transfers, Early
Retirement, and Retrenchment," in Gary Burtless and Joseph Pechman, eds., *Retirement and
Aging* (Washington, D.C.: The Brookings Institution, 1984) for an analysis of the effects of
Reagan retrenchment policies in the disability area on the income and earnings of disabled
workers affected by them.

10. Sally Davies, "The Effects of the 1981 Omnibus Budget Reconciliation Act on the
Well-being of AFDC Recipients in Wisconsin: A Simulation Analysis," mimeographed, University of Wisconsin—Madison, 1983.

training and public service employment. In the case of reductions in support for postsecondary schooling and training, the program changes decrease the attractiveness of non-labor-force options relative to working, and hence, are likely to increase labor-force participation. In the case of the education programs, however, the cuts are targeted at students from higher-income families. Hence, the positive labor-supply effects are likely to be small. The reductions in support for training are not so targeted, but the cuts are not enormous in either case—less than $15 billion over four years for both programs. The effect of the elimination of public service employment on work incentives is difficult to gauge. People employed in PSE jobs are labor-force participants. For some of these people, the elimination of PSE jobs will lead to alternative employment and no change in participation. For others, loss of PSE jobs may lead to increased reliance on income transfers (or other sources of support) and reductions in desired market work.

Men and Women Ages Twenty-Five through Sixty-One.   The Reagan administration's program changes have had the smallest impact on the work incentives facing this group. The reductions in training opportunities and the elimination of PSE jobs will have the same effects on this group as on youths. The changes in the Unemployment Compensation program, however, are targeted on this group. Because of periodic extensions of supplemental compensation, however, unemployment benefits have not been substantially reduced. The reductions that have occurred are likely to stimulate some additional job search and work effort, as is the taxation of unemployment benefits for higher-income recipients.

Personal Income Tax Reductions and Work Incentives

The Reagan administration's tax cuts are not targeted on any particular population group, although low-income families who are not liable for taxes do not benefit from the cuts. Because of the simplicity of the change enacted, the nature of the work-incentive effect is clear. By increasing disposable income, the tax cuts would be expected to increase the demand for leisure, on the presumption that leisure is a normal consumption good. The resulting reduction in labor supply would tend to be offset by the increase in the net wage associated with the reduced marginal tax rates. However, a full evaluation would also have to consider the effects on desired labor supply from equivalent reductions in net revenue through cuts in other taxes or borrowing, or the reduced size of government programs triggered by the tax cuts. Moreover, to the extent that the tax cuts do affect labor supply, general equilibrium changes in factor prices may result. For example, wage rates might be depressed in the relatively short run, attenuating the reduction in desired labor supply due to the tax cut. The net effect on labor supply could be either positive or negative, depending on the magnitude of the response generated by these various effects.

Work-Effort Responses to the Policy Changes

Identifying changes in the incentives to work caused by the policies is only the first step in assessing their impact on work effort. The next question is: How do various groups respond to these changes in incentives? The labor-supply estimation literature is voluminous, and some consistency in the estimated pattern of responses is now evident. For example, a study by Masters and Garfinkel[11] concluded that the labor-supply effect of an increase in expected income from transfer programs (holding benefit reduction rates constant) was about ten times greater for the aged than for prime-age men, and about four times greater for women and young people than for prime-age men. For prime-age men, the response to the guarantee was very small— about a 1 percent reduction in work effort for a $1,000 increase in the guarantee. The Masters-Garfinkel results also indicate that prime-age men and women are quite insensitive to changes in benefit reduction rates (net wages), but that a ten-percentage point increase in the benefit reduction rate would lead to a 2 percent reduction in work effort of female family heads with children, and a reduction of about twice that size for married women. Although other studies estimate somewhat different degrees of response,[12] these basic patterns are generally supported in the literature.

Response to Social Policy Changes

Table 4 presents the implications of the incentive changes caused by the social policy shifts attributable to the Reagan administration, and the expected responses to these incentive changes. The "counterfactual" on which these estimates rest is essential to their interpretation. In particular, it is assumed that (1) the legislation existing at the start of the Reagan administration would have remained unchanged over the succeeding four years, (2) the economy's performance from 1981 to 1983 would have been what was observed, and (3) economic performance from 1983 to 1985 would have been that projected

---

11. Stanley Masters and Irwin Garfinkel, *Estimating the Labor Supply of Income Maintenance Alternatives* (New York: Academic Press, 1977).

12. Michael Keeley, *Labor Supply and Public Policy* (New York: Academic Press, 1981).

TABLE 4

ROUGH ESTIMATES OF LABOR-SUPPLY EFFECTS OF THE REAGAN ADMINISTRATION'S SOCIAL POLICY CHANGES

Population Group	Number in Population, 1980 (Millions) (1)	Number in Civilian Labor Force, 1980 (Millions) (2)	FY 1981–FY 1985 Change in Work Incentives (3)	Responsiveness to Changes in Incentives (4)	Best-Guess Change in Full-Time Equivalents in Labor Force Due to Reagan Program Changes (Millions) (5)
1. Persons age 62 and older	30.5	5.4	Very small increase	High	0 to +.1
2. Disabled persons under age 62	7.1	2.5	Substantial increase	Moderate	+ .2 to +.4
3. Female family heads with children	6.6	4.6	Ambiguous	High	−0.6 to +.03
4. Persons ages 16–24 not in categories (2) or (3)	35.4	23.2	Very small increase	Moderate	0 to +.15
5. Women ages 25–61 not in categories (2) or (3)	43.9	27.8	Very small increase	Moderate	0 to +.2
6. Men ages 25–61 not in category (2)	45.7	43.7	De minimus	Low	0 to +.1
TOTAL	169.0	107.4			Upper bound = +.95 Lower bound = +.14

SOURCE: Columns (1) and (2), U.S. Census; columns (3)–(5), calculations by author.

in 1983.[13] Columns 1 and 2 show the size of the population and the size of the work force for each of the six groups in 1980. Column 3 shows the changes in work incentives implicit in the Reagan human resources budget cuts and program restructuring. (This assessment rests on the discussion in the previous section.) The extent of individual response to these incentive shifts, based primarily on the general patterns mentioned earlier, is suggested in column 4.[14] Column 5 presents a rough, back-of-the-envelope estimate of the changes in desired labor supply attributable to the Reagan administration's social policy changes.[15]

Overall, the changes associated with Reagan policies are likely to increase labor supply. Our upper-bound estimate of the work effort response to the social policy changes is an increase of 950,000 full-time-equivalent workers, about a 0.9 percent increase in aggregate labor supply. Two groups account for the bulk of this increase—disabled persons younger than sixty-two years of age who are eliminated from the disability rolls or denied access to them, and prime-age women, some of whom might enter the work force to offset income and benefit losses to members of their families. Our lower-bound estimate is an increase of 140,000 persons, or about 0.1 percent of the labor force. A reasonable intermediate estimate would be *an addition of about 400,000 to 500,000 person years in desired labor supply*, which represents about *a 0.3 to 0.4 percent increase in desired work effort*.

The group-specific estimates presented in column 5 of table 4 reflect both the nature of the policy changes affecting each group and the likely

---

13. CBO, "*Major Legislative Changes.*"

14. If the labor-supply results from the Seattle-Denver experiment are substituted for those in column 4, a somewhat different pattern would be indicated. See U.S. Department of Health and Human Services, Office of Income Security Policy, Assistant Secretary for Planning and Evaluation, *Final Report of the Seattle-Denver Income Maintenance Experiment* (Washington, D.C.: U.S. Government Printing Office, 1983). In response to experimental programs of the negative income tax type, working-age married men were found to reduce their desired labor supply by about 9 percent, working-age married women by about 20 percent, female family heads by about 14 percent, youths by well over 20 percent. If these response patterns had been relied upon in column 4, the pattern would read:

Persons Age 62 and Older	High
Disabled Persons under Age 62	Moderate
Female Family Heads with Children	Moderate
Persons Ages 16–24	High
Women Ages 25–61	High-moderate
Men Ages 25–61	Low

15. The estimates presented here are of *desired* labor supply. While labor supply desires can change almost instantaneously to a change in incentives, actual labor supply may adjust fairly slowly. For example, to make a change in work hours may require a change in employers. Because of the costs of making such changes (including the loss of seniority and job-specific human capital), the observed change in actual hours may lag well behind the change in desired hours of work.

response of the group to these changes. With the exception of female family heads with children, all the groups would be expected to increase their labor supply because of the changes. A large portion of this increase is due to reduced benefits—with leisure a normal good, reduced disposable income from reduced benefits implies a somewhat smaller demand for nonwork. A second sizable impact is due to the denial of access to support from transfer programs for persons with health problems (e.g., elimination of people from disability rolls) or persons with employment handicaps (e.g., low-skill youths or women with children), or a reduction in the attractiveness of alternatives to working (e.g., college attendance for youths). Reagan administration policies have not tended to cut benefit reduction rates; hence little increased labor supply can be expected from this effect. On the contrary, in the AFDC, Food Stamp, housing, and student aid areas, benefit reduction rates have been increased. For this reason, the lower-bound estimate for female family heads with children is shown to be negative. The appendix describes in more detail the basis for the estimates of each of the groups.

A rough check on the reasonableness of the 0.3 to 0.4 percent estimated labor-supply increase attributed to the Reagan administration's human resources and social policy changes can be obtained by comparing that figure to estimates of the change in labor supply attributed to the growth in income transfers during the 1960s and 1970s. Danziger, Haveman, and Plotnick[16] estimated that aggregate labor supply was reduced by about 5 percent because of the presence of income transfers equal to about 10 percent of GNP. The reduction in human resources outlays attributable to Reagan policies averages about $30 billion per year over the FY 1981–FY 1985 period, about 0.1 percent of GNP. If the Reagan budget cuts were similar to the growth of income transfers in terms of their effect on the shape and position of the budget constraint facing individuals, the cuts would imply an increase in labor supply of less than 0.1 percent. However, the Reagan administration's changes have been substantially different in a number of respects. Whereas the expansion in transfer policies was designed in part to minimize the adverse effect on labor supply, the Reagan administration's policies have been designed to secure large reductions in benefit recipiency and, hence, increases in work effort. For example, the Reagan administration has used administrative decisions and inflexible caps to eliminate people from transfer program recipiency (e.g., SSDI, AFDC, and PSE), directly forcing increased reliance on work effort and labor supply. Viewed in this context, the 0.3 to 0.4 percent estimated increase in labor supply seems reasonable.

---

16. "How Income Transfer Programs Affect Work, Savings, and the Income Distribution."

Response to Reductions in Income Tax Rates

The reductions in personal income tax rates sponsored by the Reagan administration affect all taxpayers, increasing disposable incomes and reducing marginal tax rates. The magnitude of the labor-supply impact of these changes, however, is likely to vary substantially across the income distribution. One approach to estimating the labor-supply effects of these changes in tax rates would follow the procedure used earlier for analyzing the response to spending program changes. Estimates of relevant labor-supply coefficients could be used in conjunction with calculated wage and income changes stemming from the tax cuts, and the implied change in labor supply calculated. If the relevant coefficients were available for all of the income and demographic groups, such a calculation could yield group-specific estimates of labor-supply responses, and hence the effect of the tax cut on aggregate desired labor supply.[17]

A better approach would be to model the labor-supply effects of taxation directly, taking explicit account of the characteristics of the tax system and their impact on the budget constraint of various individuals. This approach has been followed in a series of studies by Hausman[18] and by Hausman and Ruud.[19] In the work by Hausman and Hausman and Ruud, the effect of both the existing tax structure (as of 1975) and changes in the tax (and welfare) systems on the work effort of married men, their wives, and female-headed families with children have been directly estimated. These analyses take explicit account of the nonlinearity (and perhaps, nonconvexity) of the budget constraints people face as a result of progressive income taxes—together with payroll taxes, and transfer payments—and of the fixed costs of working.

17. Such a procedure has been followed in estimating the labor-supply response to negative and credit income tax proposals using the "KGB" microdata simulation model developed at the U.S. Department of Health and Human Services. See David Betson, David Greenberg, and Richard Kasten, "A Microsimulation Model for Analyzing Alternative Welfare Reform Proposals: An Application to the Program for Better Jobs and Income," in R. Haveman and K. Hollenbeck, *Microeconomic Simulation Models for Public Policy Analysis* (New York: Academic Press, 1980); and "A Simulation Analysis of the Economic Efficiency and Distributional Effects of Alternative Program Structures: The Negative Income Tax versus the Credit Income Tax," in I. Garfinkel, ed., *Income-Tested Transfer Programs: The Case For and Against* (New York: Academic Press, 1982).

18. Jerry Hausman, "The Effects of Taxes on Labor Supply," in H. Aaron and J. Pechman, eds., *How Taxes Affect Economic Behavior* (Washington, D.C.: The Brookings Institution, 1981); and Hausman, "Income and Payroll Tax Policy and Labor Supply," in L. Meyer, ed., *The Supply-Side Effects of Economic Policy* (St. Louis: Center for the Study of American Business, 1981).

19. Jerry Hausman and Paul Ruud, "Family Labor Supply with Taxes," National Bureau of Economic Research, Working Paper 1271, February 1984.

Moreover, Hausman's model explicitly allows for the diversity of tastes among the population in estimating labor-supply behavior. A key measurement technique is what Hausman calls "virtual income"—the income a person would receive if his or her marginal tax rate were fixed on a segment of the budget constraint, but work hours equaled zero. This virtual income is, in effect, Hausman's nonlabor income through which the labor-supply response to income changes from taxation is measured. The method and conceptual basis of Hausman's approach have gained widespread acceptance.

This framework was used by Hausman to estimate a labor-supply function for a sample of about 1,100 married men ages twenty-five to fifty-five from the Michigan Panel Study of Income Dynamics (PSID) data for 1975.[20] The uncompensated wage coefficients Hausman obtained differ somewhat from those obtained in other studies, but they are not sorely deviant. The estimated income elasticities are very large compared with those that other researchers found. And when they are applied using Hausman's approach, they yield much larger estimated reductions in labor supply due to the tax and transfer programs than do other studies. Indeed, the total response to Hausman's estimated income and wage coefficients must be viewed as an upper-bound estimate.

Table 5 presents the estimated wage and income coefficients from Hausman's studies for married men and their wives who work. It also summarizes his estimates of the effect of the existing federal tax system on the labor supply of both husbands and wives and of 10 and 30 percent cuts in personal income tax rates on the labor supply of these men and their wives.

Hausman concludes that for the husband with average tastes who is in the $8,000 to $12,000 income bracket, the *existing federal tax system* results in an 8.5 percent[21] reduction in work effort; Hausman claims that the tax system reduces the labor supply of working wives by more than 18 percent.[22]

This extremely large estimate of the labor-supply response of wives to the existing (pre-Reagan) federal tax system is suspect. First, the underlying estimation framework does not reflect the joint nature of the family labor-supply decision. It assumes that wives are secondary earners, and estimates their marginal tax rate by adding their income to that of their husbands. Moreover, because of the joint nature of the family work-leisure decision, the simulation model Hausman employed does not accurately reflect the effect of taxes operating through the change in their husbands' budget constraint on the virtual income of the wives. The effect of these considerations on the

---

20. Farmers, the self-employed, and the severely disabled were excluded from the sample.
21. This represents a reduction of about 188 hours per year.
22. Hausman, "Income and Payroll Tax Policy and Labor Supply," p. 194.

TABLE 5

ESTIMATES OF LABOR-SUPPLY ELASTICITIES AND SIMULATED LABOR-SUPPLY
RESPONSES TO FEDERAL TAX REGIMES

	Husbands, Ages 25–55	Working Wives
1. Uncompensated wage elasticity	≈ 0	≈ .91
2. Income elasticity	− ≈ .9	− ≈ .4
3. Change in hours worked per year due to federal tax system[a]	− ≈188	− ≈350
4. Percentage change in hours worked per year due to federal tax system[a]	− ≈ 8.5	− 18.2
5. Change in labor supply due to rate cuts (in hours per year):[a]		
10 percent cut	+ ≈ 24	+ ≈ 50
30 percent cut	+ ≈ 59	+ ≈117
6. Percentage change in labor supply due to rate cuts:[a]		
10 percent cut	+ 1.1	+ 4.1
30 percent cut	+ 2.7	+ 9.4

SOURCE: Jerry Hausman, "The Effects of Taxes on Labor Supply," and idem, "Income and Payroll Tax Policy and Labor Supply."
  a. Estimated at the mean.

estimated impact of the federal tax system on the aggregate labor supply of couples is unclear. However, Hausman's estimate for wives' response to federal taxes—the 18 percent figure—seems far too high. In its place, we substitute an upper-bound response for wives—10 percent—that is somewhat larger than the upper-bound estimate for husbands—8.5 percent. To obtain a lower-bound estimate of the effect of federal taxes on wives' labor supply, we use the same percentage response as that reported by Hausman for husbands—8.5 percent. The direction of this adjustment is corroborated in additional calculations based on a respecification of the basic model to reflect the joint character of family labor-supply decisions.[23]

    Hausman's estimated response of married men to federal taxes is also large relative to estimates in other studies. These large estimates are, in part, due to the large estimated income coefficient in the Hausman study. In obtaining a lower-bound estimate of married men's labor-supply response to federal taxes, we substitute an income coefficient from alternative studies for the large value measured by Hausman.

---

    23. Hausman and Ruud, "Family Labor Supply with Taxes."

While Hausman's estimates provide an assessment of the labor-supply response of prime-age men and their wives to federal taxation, other studies are required to evaluate the effect of taxes on young people and the aged. These studies indicate that the responsiveness of the aged to wage and income incentives are relatively large—perhaps on the same order as that of married women.[24] The few existing studies on the labor-supply response of youths and women without children indicate that both groups have responses which are closer to those of prime-age married men than to their working wives.[25]

According to Hausman's estimates, a 10 (30) percent tax reduction similar to that enacted in ERTA would avoid about 13 (34) percent of the decrease in labor supply from the existing tax system for husbands. Assuming that the wives of these husbands are all secondary earners and that their wage rate is insensitive to the number of hours that they work, the 10 (30) percent rate cuts are estimated to eliminate about 23 (52) percent of the labor-supply reductions caused by the existing federal tax system.[26] Again, the magnitude of this response estimate for wives is suspect because of the specification problems referred to earlier.

Using Hausman's estimates for prime-age men and married women, we can estimate an upper bound to the labor-supply effects of the Reagan administration's tax cuts. In making this estimate, we will assume, first, that the Reagan administration's tax cuts effective by 1982 (a 10 percent cut) were in effect in 1980 and, second, that the full set of reductions experienced in the years after 1983 (a 23 percent cut) were in effect in 1980. The lower-bound estimate for the response of men to the cuts is based on the aggregate labor-supply effects of federal taxes obtained by substituting an estimate of the income coefficient from other studies for the very large responses estimated by Hausman. As indicated previously, the upper-bound estimate of the response of wives to the tax cuts is adjusted downward from Hausman's estimate for wives, but is above his estimate of the response for husbands. The lower-bound estimate for wives assumes that Hausman's estimate of the response of husbands to the tax cuts applies to their wives as well.

Labor-Supply Effects of the Total Federal Tax System—Upper and Lower Bounds. We first provide an *upper-bound estimate* of the size of the work force in 1980 if no federal income or payroll taxes had been in effect in that year. This upper-bound estimate of the no-tax labor force in

---

24. Masters and Garfinkel, *Estimating the Labor Supply of Income Maintenance Alternatives.*

25. This statement should be interpreted with caution. A substantial proportion of Hausman's estimate of the labor-supply reduction of married women attributable to the tax system is due to the high marginal tax rates they confront because of their treatment as secondary workers.

26. Hausman, "Income and Payroll Tax Policy and Labor Supply."

TABLE 6

ROUGH ESTIMATES OF LABOR-SUPPLY EFFECTS OF FEDERAL TAXES AND THE REAGAN ADMINISTRATION'S CHANGES IN PERSONAL TAX POLICY

(Millions of workers)

	Actual Civilian Labor Force, 1980 (1)	Upper-Bound Estimate of No-Tax Civilian Labor Force, 1980 (2)	Lower-Bound Estimate of No-Tax Civilian Labor Force, 1980 (3)	Upper-Bound Change in the Labor Force Due to Federal Taxes (col. (2)–col.(1)) (4)	Lower-Bound Change in the Labor Force Due to Federal Taxes (col. (3)–col. (1)) (5)	Upper-Bound Change in Labor Force Attributable to 10 Percent Reagan Tax Cuts (6)	Lower-Bound Change in Labor Force Attributable to 10 Percent Reagan Tax Cuts (7)	Upper-Bound Change in Labor Force Attributable to 23 Percent Reagan Tax Cuts (8)	Lower-Bound Change in Labor Force Attributable to 23 Percent Reagan Tax Cuts (9)
1. Persons age 62 and older	5.4	6.1	5.8	–.7	–.4	+.2	+.2	+.3	+.2
2. Disabled persons under age 62	2.5	2.6	2.6	–.1	–.1	—	—	—	—
3. Female family heads with children	4.6	4.8	4.7	–.2	–.1	—	—	—	—

4. Persons ages 16–24 not in categories (2) or (3)	23.2	25.4	23.7	−2.2	−.5	+.3	+.1	+.6	+.2
5. Women ages 25–61 not in categories (2) or (3)	27.8	30.8	30.4	−3.0	−2.6	+.7	+.3	+1.2	+.7
6. Men ages 25–61 not in category (2)	43.7	47.8	44.7	−4.1	−1.0	+.5	+.1	+1.0	+.2
TOTAL	107.2	117.5	111.9	−10.3	−4.7	+1.7	+.7	+3.1	+1.3

SOURCE: Column (1), U.S. Census; Columns (2)–(9), calculations by author.

1980 is shown in table 6, column 2 (column 4 shows the upper-bound reduction due to federal taxes). The no-tax labor force of prime-age men is greater than the actual by an amount that reflects Hausman's estimate of an 8.5 percent reduction in labor supply of prime-age married men attributable to the federal tax system (see table 5).[27] Of the population of prime-age women (group 5), about 80 percent are married. For this married group, our upper-bound estimate suggests that actual labor supply is about 10 percent below what it would be in the absence of federal taxes. Assuming that the nonmarried 20 percent of this group has a behavioral response similar to that estimated for prime-age men, the combined effect implies a work force of 30.8 million prime-age women in the absence of federal taxes.

Reliable estimates of wage and income responses are unavailable for young adults—group 4. Assuming that total federal taxes have altered their work-effort choices in much the same way that taxes altered the choices for prime-age men, we rely again on the 8.5 percent estimate of Hausman to calculate the no-tax work force of 25.4 million for this group. The work-effort choices of female-headed families with children (group 3) appears to be dominated by the incentives and other constraints of transfer programs (largely AFDC), with federal taxes playing a marginal role. We assume a 5 percent reduction in labor supply because of the existence of federal taxes. The level of work effort of disabled persons is also governed largely by transfer program possibilities and health constraints, rather than by the incentives from federal taxes; we again assume a 5 percent reduction because of the federal tax system for this group. As with youth, reliable estimates of the wage and income responses of the older population (group 1) are not available, but most estimates indicate a rather large response to changes in labor-supply incentives. We assume a slightly larger response than that used for married women—12 percent—which yields a no-tax labor force of workers age sixty-two and older of 6.1 million. These calculations imply that, in the absence of federal income and payroll taxes, the aggregate work force in 1980 would total about 117.5 million persons—implying an *upper-bound* reduction of about 8.6 percent in the total work force due to federal payroll and income taxes.

A *lower-bound estimate* of the total work-effort response to federal taxes is shown in table 6, column 3 (column 5 shows the lower-bound reduction in work effort due to federal taxes). By substituting estimates of labor-supply

---

27. This procedure assumes that (1) Hausman's estimate of the labor-supply response to the federal tax system in 1975 is applicable to 1980, and (2) estimated percentage changes in labor supply measured in terms of hours of work can be translated into percentage changes in labor supply measured in terms of number of workers.

responses of men to income changes from other studies for the very large effects estimated by Hausman,[28] we can crudely adjust his estimates. The adjustment indicates a lower-bound estimate of the negative impact of federal taxes on the labor supply of prime-age men (group 6) of 1.0 million persons (as opposed to the upper-bound estimate of 4.1 million persons). Because the estimated impact for youths ages sixteen through twenty-four (group 4) is also sensitive to the estimated income coefficient for men, the lower-bound estimate for this group is also substantially below the upper-bound estimate. Only the nonmarried portion of prime-age women (group 5) is affected by this adjustment in the income coefficients. Because the 10 percent response for the married portion (from the upper-bound estimate) is reduced only to 8.5 percent here, the lower-bound estimate for the entire group does not deviate far from the upper-bound estimate. A 2.5 percent reduction replaces the 5 percent estimate for disabled persons (group 2) and female family heads with children (group 3) in the lower-bound estimate, and for the aged (group 1), a 7.5 percent reduction is substituted for the upper-bound 12 percent figure. The *lower-bound* estimate attributes to the pre-Reagan tax system a reduction in labor supply of 4.7 million workers in 1980, about 4 percent of the labor force.

Labor-Supply Effects of the Reagan Administration's Tax Cuts— Upper and Lower Bounds. Given these estimates of reductions in labor supply induced by the entire federal system existing in 1980, the next task is to evaluate the decrease in these impacts attributable to the Reagan administration's tax policy changes.

By calendar-year 1982, a 10 percent reduction in marginal tax rates had been effected, similar to the 10 percent Kemp-Roth type of cuts simulated by Hausman. For married men, Hausman estimated that about 13 percent of the labor-supply reduction induced by federal taxes would be avoided by the

---

28. Hausman's income (β) coefficient at the mean is -0.153 for working age married men (Hausman, "The Effects of Taxes on Labor Supply"). The negative estimated income coefficients for working-age men range from 0 to -0.07 in studies reported in Glen Cain and Harold Watts, eds., *Income Maintenance and Labor Supply* (Chicago: Markham, 1973). These include the following: Ashenfelter and Heckman (-0.065 to -0.070); Boskin (≈ -0.055); Fleisher, Parsons, and Porter (-0.031); Garfinkel (≈ 0); Rosen and Welch (0 to -0.07). Excluding zero, the effective range is -0.03 to -0.07. In the lower-bound estimate, an income coefficient for men of -0.03 was substituted for Hausman's -0.153. This lower coefficient was introduced into the calculation of labor-supply effects for the average husband, using Hausman's method. The resulting percentage reduction in estimated response was assumed to be equal over the income distribution, and, hence the aggregate labor response attributable to the "virtual income" calculation was reduced equivalently.

Hausman's income (β) coefficient at the mean is -0.12 for wives, an estimate that is within the range of estimates in other studies presented in Cain and Watts.

10 percent Kemp-Roth cuts.[29] In table 6, column 6, this translates into an upper-bound estimate of the increase in the prime-age male labor force (group 6) of 500,000 attributable to the 10 percent Reagan tax cut. The lower-bound estimate for prime-age men is based on the alternative income coefficients, and it is shown in column 7. It is a much smaller 100,000.

For married women, Hausman estimates that 23 percent of the labor-supply reduction attributable to the federal tax system is avoided by a 10 percent Kemp-Roth type of tax cut.[30] This 23 percent offset estimate, while suspect, is used in the upper-bound calculation and represents an increase of 600,000 prime-age working wives. The percentage offset estimate for the nonmarried 20 percent of group 5 is taken to be equal to that of prime-age men (namely, the avoidance of 13 percent of the labor-supply loss of total federal taxes from a 10 percent cut in the personal income tax). For both married and nonmarried prime-age women, then, we estimate, as an upper bound, an increase of 700,000 prime-age female workers due to the 10 percent Reagan cut (column 6). The lower-bound estimate (column 7) is attributable to the assumption that all prime-age women have a labor-supply response to tax cuts similar to the response of men—namely, a 13 percent offset to the reduction in labor supply due to federal taxes from a 10 percent, Kemp-Roth type of tax cut—and is an increase of 300,000 workers.

Finally, we estimate the increase in labor supply in 1980 if the full 23 percent cut in marginal income tax rates scheduled to go into effect in 1984 had been in effect in 1980. The procedures for this calculation parallel those for the 10 percent cut. In this case, however, the effects of the 30 percent Kemp-Roth type of cuts estimated by Hausman—which serve as the basis of the calculation—are reduced proportionately.[31] The upper- and lower-bound results of this calculation are shown in columns 8 and 9 of table 6. The upper-bound estimate suggests that 3.1 million additional workers would have been in the work force in 1980 if the 23 percent cut in marginal income tax rates attributed to the Reagan initiative had been in effect in that year. This represents an increase in labor supply of 3.0 percent attributable to the full change in personal tax rates initiated by the Reagan administration. The lower-bound

---

29. For the 10 percent Kemp-Roth type of tax cut, Hausman estimated that, at the mean, hours of labor supply would rise by 1.1 percent for married men. This represents a 13 percent offset to the total labor-supply reduction of married men attributed to the federal tax system ($1.1 \div 8.5 = 0.13$).

30. For the 10 percent Kemp-Roth type of tax cut, Hausman estimated that, at the mean, hours of married women's labor supply would rise by 4.1 percent. This represents a 23 percent offset to the total labor-supply reduction of married women attributed to the federal tax system ($4.1 \div 18.2 = 0.23$).

31. The calculation was done for the 30 percent tax rate reduction simulated by Hausman and then scaled down by a factor equal to $23 \div 30 = 0.77$.

estimate attributes an increase of 1.3 million workers to the 23 percent personal income tax cut—a 1.2 percent increase in the 1980 labor force.

Summary and Caveats

The program and policy changes analyzed in this paper include most of those sponsored by the Reagan administration that are likely to affect labor supply. The upper- and lower-bound estimates of the labor-supply response to these policies are summarized in table 7.

We conclude that, at most, the combined effect of the $112 billion of cumulative 1982–1985 spending cuts and $360 billion of cumulative tax cuts may increase the aggregate labor supply by 4.1 million workers, or *3.8 percent.* This calculation assumes that the full 23 percent tax cut effective by 1983 was in effect in 1980, an assumption that implies a counterfactual of *no cuts in federal taxes* in the absence of the Reagan election. In fact, tax cuts had been proposed by the Carter administration. If we assume that the proposed cuts would have been enacted, the 10 percent tax cut scenario closely approximates the *additional* cuts appropriately attributed to the Reagan ad-

TABLE 7

UPPER- AND LOWER-BOUND ESTIMATED INCREASES IN LABOR SUPPLY
ATTRIBUTABLE TO THE REAGAN ADMINISTRATION'S HUMAN RESOURCES AND
PERSONAL INCOME TAX POLICIES

	Upper-Bound		*Lower-Bound*	
	Number of Workers (Millions)	*Percentage Change in Labor Force*	*Number of Workers (Millions)*	*Percentage Change in Labor Force*
Human Resources				
Policies	1.0	+.9	.1	+.1
Personal Tax Policies				
10 percent reduction in rates effective in 1982	1.7	+1.6	.7	+.7
23 percent reduction in rates effective in 1984	3.1	+2.9	1.3	+1.2
Combined Reagan administration's human resources and personal tax policies beyond those proposed by Carter administration	2.7	+2.5	.8	+.8

SOURCE: Author's calculations.

ministration. Using the upper-bound estimate of the labor-supply impact of the 10 percent cut, along with the upper-bound estimate of the work-effort response to changes in the human resources programs, yields an upper-bound estimate of an increase in aggregate labor supply of 2.7 million workers, about *2.5 percent*, to the Reagan policies over and above those proposed by the Carter administration. The lower-bound estimate attributed to this "Reagan minus Carter" scenario is 800,000 workers, a *0.7 percent* increase in labor supply. A reasonable best guess of the labor-supply response to the Reagan program, relying on this second counterfactual, would be on the order of *1.5 percent*. This response, it should be noted, is far from what has been suggested by the administration, and not close to that required to make even the tax cuts self-financing.

These estimates, it must be emphasized, are rough, and must be interpreted with caution.

First, judged against the magnitude of the tax cuts and their impact on average after-tax income, even our 1.5 percent estimate may be exaggerated.[32]

Second, the estimates implicitly assume that the strength of labor demand in 1980 persisted through the four years of the Reagan administration. In fact, a serious recession followed the Reagan election, and the discouraged workers who left the labor force in response to high unemployment are not reflected in the estimates. Our estimates are of the changes in desired labor supply attributable only to the changes in human resources and tax policies.

Third, the estimates of desired work effort are couched in terms of numbers of labor-force participants. Because they are in part based on estimated labor supply in terms of "hours worked" coefficients, we are assuming that changes in the labor force and in desired hours worked are proportional.

Fourth, many of the human resources policy changes are complex and interact with still other policy changes. Moreover, many require estimates of behavioral responses that are simply not available and were judgmentally assigned. We have, however, specified the assumptions underlying our analysis so that alternative judgments can be substituted.

---

32. For 1982, the revenue loss from ERTA due to personal tax rate changes was estimated by the Joint Committee on Taxation at the time of enactment to be $26.9 billion (Joseph Minarek, "Tax Policy in the Budgetary Context of the 1980s," Urban Institute Discussion Paper, September 1983). This is about 5 percent of 1982 total federal personal and payroll tax revenues without ERTA forecast by the administration in February 1981. This percentage reduction in tax liability represents an increase in after-tax income of about *1.2 percent*. For 1984, the revenue loss from ERTA due to personal tax rate changes was estimated by the Joint Committee on Taxation at the time ERTA was enacted to be $114.7 billion. This is about 15 percent of 1984 total federal personal and payroll tax revenues without ERTA forecast by the administration in February 1981. This percentage reduction in tax liability represents an increase in after-tax income of about *4 to 4.5 percent*.

Fifth, the econometric measurements that serve as the primary basis for the estimated labor-supply response to the tax cuts are based on a complex methodology developed by Hausman. This procedure has been subject to important methodological criticisms having to do with (1) the extremely large income coefficient for males, (2) the potential effect on the estimate of permitting a limited number of observations to have extremely large income elasticities (as a result of Hausman's introduction of a distribution of preferences reflected in the income coefficient),[33] (3) the truncation of the distribution of income coefficients at zero, and (4) the potential unreliability of estimates far from the mean of the distribution (i.e., precisely where the large labor-supply impacts estimated by Hausman are located).[34] As already indicated, the response estimates that Hausman's procedure yields are larger than those that would be or have been derived from the plethora of other labor-supply studies.

Sixth, reliable estimates of labor-supply responses for some of the groups other than couples are unavailable. Our calculations for these groups rest on both extrapolations from Hausman's estimates and estimates for these groups reported in other studies.

Finally, the estimates presented here presume that the reduction in tax revenues generated by the tax cuts does not result in a reduction in the level of goods and services provided by government. Hence, both income and substitution effects are considered. An alternative view argues that, in a general equilibrium world, only substitution effects should be considered, in that the economy's production possibilities frontier is not altered by the policy change.[35] Hausman and Ruud[36] provide a critique of this position.

---

33. A recent paper by Blomquist concludes that the imposition of a distribution of preferences yields a mean value of the income coefficient that is very close to the value when it is estimated without an imposed distribution. However, Blomquist's estimated income coefficient for men is only about one-tenth of Hausman's. See N. Sören Blomquist, "The Effect of Income Taxation on the Labor Supply of Married Men in Sweden," *Journal of Public Economics*, vol. 22, 1983, pp. 169–197.

34. Gary Burtless, "Comment," in H. Aaron and J. Pechman, eds., *How Taxes Affect Economic Behavior* (Washington, D.C.: The Brookings Institution, 1981).

35. James Gwartney and Richard Stroup, "Labor Supply and Tax Rates: A Correction of the Record," *American Economic Review*, vol. 73, June 1983, pp. 446–451.

36. "Family Labor Supply with Taxes."

Persons Age Sixty-Two and Older

Table 3 suggests that annual expected program benefits to persons age sixty-two and older decreased, on average, by about $350. Up to $150 of these benefits, however, are not associated with cuts in Social Security and are not work conditioned. The Masters-Garfinkel coefficients applied to a $200 change in expected income (interpreted as a change in the guarantee of the mix of programs available to the aged) indicates a 2 percent increase in the labor supply of this group, or the equivalent of 190,000 full-time workers. This estimate is taken as an upper bound. Because of the very small size of the change, the lower bound is taken to be zero.

Disabled Persons under Age Sixty-Two

For disabled persons under age sixty-two, the work effects of program changes have come largely from administrative elimination of individuals from the rolls after caseload investigations, and from increased administrative stringency in applying eligibility criteria to new applicants. In 1980, new awards in the SSDI program totaled 400,000; by 1982, new awards fell to 300,000.[1] On this basis, we assume that 100,000 persons per year, from 1981 through 1985, who would have obtained benefits under the procedures in effect before the Reagan administration changed them do not, in fact, obtain benefits under the post-Reagan procedures. Furthermore, in the pre-Reagan period from 1977 through 1980, the number of cases terminated after investigation ranged from 38,000 to 45,000 each year; in 1982, the number terminated after investigation was 180,000. Assuming that the increase in terminations averages 100,000 per year over the Reagan years, another 100,000

---

1. U.S. Congress, House Ways and Means Committee, *Background Material and Data on Major Programs within the Jurisdiction of the Committee on Ways and Means*, February 1983.

persons per year are eliminated from benefit recipiency. The sum of these two effects amounts to 200,000 persons per year who were denied benefits under the Reagan policy, but who would have been recipients under pre-Reagan policy. Over the four years, the total comes to 800,000 persons.

Research on administrative elimination from the rolls of SSDI recipients ages sixty-two through sixty-five indicates that about one-third of those eliminated find income support by working and the remainder obtain transfer income from other programs (especially early retirement).[2] The share of disabled persons under age sixty-two eliminated from the rolls who return to the work force is likely to exceed one-third—we choose 50 percent. Hence our upper-bound estimate attributes an increase in the work force of 400,000 persons in this population group to Reagan policies (800,000 × 0.5). This number amounts to about 16 percent of the 1980 disabled working population.

Because the peak intensity of denial of benefits reached in 1982 is unlikely to continue in 1984 and 1985 because of congressional action,[3] our lower-bound estimate is 200,000 over the four-year period—one-half of the upper-bound estimates.

Female Family Heads with Children

Average annual expected benefits from AFDC, Food Stamps, housing, and the like are estimated to fall about $325 because of Reagan policies (see table 3). This reduction is combined with significantly increased benefit reduction rates for a number of AFDC recipients (implying reduced labor supply), and the termination of other people with relatively high earnings from AFDC (implying either increased work to offset the eliminated benefits or decreased work to retain benefit and Medicaid eligibility). Assuming the latter impact to be zero, the Masters-Garfinkel coefficients applied to the reduced benefits (interpreted as a guarantee) suggest an increase in labor supply of 1.3 percent—the equivalent of 60,000 persons. Assuming an increase in benefit reduction rates of 30 percentage points, the Masters-Garfinkel coefficients suggest a decrease in the labor supply of about 6 percent of the relevant working AFDC population (15 percent of the total caseload of 3.8 million in 1980)—about 35,000 persons (3.8 million × .15 × .06). We take the net effect to be an *increase* in labor supply of 25,000 persons and accept it as the upper bound.

---

2. Robert Haveman, Barbara Wolfe, and Jennifer Warlick, "Incentive and Economic Status Effects of Social Security Retrenchment," mimeographed, University of Wisconsin—Madison, 1983.

3. *Wall Street Journal*, September 28, 1983, p. 4.

Although early reports suggested a major reduction in the labor supply of AFDC recipients because of efforts to avoid the cap,[4] only about 550,000 recipients have earnings. A study of Wisconsin AFDC recipients indicated that 4.5 percent of all recipients are made ineligible because of the income cap, and that one-third of these stay on rolls by reducing work effort.[5] Assuming that all of these persons remaining on the rolls cease working, and that this is the only labor-supply response, the lower-bound estimate is a *reduction* in labor supply of 56,000 persons (3.8 million × 0.045 × 0.33).

Youths, Ages Sixteen through Twenty-Four

Any labor-supply effects of Reagan social policies on youths ages sixteen through twenty-four would stem from budget cuts for student aid, training, and public service employment programs. Research on the effect of public subsidies for college attendance suggests that the rate of college enrollment has been little affected by the programs. In particular, the relative rate of enrollment of students from below median income families appears not to have been affected by the rapid growth in direct student aid in the 1970s.[6] Because the changes in the student loan and student aid programs under the Reagan administration were designed primarily to reduce the subsidy for students from higher-income families, it seems unlikely that a major reduction in college attendance—or a concomitant increase in labor supply—is attributable to this change. Assigning an increase in labor supply of 100,000 youths to these reductions would, it appears, be an upper bound.[7] Zero is our lower-bound estimate.

The effect of the cuts in employment and training programs on youth labor supply is difficult to appraise. In the short run, some increase in desired labor supply is likely to result as training opportunities are reduced. In the longer run, however, people who would have received training in the absence

4. Tom Joe, "Profiles of Families in Poverty: Effects of the FY 1983 Budget Proposals on the Poor," Center for the Study of Social Policy, Washington, D.C., 1982.

5. Davies, "The Effects of the 1981 Omnibus Budget Reconciliation Act on the Well-being of AFDC Recipients in Wisconsin."

6. W. Lee Hansen, "Economic Growth and Equality of Educational Opportunity," in E. Dean, ed., *Education and Economic Productivity* (Cambridge: Ballinger, 1984); and W. Lee Hansen and Robert Lampman, "Basic Opportunity Grants for Higher Education: Good Intentions and Mixed Results," in R. Haveman and J. Margolis, *Public Expenditure and Policy Analysis* (Boston: Houghton-Mifflin, 1983).

7. Preliminary statistics indicate some discernable reduction in enrollment in black colleges and other institutions with a high proportion of students from lower-income families. A syndicated column by Jane Bryant Quinn in November 1983 stated that independent black institutions reported an average drop in enrollments of 12.7 percent in 1982.

of cuts will be less employable and probably more dependent on nonmarket sources of income. We assign to these cuts an upper-bound estimate of an increase of 50,000 in the youth labor force; again, zero is the lower bound.

The elimination of public service employment also has a mixed effect on labor supply. Of the 600,000 PSE jobs per year eliminated, about one-fourth were filled by youths. If all these people should find alternative employment or continue to seek work, there would be no change in labor supply. Some, however, may return to school or cease looking for work. In the absence of evidence on these patterns, we assign a zero labor-supply effect to the elimination of the PSE program.

Women, Ages Twenty-Five through Sixty-One

Very few of the changes in human resources policy are likely to directly affect the work effort of women ages twenty-five through sixty-one who do not head families. However, some women will be affected by the loss of food stamps and housing benefits (in the form of increased rents), school lunch and higher education subsidies for their children, and the net reductions in unemployment benefits (e.g., the taxation of benefits received by higher-income families), and they may seek work to offset these losses. Given the substantial responsiveness of prime-age married women to changes in work incentives, we assign an arbitrary increase in labor supply of 200,000 to this population, sufficient to increase their labor-force participation rate by 0.5 percentage point. The lower bound is zero.

Men, Ages Twenty-Five through Sixty-One

The labor-force participation rate of men ages twenty-five through sixty-one is very high—96 percent. The only change in human resources policy likely to affect the work effort of this group is a change in unemployment compensation and employment and training. Because the Reagan administration somewhat reduced both unemployment benefits and training opportunities, some small increase in job search and work effort could be expected. We assign an arbitrary increase of 100,000 persons as an upper-bound estimate, and zero as a lower bound.

THE EFFECTS OF INTERNATIONAL COMPETITION ON U.S. ECONOMIC GROWTH

Paul Krugman

Not too long ago, it was possible to discuss economic issues in the United States with only minor attention to international dimensions. In the last decade, this insularity has vanished. In part, this shift reflects changing realities: the export market plays an increasingly important role in domestic production, and imports figure more prominently in domestic consumption. However, more important than these facts is a change in perception: International competition now looms as a constant concern.

This concern focuses on the fear that U.S. industry is losing its ability to compete in world markets, and that this loss of competitiveness is threatening the basis for long-term U.S. economic growth. Indeed, many argue that U.S. failure to keep up with foreign competition will lead not only to slowing growth, but actually to declining living standards.

However, in spite of increasing public debate about U.S. competitiveness, the Reagan administration has, like its predecessors, adhered to a basic policy of free trade, tempered by occasional concessions to influential interest groups—for example, steel and automobiles. Thus to assess the administration's policies towards international competition is really to estimate the consequences of what it has *not* done. The central question is whether we have entered a new era in which foreign competition, unless countered by activist U.S. policy, will threaten long-term U.S. growth.

This paper suggests the following answer to that question. The United States is entering a new era of international competition because it is losing its position of technological dominance. As a result of this loss, the U.S. economy has been squeezed into producing a narrowing range of increasingly technologically sophisticated products. The gradual closing of the technology gap has also fostered a distinctive dynamic of international competition in

127

which foreign firms target particular market segments and aggressively undercut established U.S. firms. However, this analysis finds no supporting evidence for the belief that foreign competition is threatening U.S. economic growth.

The discussion has four parts. First, the paper briefly reviews what is known about the nature of declining U.S. technological superiority and sketches a model of the relationship between technology and comparative advantage in international trade. In the second section, this framework is used to analyze how the diminishing technological lead affects the United States; then, the discussion moves to the micro level to encompass the effects of the U.S. relative decline on the competitive strategies and positions of both U.S. and foreign firms. The third section considers the effects of government action, particularly the policy of targeting certain industries for intensive competition and the notion of defining *key* sectors. The concluding section assesses the overall effects of foreign competition on U.S. growth and suggests that the traditional, free-trade stance is still appropriate.

The Narrowing U.S. Technological Lead

From the U.S. point of view, the most important international trend of the last generation has been the steady erosion of U.S. technological superiority. This erosion is reflected in a variety of measures, some of which are summarized in figures 1 and 2.

Measures and Causes

Real Gross Domestic Product (GDP) per employed person is a common measure of labor productivity. It is also indirectly a measure of technological sophistication because, all other things being equal, greater productivity is associated with better technology. As figure 1 indicates, over the last twenty years GDP per employed person in Japan, France, and Germany has gradually approached the U.S. level. From this we can deduce that the technological sophistication of these countries is increasing relative to the United States.

Another indicator of relative levels of technology is the direction in which trade in patents and in research intensive goods flows. Table 1 shows the pattern of high technology trade between 1962 and 1980. What was once predominantly a U.S. export flow has become substantial trade in both directions: the export-import ratio is now only 2 to 1. Such numbers confirm

FIGURE 1

GROSS DOMESTIC PRODUCT PER EMPLOYED PERSON

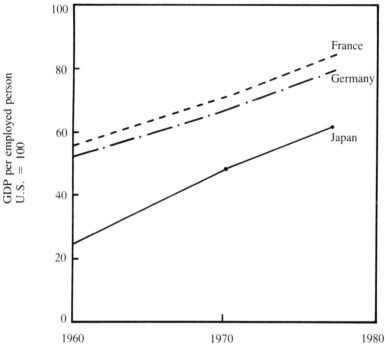

SOURCE: National Science Board, Science Indicators 1978.

the general impression that a once overwhelming U.S. superiority has been substantially reduced.

Why is the U.S. losing its technological lead? The simplest answer yet proposed is that international diffusion of technology is natural. Thus it is the lead, not its narrowing, that needs explaining. From this perspective, the early post-war U.S. technological superiority was an unusual position that could not have been expected to persist.

Other countries have also accumulated physical and human capital more rapidly than the United States. As figure 2 shows, during the 1970s the United States had the lowest investment rate and the highest labor force growth rate among the industrial countries; as a consequence, the capital necessary for industrial expansion may have been more costly here than elsewhere. At the

FIGURE 2

INVESTMENT AND LABOR FORCE GROWTH

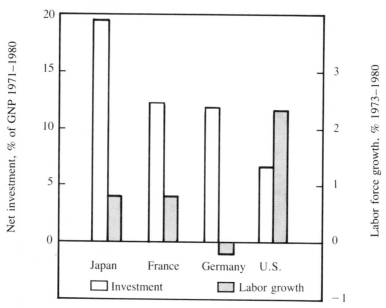

SOURCE: Organization for Economic Cooperation and Development, *Historical Statistics, 1960–1980.*

TABLE 1

U.S. TRADE IN HIGH TECHNOLOGY PRODUCTS
(*In billions of current dollars*)

	Exports	Imports	Ratio of Imports to Exports
1962	4.6	1.0	0.22
1973	18.8	9.4	0.50
1980	63.3	32.8	0.52

SOURCE: U.S. Department of Commerce, *An Assessment of U.S. Competitiveness in High-Technology Industries*, 1983.

same time, the United States is reputed to have been less effective than other countries in educating its work force. Other reasons for lagging U.S. productivity may be persistently poor labor-management relations and a weakly motivated work force.

It has also been suggested that U.S. management suffers from chronic shortsightedness by focusing on near-term profits at the expense of longer-term growth and market share. U.S. and foreign firms may well differ on this score; however, as we shall see below, U.S. practice may reflect a rational response to circumstances rather than lack of vision.

Finally, many believe that foreign governments have inhibited U.S. growth by targeting certain industries or products for special competition and subsidizing that competition as necessary. In the third section of this paper, we will consider some of the evidence for this belief.

Whatever its causes, the declining U.S. technological lead is key to understanding how international competition affects the U.S. economy. The fact that other industrial countries are catching up dictates both the nature of changes in the U.S. economy and the process by which those changes come about.

Technology and Comparative Advantage

In thinking about how a declining technological lead affects the U.S. economy, it is useful to begin with a simple model of the effects of technology on comparative advantage—that is, the relative cost advantage a country has in producing and selling a certain good. This model provides an unambiguous definition of national level of technology, and differences in national levels of technology determine the patterns of international trade and specialization.

Assume a world in which there are well-defined *best practice* technologies for producing goods. These technologies progress over time, but at different rates for different industries. For example, in technologically progressive industries, best practice technology improves very rapidly, and labor productivity may double every few years. In technologically stagnant industries, best practice technology may vary little from year to year. For purposes of the model, we will assume that there is an unambiguous ranking of industries from most to least progressive.

Every country will, to some extent, lag behind best practice technology. In reality, countries may be closer to the frontier in some sectors than in others, but suppose for the moment that the lag is uniform: the United States always takes two years to adopt the latest innovations, Japan takes three, Germany takes five, etc. The extent of the lag is an index of a country's level of technology; it reflects the determinants of technological capacity. We will also assume an unambiguous ranking of countries from shortest to longest lag.

These two rankings—the scale of industries (and goods) and the ladder of countries—can be used to describe the pattern of comparative advantage.

For example, a technologically advanced country will be highly productive in all industries, but its productivity advantage will be greater for goods high on the scale of industries. On the other hand, an advanced country's higher productivity will be reflected in a high wage rate. For sufficiently progressive industries, where the productivity rate grows very rapidly, the advanced country's productivity advantage will more than outweigh its high labor costs. For technologically stagnant industries, the reverse will be true. Thus, technologically advanced countries will have a comparative cost advantage in technologically progressive goods.

If we translate this definition of comparative advantage into a pattern of trade, we would expect correspondence between a country's level of technology and its exports. Each country will have a niche in the scale of goods; the higher the country's position on the ladder of countries, the higher on the scale of goods its niche of cost advantage will lie.

How adequate is this model of comparative advantage? Substantial case study evidence supports the proposition that, at any given point in time, countries can be rather clearly ranked by technological level. For example, in the 1960s, a new innovation was most likely to be adopted first in the United States, then in Europe, and then in Japan. Quantitative evidence is harder to produce because technological progressiveness is hard to measure. However, if we use R&D intensity (the ratio of the amount spent on R&D to the value of a finished good minus the value of the raw materials needed to produce it) as a (not very good) proxy, we find some patterns that seem roughly consonant with our model.

Figure 3 illustrates levels and changes in the composition of U.S. and Japanese manufactures exports in 1970 and 1980. Industries are grouped in the following way: *High* technology industries spend 10 percent of their value-added or more on R&D, and/or 10 percent or more of their employment consists of scientists, engineers, and technicians. For *medium* technology industries the criterion is 5 percent. *Low* technology industries are the residual. Each category has been assigned an index of the country's revealed comparative advantage.[1] The index is based on the ratio of two shares: the country's share of OECD (Organization for Economic Cooperation and Development) exports in the particular industry, and the country's share of all OECD manufactures exports. Figure 3 shows the totals of the indexes for all the industries in each category. Table 2 gives the indexes for some representative industries within each category. When the index is 0, it indicates that a country has equal shares of total OECD exports and exports in a particular area. Plus

---

1. The logarithm of the ratio is actually used.

FIGURE 3

U.S. AND JAPAN REVEALED COMPARATIVE ADVANTAGE

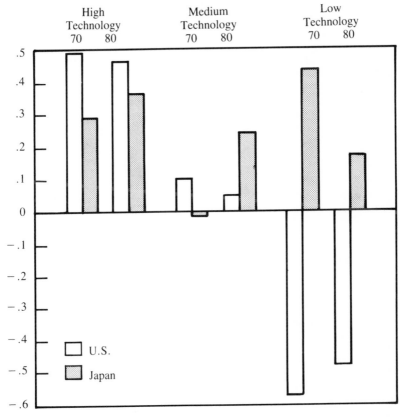

SOURCE: U.S. Department of Commerce, *An Assessment of U.S. Competitiveness in High-Technology Industries,* 1983.

values indicate that a country has a relatively higher share in a particular industry than in total trade; minus values indicate a relatively smaller share.

In 1970, the United States had its comparative advantage in high technology goods while the center of gravity for Japan's exports lay at the low technology end of the scale. In 1980, the United States still specialized in high technology exports, and the U.S. comparative advantage in most high technology industries remained unchanged, or as in computers and business machines, increased slightly. However, Japan's trade pattern shifted sub-

TABLE 2

U.S. AND JAPAN REVEALED COMPARATIVE ADVANTAGE

Technology	United States		Japan	
	1970	1980	1970	1980
High Technology				
Drugs and Medicinals	− .07	− .04	− 1.19	− 1.56
Business Machines	+ .72	+ .81	− .11	− .11
Computers	+ .54	+ .77	+ .22	+ .11
Electrical Machines	+ .16	+ .09	+ .15	+ .53
Telecommunications				
Equipment	+ .17	+ .10	+ .29	+ .74
Electronic Components	+ .77	+ .52	− .35	+ .90
Jet Engines	+ .79	+ .67	− 4.49	− 4.70
Aircraft	+ 1.28	+ 1.17	− 2.41	− 3.31
Scientific Instruments	+ .47	+ .49	− .02	− .06
Consumer Electronics	− .68	− .50	+ 1.71	+ 1.57
Medium Technology				
Metalworking Machinery	− .11	− .40	− .62	+ .38
Road Vehicles	− .06	− .30	+ .03	+ .76
Steel	− .72	− 1.19	+ .88	+ .84
Low Technology				
Textiles	− 1.02		+ .74	+ .22
Apparel	− 1.39		+ .24	− 1.61

SOURCE: U.S. Department of Commerce, *An Assessment of U.S. Competitiveness in High-Technology Industries*, 1983.

stantially. The comparative advantage for the whole medium technology category is dramatically increased as are several high technology industries—for example, electrical machines, telecommunications equipment, and electronic components.

These patterns are consistent with the predictions of our model. In 1970, the United States was still clearly the technological leader of the industrial nations—at the top of the ladder of countries—and its comparative cost advantage was in goods at the top of the scale of industries. By 1980, Japan had moved up in the technological world, and so its cost advantage is in goods increasingly more progressive.

Although our model falls far short of providing full account of the factors that determine trade patterns, it is a useful way to think about international competition. The next step in our assessment is to ask how we expect the erosion of technological leadership to affect the U.S. economy.

The Effects of a Narrowing Gap

Let us begin by returning to the analytical framework. How would our model describe the effect on an advanced country if its technological lead over a competitor is reduced?

The High Technology Squeeze

Unless other factors support an overvalued exchange rate, the first effect will be a fall in the advanced country's relative wage. If relative wages did not fall, the diminished technological advantage of the advanced country would be reflected in a smaller range of products in which the country is competitive. The fall in relative wage will limit, but not completely offset, the extent to which the advanced country loses its advantage in lower-technology goods. Thus, the second effect of a narrowing technological gap will be a structural change in the economy of the advanced country.

The nature of this change is somewhat paradoxical. As the advanced country loses its technological edge, the first goods to become uncompetitive are the least progressive goods that the country produces. In other words, as an advanced country slips on the ladder of countries, it will become increasingly specialized in high technology goods. In effect, the country is squeezed into industries high on the scale of goods.

Figure 4 presents suggestive evidence that the United States in the 1970s experienced something like this squeeze. If we use the admittedly imperfect proxy of R&D intensity to measure the technological sophistication of goods, we see a trend towards increasing net export of high technology goods, and an increasing net import of technologically less sophisticated products.

If this technological squeeze persists, could the United States be squeezed out of a competitive position altogether? According to our model, the answer depends on the behavior of wages. If a country reduces its labor costs sufficiently—for example, by adjusting the currency exchange rate—then a diminishing technological edge need not pose any overall problems of competitiveness.

We can test the validity of this assumption by examining the U.S. trade position during the 1970s—the same period in which we noted the trend towards increasing net export of high technology goods.

The United States maintained its aggregate trading position remarkably well during this era. Figure 5 shows three measures of U.S. performance

FIGURE 4

U.S. TRADE BALANCES, INTENSIVE MANUFACTURES

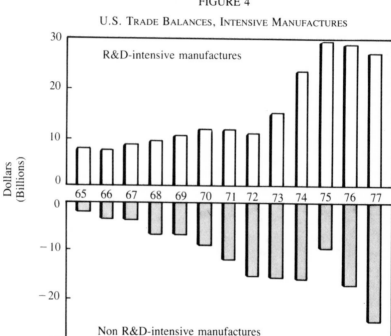

SOURCE: National Science Board, *Science Indicators,* 1978.

against competitors. The first is the trade balance in manufactures. During the 1970s, the United States trade balance fluctuated between deficit and surplus, but averaged out to a small surplus. The fluctuations partly reflect business cycles at home and abroad and partly movement in exchange rates.

These trade patterns do not support the common image of the U.S. manufacturing base being steadily eroded by foreign competition.[2] Why, then, is this image so widespread? In part, it springs from the well-publicized difficulties of the steel and automobile industries. Another source is the basis on which the trade balance is calculated: U.S. manufactures trade has been roughly balanced with the world as a whole, but has showed a huge bilateral

2. Because of the increased price of imported oil, the United States did experience a downward trend in its overall trade balance. In the overall balance of payments, this downward trend was offset by increased exports of services and by reduced exports of capital.

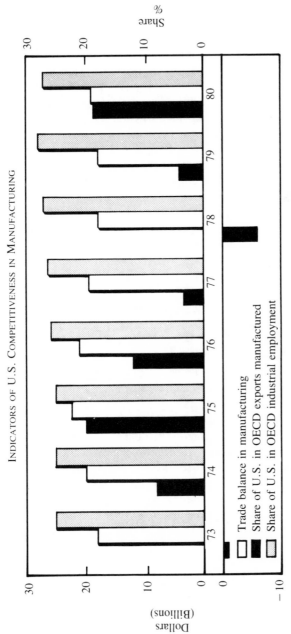

FIGURE 5

INDICATORS OF U.S. COMPETITIVENESS IN MANUFACTURING

Trade balance in manufacturing

Share of U.S. in OECD exports manufactured

Share of U.S. in OECD industrial employment

SOURCE: *Economic Report of the President, 1983*, and Organization for Economic Cooperation and Development, *Historical Statistics, 1960–1980.*

deficit with Japan. The reasons for this deficit are largely independent of the general issues of foreign competition; they are discussed in Appendix A.

A second measure of U.S. manufacturing performance is market share, defined here as the share of OECD manufactures exports. The U.S. market share, after declining in the 1960s and early 1970s, stabilized and even rose slightly after 1973 when the dollar began floating. This performance is better than our model would suggest; other things being equal, a country whose technological lead is eroding should expect to have a declining market share simply because it will account for a smaller part of the gross world product. However, the reason for the strong U.S. performance is straightforward. Although the U.S. lagged behind its competitors in growth of productivity, it had much more rapid growth in labor force—and it succeeded in employing the new entrants. The net result was that U.S. manufacturing output grew at about the same rate as output in other industrial countries.

Indeed, relative U.S. employment performance during this period is the most surprising fact of all. As figure 5 shows, the U.S. share of OECD manufacturing employment shows a consistent upward trend.

Our model suggests that to maintain employment in the face of shrinking technological lead, a country must accept a reduction in relative wages. Figure 6 shows that this was indeed the case for the United States in the 1970s. Wage rates of our major competitors rose relative to U.S. rates. In part, U.S. relative wages fell because they were growing more slowly than those of Germany and Japan, but the primary cause was a weaker dollar. The resulting decline in relative U.S. labor input costs was not fully reflected in a lower relative price for U.S. goods because it was partly offset by the quicker rise in foreign productivity. Nevertheless, U.S. terms of trade—that is, the real price of exports compared to the real price of imports—declined significantly during this period. Nonagricultural, nonoil terms of trade[3] deteriorated by 11 percent between 1970 and 1979.

We should note that all of the measures of the competitive position of U.S. industry shown in figure 5 are likely to turn down sharply in the next few years. However, this trend will not be a manifestation of a long-term problem of competitiveness; instead, it will reflect the extraordinary appreciation of the dollar between 1980 and 1983, which in turn reflects the unusual combination of very loose fiscal and very tight monetary policies. Theory and experience both suggest that the dollar will eventually return to more normal levels, and that the competitiveness of U.S. industry will—with a

---

3. That is, the effects of rising oil prices and other commodity price fluctuations have been removed.

FIGURE 6

THE DECLINING U.S. RELATIVE WAGE RATE, 1970–1979

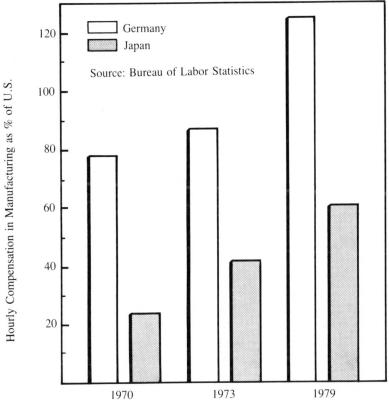

SOURCE: Bureau of Labor Statistics, *Handbook of Labor Statistics, 1982.*

lag—be restored. But U.S. trade performance will be adversely affected by macroeconomic policies at least through the first half of the 1980s.

We have suggested that a narrowing technological lead need not threaten overall competitiveness. However, the structural change that accompanies the technological catchup may cause adjustment problems. For example, an advanced country with an eroding technological advantage will become more specialized in high technology goods, thus requiring a redistribution of labor from less progressive to more progressive industrial sectors. Within the framework we have been using, U.S. structural change in this situation has been gradual. However, there are good reasons to expect that firms in the challenging countries will seek strategies to produce rapid changes in particular industries and to anticipate changes in comparative advantage.

The Process of International Competition

If the United States is losing its technological advantage over other countries, they will be producing similar products and taking a share of markets that the United States once dominated. Although it is possible that U.S. market shares will decline gradually across the board, it is much more likely that competing countries will achieve deeper penetration on narrower fronts. For example, it is more reasonable to expect Japan to achieve a dominant share in 25 percent of high technology products than to have a 25 percent share in all of them.

The basic reason for this expectation is the importance of *learning*. There is substantial evidence that, in many industries, the average cost of production for an individual firm falls with the firm's cumulative production. This *learning curve* reflects the accumulation of firm-specific knowledge with experience. The learning curve provides an incentive for a firm to focus its efforts. It is not in the firm's interest to seek a small share in many markets because this will do nothing to challenge the advantage of the cumulative experience held by the established firms. Instead, the challenging firm should choose a few market segments, concentrate its efforts, and quickly achieve a large market share in order to match the experience of firms already in the market.

The postwar period has many examples of firms behaving in this way. Because the United States was once the dominant producer of many manufactured goods, foreign firms were usually the challengers, and they sought large shares in a few market segments. Rapid surges of foreign firms into traditional U.S. markets are an inevitable consequence of the logic of competition. However, these surges mean that structural change viewed from the perspective of individual markets is much more dramatic and dynamic than the gradual, aggregate view.

Learning is also important when assessing changes in comparative advantage. For example, even if the broad pattern of international specialization reflects underlying factors such as the education of the labor force, the detailed process of competition will often involve shifts in market share that anticipate the shift in comparative advantage. Suppose that technological sophistication, the gradually shifting costs of capital, and so forth are tending toward an eventual Japanese comparative advantage in some product line. Even if U.S. firms currently have a cost advantage, it may be worthwhile for Japanese firms to enter the market, pricing below cost so as to gain market share.

Eventually, the combined effects of the learning curve and the underlying shift in comparative advantage will give the entering firms the cost advantage, and they may be able to recoup their initial losses. Not only is this strategy of *forward pricing* possible. Competition among Japanese firms will actually force them to adopt this strategy because a firm who fails to do so will have conceded an irreversible advantage to its domestic competitors.

This analysis suggests that the aggregate and the microlevel views of international competition and structural change are very different. The underlying factors that determine broad patterns of specialization shift only gradually, but microlevel shifts in market share occur rapidly and may seem to create comparative advantage rather than respond to it.

The microlevel perspective on competition also sheds light on the contrast mentioned earlier between present-oriented domestic and future-oriented foreign firms. As the U.S. technological lead erodes, we expect to see foreign firms targeting particular sectors and accepting initial losses to establish a market position. (This behavior is often cited as evidence that foreign governments are directing economic activity.) On the other hand, U.S. firms have less incentive to trade lower current profits for future market share because they have already exhausted most of the gains from experience.

If this analysis is correct, we can predict the following: As other countries catch up with the United States, the differences in managerial strategies will disappear. The past asymmetry in roles—U.S. firm the established defender, foreign firm the entering challenger—will be less marked. Increasingly often, U.S. firms will be challengers, and U.S. managers will be emphasizing the longer run.

The Role of Government Policy

So far, this account of technology and competition has made no mention of government policy. This omission is deliberate: Government policies have probably not played a decisive role. It is hard to believe that Japan would not have grown rapidly in the postwar period even without its industrial policy, and this rapid growth would have produced the characteristic features of Japanese-U.S. competition without government intervention. Japan's production would still have increased steadily in technological sophistication, and Japanese firms would still have aggressively targeted narrow market segments.

Targeting

Nevertheless, Japan does have a government policy of industrial targeting, and this policy is widely credited with playing a major role in Japan's
success. The logic of this attribution is simplistic and based on aggregate
results: Japan has had a government policy of industrial targeting, Japan has
had rapid growth, therefore the government policy must work. In addition to
this sort of argument, there is the fact that some targeted sectors have eventually become effective international competitors. The crucial point to remember is that Japan has been playing catchup to the United States, and
would have been doing so even without targeting. Many characteristics of
U.S.-Japanese competition which have been attributed to government policies
are probably simply inherent in this process.

As we have just discussed, Japan has been moving up the ladder of
countries for reasons that have nothing to do with government policy. And
policy has been formulated to take advantage of this trend. The typical Japanese policy has been to target industries that are somewhat more technologically sophisticated than the current specialization: steel in the 1950s,
semiconductors in the 1970s. Because the economy was moving in the direction of more technological sophistication anyway, this policy has a good
chance of appearing successful in the sense that the targeted industries eventually became competitive—even if the targeting had nothing to do with the
result.

This does not mean that targeting was completely ineffectual. A combination of subsidies and protection for infant industries surely enabled some
targeted industries to move down their learning curve and become competitive
more quickly than they would have otherwise. (Remember that Japanese firms
would have tended to anticipate comparative advantage in any case.) Although
the effects of targeting may be exaggerated, this policy probably helped to
push Japan's production more quickly towards high technology goods. But
this does not necessarily mean that the targeting has actually promoted Japan's
growth, or hurt that of the U.S.

To make a persuasive case that industrial targeting has indeed helped
Japan—and hurt the United States—it is necessary to argue that the contributions of the targeted industries to the economy as a whole substantially
exceeded their market return—that is, that the social rate of return from these
industries is greater than the private rate of return. If such *key* or strategic
industries exist and can be identified, a country can accelerate its growth by
targeting them, thus to some extent achieving this more rapid growth at other
countries' expense. For this reason, the concept of key industries provides
not only a role for industrial targeting but a justification for concern about

the effects of international competition on growth. If competition might cause key sectors of the U.S. economy to disappear, then there is good reason to be concerned about the effects of competition on long-term U.S. growth. The problem posed by the threat of competition to key U.S. industries would not be one of competitiveness, broadly defined as U.S. industry's inability to export or compete with imports. Rather, the problem would be one of the *structure* of trade, in which investment would be discouraged in sectors in which the United States, with its lack of appropriate industrial policy, would have already invested too little.

The issue is whether we can identify key industries and, if so, whether key U.S. industries are threatened by foreign competition.

Key Industries and International Competition

The criteria for defining a key industry are by no means clear. Those most often proposed are either based on faulty logic or are difficult to operationalize.

Perhaps the most influential criterion for choosing key industries is the idea of *linkage*: some sectors are more important than others because their output is an input to many other industries. Historically, this argument has been used to support government promotion of such industries as steel and petrochemicals; it is now being used to argue for special concern over electronics and other high technology industries.

However, careful analysis shows that linkage *per se* does not justify special concern over an industry. In an economy without other market failures, there would not be an exceptionally high social rate of return for industries producing intermediate goods, nor would there be any reason to prefer domestic production of these goods if it is cheaper to import them. Market failures caused by externalities—social payoff, such as the generation of knowledge, which cannot be captured by firms—might lead to underinvestment in linkage industries. But they might just as easily lead to overinvestment in these sectors. It is simply not true that linkage itself creates a divergence between private and social rates of return.

Another popular criterion of keyness is high value-added per employee— that is, a large amount of national income generated per worker. The numbers on this actually point to sectors few would regard as key. Petroleum refining and cigarette manufacture are among the highest value-added sectors in the U.S. economy; steel and electronics have only moderate value-added. In any case, high value-added per employee is not a free good. It results from high inputs per worker of both human and physical capital. Since these are scarce resources, it is far from clear that promoting sectors with high value-added per worker will raise national income. As in the case with linkages, the fact that sectors differ in value-added per worker does not, by itself, create any presumption of a divergence between private and social rates of return.

Although these popular criteria for defining key industries are questionable, there are some valid reasons for believing that certain sectors yield especially high social returns. The most important of these reasons is that when firms invest in knowledge—either by explicit R&D or by accepting low initial profits in order to move down the learning curve—they inevitably generate knowledge for other firms as well. This fact implies that international competition will have both benefits and costs. On the positive side, foreign firms generate knowledge that is useful to U.S. firms, and as other countries approach the U.S. level of technology, U.S. technological borrowing will become increasingly important. On the negative side, it is possible that competition could shrink, or destroy, industries that provide valuable information to other sectors. For example, it is sometimes argued that the competitiveness of the computer industry requires proximity to a national semiconductor industry so that computer manufacturers are aware of the latest advances in technology. If this is true, then foreign competition that causes U.S. innovation in semiconductors to lag could hurt U.S. growth prospects—whether or not the competition results from deliberate government targeting.

These kinds of arguments suggest the desirability of providing special support and encouragement for industries that are R&D intensive and employ highly progressive technology. (The complexities of this issue are discussed in more detail in Appendix B.) But it is unclear whether increased international competition in these industries hurts or benefits U.S. growth.

It is important to note that the U.S. industries having the best claim to being keys to long-term growth—for example, computers and semiconductors—have only recently begun to be seriously challenged by foreign competition. This means that foreign competition could have a negative effect on U.S. growth through this channel in the future, but it cannot have mattered much in the past.

Effects of Foreign Competition on U.S. Economic Growth

This paper has proposed a model of foreign competition. The model suggests that the technological gap between the United States and other advanced countries is narrowing. The final question in our assessment is whether this narrowing gap threatens U.S. growth.

There are three channels through which increased foreign technological prowess could, in principle, slow U.S. economic growth.

- *Unemployment*: If the United States wishes to maintain high employment rates in the face of increasing foreign technological parity, it must reduce relative U.S. wages and, to some extent, prices. If the United States is unable or unwilling to accept these adjustments, U.S. unemployment could rise.

- *Deterioration of the terms of trade*: To the extent that the United States does reduce wages and prices to maintain employment, U.S. terms of trade will worsen. This deterioration will not, by itself, slow the rate of growth of real production, but it could slow or reverse improvement in U.S. living standards.

- *Slowing of U.S. technological progress*: If foreign competition leads to reduced U.S. production or investment in key sectors that provide valuable technological information, the rate of U.S. growth could be slowed. Targeting by foreign governments could aggravate this effect.

How important have these concerns been in practice?

The fear that foreign competition will lead to higher U.S. unemployment finds virtually no support in aggregate experience. We have already examined data from the 1970s (figure 5) when the United States increased employment and maintained its share of manufacturing output and exports, despite relatively slow growth in productivity. The price of this success was, of course, a decline in relative U.S. wages and a deterioration of the U.S. terms of trade. But the evidence suggests that as long as macroeconomic policies are sensible—which they have not been recently—foreign competition will not be a source of mass unemployment.

Aggregate adjustment is, however, not the whole story, since foreign competition tends to focus on a limited range of products. If U.S. labor cannot move easily out of the targeted sectors, then a drop in the overall relative U.S. wage rate will not suffice. It will also be necessary, at least temporarily, for wages in the targeted sectors to fall relative to those in the U.S. economy as a whole. If this does not happen, the result will be pockets of structural unemployment. In other words, the special sectoral problems of steel, automobiles, and a few other industries could be keeping the general unemployment rate higher than it would otherwise be.

Although this argument probably contains an element of truth, its real importance is questionable. Presumably this kind of structural unemployment would show up as long-term unemployment. Yet in 1978-9, before the recent double recession, long-term unemployment averaged less than 0.6 percent of the labor force. Since not all of this can have been caused by foreign competition, it is difficult to assign competition a major role in driving up un-employment rates.

The deterioration of the U.S. terms of trade as a result of increasing foreign technological capacity makes theoretical sense and has empirical support. However, its importance should not be overstated. Between 1970 and 1979, the U.S. nonagricultural, nonoil terms of trade deteriorated by about 11 percent. Nonoil imports accounted for 7 percent of U.S. GNP in 1980, so the total effect of this deterioration was to reduce U.S. real income by 0.8 percent over the course of a decade. This is by no means an insignificant amount—it is comparable to the effects of a 40 percent increase in the price of oil—but it is not enough to be a central concern in U.S. economic policy.

Finally, as we have pointed out, the basic problem with assuming that competition will adversely affect key sectors is that no one knows what constitutes a key sector. In addition, there is no evidence that foreign competition has retarded U.S. technological progress. Indeed, it can be argued that increasing technological prowess abroad provides the United States with increasing opportunities to acquire information.

In sum, we find no evidence that U.S. economic growth is being undermined by foreign competition, either market driven or the result of foreign industrial policies. The only clear-cut negative effect of foreign competition on U.S. growth has been deterioration in U.S. terms of trade, resulting in a significant but not dramatic drag on the U.S. standard of living. The United States has indeed entered a new era of international competition, but the experience to date does not suggest the need for an activist U.S. policy to combat the threatening effects of competition. So far, the Reagan policy of free trade has remained appropriate.

For many U.S. industries and for the public at large, the focus of concern about international competition is competition with Japan. Japanese manufacturing appears to have an overwhelming competitive edge, reflected in a huge manufacturing trade surplus. The size of this surplus has led to accusations that the yen has been undervalued, perhaps deliberately.

The Japanese cost advantage has been persistent. As figure 6 indicates, Japanese labor compensation has remained well below U.S. rates, despite comparable and often higher labor productivity. Many businessmen in both Japan and the United States feel that rough parity in manufacturing costs would obtain only at a rate of 180–200 yen to the dollar. However, as table A.1 shows, the actual yen rate, adjusted for differences in inflation, has for the most part remained much higher.

This persistent Japanese cost advantage has been reflected in a persistent large Japanese trade surplus in manufactures. However, this surplus has not exerted upward pressure on the yen because it has been offset by large deficits

TABLE A.1

AVERAGE REAL YEN-DOLLAR EXCHANGE RATE
(*Adjusted to 1982 consumer prices*)

1973	257
1974	246
1975	245
1976	236
1977	211
1978	171
1979	192
1980	209
1981	213
1982	249

SOURCE: *Economic Report of the President*, 1983.

in other parts of Japan's trade, especially in raw materials and, to some extent, in services.

Tables A.2 and A.3 illustrate this point by comparing the structure of U.S. and Japanese balances of payments in 1981—a year in which both were roughly in current account balance. What is clear, especially from table A.3, is the extraordinary extent to which Japan's competitive advantage in manufacturing is simply needed to pay for raw materials. In effect, the yen must be kept weak enough to induce a manufacturing surplus of more than $100 billion in order to offset a lack of natural resources. The problem is that the rest of the world may simply not be willing to accept a collective manufacturing deficit of that magnitude.

TABLE A.2

U.S. AND JAPANESE TRADE BALANCES 1981
(In billions of dollars)

	United States	Japan
Manufactures	+5	+118
Raw materials	−50	−105
Services	+39	−14

SOURCE: Organization for Economic Cooperation and Development, *Historical Statistics, 1960–1980.*

TABLE A.3

U.S. AND JAPANESE TRADE BALANCES 1981
(Percentage of GDP)

	United States	Japan
Manufactures	+0.2	+10.4
Raw materials	−1.7	−9.2
Services	+1.3	−1.3

In this paper we suggested that the technological information generated by certain sectors constituted the best argument for designating *key* industries, suitable for targeting. Unfortunately, there are several reasons why high technology targeting could be counterproductive. On one hand, despite the fact that the information generated has value outside the industry, it is possible that too much R&D will be done in some industries; on the other hand, encouraging research might distort it rather than increase its volume.

The possibility of too much R&D derives from the fact that knowledge-intensive industries, because of the importance of economies of scale, are also imperfectly competitive. As a result, firms in these industries may have incentives to overinvest. From society's point of view, they may overinvest in two ways. First, if firms are in a close race to get there first with a profitable technology, they may invest too much in unnecessary duplication of research. Having a product six months earlier may not be worth very much to society as a whole, but getting there six months sooner may be critical for a firm's competitive position, and the firm may spend heavily to accelerate its progress. Second, an established firm may use heavy R&D expenditure to obtain such a lead that potential rivals are deterred from entering the industry.

In either of these cases, the marginal *social* returns to R&D may be quite low. Thus subsidizing R&D or otherwise encouraging it could be a poor policy.

A different sort of difficulty arises from the inevitable imperfections of any promotion scheme. Any effort to promote innovation will have biases. For example, a program that subsidizes R&D may tend to favor larger firms with formal research departments over smaller, less formally structured enterprises. Yet both kinds of firms will be competing for some of the same scarce resources, such as skilled workers and managerial talent. Thus one could argue that efforts to promote R&D will merely redistribute the research rather than increase it.

None of these objections is wholly compelling. There is still a respectable case to be made for giving special attention to high technology industries. But it is not a simple open and shut one.

FEDERAL SPENDING PRIORITIES AND LONG-TERM ECONOMIC GROWTH

Donald A. Nichols

In part, the Reagan administration was elected to restore the economy to health. One of the symptoms of poor health during the 1970s was the lagging rate of economic growth. The administration proposed to stimulate growth through a combination of policies, but the primary strategy was to reduce marginal tax rates in order to restore the incentive to save and invest. Blinder and Olson, in papers in this volume, assess the likely success of this strategy.

In this discussion, I analyze another potential tool for stimulating economic growth: budgetary spending decisions. I argue that recent administration decisions provide little evidence of a pro-growth strategy. Instead, what we see is a strategy that is pro-defense, and explicitly designed to reduce the size of the public sector, to shrink government social programs, and to transfer responsibilities from the federal government to states and localities. Occasionally, this strategy may lead to decisions that will encourage long-term economic growth. But that characteristic of the favored programs seems to be incidental to the decision to adopt them.

The administration seems to realize that certain kinds of R&D outlays can stimulate growth, and some categories of R&D support have been increased. However, it appears to ignore federal investment as a potential tool. Ignoring federal investment is an unfortunate tactic if one's overall objective is to stimulate total investment and growth. Eisner and Nebhut have estimated that total public investment is larger in the United States than is total private investment.[1] This finding is controversial, of course, and, by itself, does not

---

1. Robert Eisner and David A. Nebhut, "An Extended Measure of Government Product: Preliminary Results for the United States, 1946–76," *Review of Income and Wealth* 27(1), 33–64, 1981.

imply that a pro-investment strategy would require increases in federal spending. But it does warn us that reducing the size of government willy-nilly, simply to provide more room for the private sector, does not necessarily lead to an increase in investment.

Which budget outlays affect economic growth? Theory tells us that the rate of economic growth is determined in the long run by the growth rates of the labor force and of technology. In the short run, the rate of investment is also important. In my discussion, I ignore the issue of population growth, since it is not subject to policy manipulation. Short-run changes in labor force participation are a feature of the Reaganomics debate, but this issue deserves separate coverage. We are left, then, with investment and technical progress as the major determinants of growth. Technical progress is affected by many things, some of which are too complicated to measure. However, the major budget outlay thought to affect technical progress is research and development.

Therefore, in this paper I concentrate on three aspects of federal spending: (1) outlays for research and development, (2) direct government investment, and (3) government spending on activities that substitute for or complement private investment. I begin by illustrating the difficulties involved in drawing firm conclusions from the available budget data. I then turn to the three major categories of budget outlay. Next, I describe research and development spending, emphasizing the historical trends as well as proposals in recent budgets. Following that description, I discuss outlays for federal investment, and finally I describe the probable effects of federal spending on private saving and investment.

Limitations of Budget Data

Before trying to draw conclusions from the available data, it is useful to note some of the problems of interpretation they pose. The basic issue can be posed as follows. In some cases, we have data, but they have been classified according to criteria that are precise in theoretical terms but may seem arbitrary in particular instances. In these instances, the data are best thought of as approximations to what is needed. In other cases, the very concepts we wish to measure defy precise quantification, and an element of ambiguity will remain no matter how careful our definitions and classifications.

To illustrate these points, I have posed the major qualifications about data in the form of two basic questions about measurement and classification.

1. How can we measure the effect of the Reagan administration on the budget?

The answer is that we do not have an exact measure of this effect.

Policy changes derive from a variety of sources, the wishes of the administration being but one of them. In any single year, an administration's proposals may be clearly identified in its budget message. But after several years, and after the original requests are modified by Congress and given close public scrutiny, the administration may change its objectives. Thus, its latest budget proposals need not reflect the intended completion of a fixed agenda but rather a new appraisal of political reality. For this reason, if our goal is to identify the administration's budget proposals, we are shooting at a moving target even if those proposals are carefully stated in budget messages. As for the historical data, they reflect decisions by Congress, of course, not the administration, even though the administration's budget may be the most important force driving congressional policy.

The outlays for highway construction illustrate the difficulties in interpreting budget numbers. In trying to assess the administration's use of the budget to encourage long-term growth, one might conclude from the 1984 budget request that an expansion of highway construction was part of that policy. Yet we know that that expansion was due to the passage of the Surface Transportation Assistance Act of 1982, which was forced on the administration by a Congress that promised to do something in that election year to combat unemployment. The same political forces that were felt by the Congress eventually caused the administration to drop its opposition to the highway construction bill and to support a similar bill of its own. Economists will remember the amusing episode engendered by this policy shift: Even after the proposal had gained administration support, administration economists released an estimate that the net effect of the highway program on employment would be negative rather than positive.

The highway example exemplifies the problem of assessing the administration's net effect on the budget. What would spending on highways be if the administration had had its way since 1981? We simply do not know. When faced with these ambiguities, we have several alternatives, and I use them in varying degrees in this discussion. One alternative is to concentrate on the 1984 proposals compared to the 1983 base, and to take these proposals as a pure measure of the administration's intent in January 1983. Another is to stop trying to determine which changes are due to the administration and which to other forces. We can simply compare the 1984 proposals to the historical data for 1980 or 1981, and take the difference as a hybrid measure of the effect of the 1980 and 1982 elections on national policy.

In general terms, we can probably agree that the major policy influence during this period was the new political philosophy brought to the White House in 1981. But because we can all point to significant variations and exceptions to that general proposition—even if we can't agree on exactly what the exceptions are—we must also conclude that we have no way to measure exactly the administration's effect on the federal budget.

2. What would the 1984 budget be if policy had not been changed in the 1980s?

We have just considered how difficult it is to determine the source of changes in budget policy. Another problem is whether changes in the historical budget data reflect changes that took place in policy, or whether they were an automatic consequence of legislation enacted years before. Basically, we lack the data to address this issue.

In discussions of budget projections for the coming year, analysts use a current-services or a current-policy budget, which projects the effect of ex- isting legislation on budget outlays. These projections are published regularly by OMB and the CBO. But no one publishes on a regular, detailed basis what the current services estimates for the 1984 budget would have been in 1980 had we known the exact inflation and unemployment rates that were to transpire between 1980 and the present. At the special request of Speaker O'Neill, the CBO did derive such an estimate for social programs.[2] Of course, it is in this area that the dependence of outlays on economic assumptions may be greatest. But the CBO has not published a similar work for research and development, or for the other investment categories that we will consider here.

Research and Development

Because of the analytic difficulties involved, the effect of federal R&D on technical progress has not been demonstrated conclusively. Nevertheless, because some studies show that *private* R&D increases productivity,[3] and because it is plausible to link technical progress to technical research, it is

---

2. U.S. Congressional Budget Office, *Major Legislative Changes in Human Resource Programs Since January 1981*, Staff Memorandum, (Washington, August 1983).

3. See Edwin Mansfield, John Rapaport, Anthony Romeo, Samuel Wagner, and George Beardsley, "Social and Private Rates of Return from Industrial Innovations," *Quarterly Journal of Economics* 91, No. 2 (May 1977), pp. 220–240.

generally granted that the most effective way for government to influence the rate of technical progress is to provide support for R&D, particularly for basic research and for research whose benefits are so diffuse that they are unlikely to be appropriable by a single firm.

Rates of return to privately financed R&D can only be estimated indirectly. The most common way to estimate them is to construct a stock of accumulated past R&D expenditures that is depreciated at various constant exponential rates, and to see which of these stocks, along with the appropriate capital and labor inputs, best explains the pattern of firm output.[4] In contrast, similarly constructed stocks of physical capital inputs often use different depreciation rates for different kinds of equipment and structures. Nevertheless, even this aggregative approach has yielded some success in estimating rates of return to R&D.

Below, we summarize some of the relevant literature.

Studies of the Effects of R&D on Technical Progress

In a summary of what is known about the effects of R&D on technical progress, Terleckyj claims that (1) estimates of the rates of return are quite high compared to returns on physical capital, (2) the estimates are not very reliable, and (3) the estimated effects of government-financed R&D on private productivity growth are far smaller than for privately financed R&D.[5] He notes that time lags and spillover effects may be greater for publicly financed research than for private, and that the estimated rates of return might, accordingly, be biased downward.

Mansfield summarizes his own research, and that of others, by saying that social rates of return to privately financed R&D are commonly over 50 percent, although the private rates of return to that same R&D are substantially less.[6]

Griliches warns us further that the estimated rates of return to R&D investment are unreliable, noting that few studies have found significant effects using post-1968 data.[7] If an effect can be found only by choosing a specific sample period, one must question whether the claimed effect is

4. See, for example Zvi Griliches, "R&D and the Productivity Slowdown," *American Economic Review* 70, no. 2 (May 1980), pp. 343–48.

5. Nestor Terleckyj, "What Do R&D Numbers Tell Us About Technological Change," *American Economic Review* 70, no. 2 (May 1980), pp. 55–61.

6. Edwin Mansfield, "Prepared Statement" in U.S. Congress, House Committee on Science and Technology, *Federal Research and Development Expenditures and the National Economy*, (Washington: U.S. Congress, 1976), pp. 41–32.

7. Griliches, op. cit.

spurious. Griliches suggests that much public investment in R&D is to support health, the environment, or products whose value is not easily measured or not easily related to the R&D outlay. Griliches finds that only one-quarter of public R&D outlays lend themselves to the commonly used estimation method noted above, and this quarter represents R&D that is done by firms on products that they produce themselves. Attempts to use econometric methods to estimate rates of return for other publicly financed R&D have been unsuccessful.

Nelson, using a different approach, reviews several case studies of the rates of technical progress in various industries, and concludes that we can make few generalizations about the relationship between technical progress and the degree of government-financed R&D support that an industry receives.[8] For example, government R&D was very important to technical developments in agriculture, aircraft, and computers, but unimportant in automobiles, semiconductors, and residential construction. In some cases, government R&D was wasteful; in others, it was quite profitable. On the basis of these cases, Nelson refuses to generalize about how an overall increase in R&D outlays is likely to affect the rate of technical progress.

In another kind of case study, Mansfield et al. estimate returns to R&D investment that are generally in the range of 50 percent per year for a group of selected innovations.[9] However, these are all cases of privately funded research, and there is no way to be sure that these rates would also apply to government-funded research. Indeed, it is not clear whether choosing to study known innovations is appropriate, even for privately financed R&D, in an area where many efforts may be unsuccessful, and some expenditures do not result in an innovation at all.

In sum, although some studies suggest substantial rates of return on publicly funded R&D, the studies also show that we have no good way to measure the return. Therefore, because it is plausible to link R&D expenditures and technical progress, we will take it on faith that a strong relationship exists.

Data Sources

Outlays for research and development are collected from the accounts of the various agencies and published in *Special Analyses*, a supplement to

---

8. Richard R. Nelson, "Government Stimulus of Technological Progress: Lessons from American History," in Richard R. Nelson (ed.), *Government and Technical Progress* (New York: Pergamon Press, 1982).

9. Edwin Mansfield, John Rapaport, Anthony Romeo, Samuel Wagner, and George Beardsley, "Social and Private Rates of Return from Industrial Innovations," *Quarterly Journal of Economics* 91, no. 2 (May 1977), pp. 222–240.

the budget.[10] This follows long-standing practice, though the tables and issues in the analysis may change from year to year. In 1984, research and development issues are discussed in Analysis K.

In Analysis K, outlays are classified according to several schemes: basic and nonbasic; defense and nondefense; and by department or agency. As one who has administered research funding in a department, I can testify to the difficulty of classifying research as basic or nonbasic. Since this classification served no departmental purpose, we made some arbitrary classification decisions to fulfill OMB's reporting requirements.

To some extent, classifying expenditures into any kind of category entails an arbitrary element. More substantively, one can question whether research, even of a basic kind, into the fundamental determinants of some aspect of current income transfer programs should be thought of as affecting the nation's long-term economic growth in the same way that basic research in science would.

This raises the awkward issue of which R&D components are most closely related to economic growth. The issue of whether defense R&D—or space exploration—helps the economy is a well known conundrum. The answer is that some defense R&D outlays have obvious commercial applications while some do not. In some cases, we can guess simply by inspecting the R&D proposals which outlays have commercial applications. In other cases, because scientific discovery is an uncertain process, we can only tell after the fact which projects will have commercial payoffs. In most cases, it is impossible to judge, even for nondefense R&D, and even for completed projects, the exact commercial value of discoveries or developments. Each reader may have a list of favorite R&D programs that he or she thinks are likely to affect growth. These lists will differ. Accordingly, I focus my attention on aggregate expenditures, with only occasional consideration of sub-aggregate accounts.

Historical Trends in R&D Funding

In recent decades, there have been several large swings in total federal support for research and development. These are shown in table 1.

The first major swing began in the mid-1950s, when total R&D outlays, measured in 1972 dollars, were about $4.0 billion. At that time, this represented about .5 percent of GNP. Knowledge that the Russians had developed

---

10. U.S. Office of Management and Budget, "Special Analysis K: Research and Development," in *Budget of the United States Government, Fiscal Year 1984, Special Analyses*, pp. K-1 to K-29.

TABLE 1

AGGREGATE FEDERAL RESEARCH AND DEVELOPMENT OUTLAYS
(*Billions of 1972$ and as a percentage of GNP*)

Year	(1972$) Defense	(1972$) All Other	(1972$) Total	(% of GNP) Defense	(% of GNP) All Other	(% of GNP) Total
1949	2.0	0.5	2.4	0.3	0.1	0.4
50	2.0	0.7	2.8	0.3	0.1	0.4
51	2.2	0.7	2.9	0.3	0.1	0.4
52	2.8	0.7	3.4	0.4	0.1	0.4
53	3.4	0.6	4.0	0.4	0.1	0.5
54	3.2	0.6	3.9	0.4	0.1	0.5
55	3.3	0.7	4.0	0.4	0.1	0.5
56	4.1	0.9	5.0	0.5	0.1	0.6
57	4.2	1.2	5.4	0.5	0.1	0.6
58	4.7	1.4	6.1	0.6	0.2	0.7
59	9.7	1.8	11.5	1.1	0.2	1.3
60	10.5	2.5	13.0	1.2	0.3	1.5
61	11.9	3.2	15.1	1.4	0.4	1.7
62	12.0	4.6	15.6	1.3	0.5	1.8
63	11.7	6.9	18.7	1.2	0.7	2.0
64	12.4	9.4	21.8	1.3	1.0	2.2
65	10.8	10.4	21.2	1.1	1.0	2.1
66	10.3	11.3	21.6	1.0	1.1	2.1
67	11.3	11.1	22.4	1.0	1.0	2.1
68	11.4	10.2	21.6	1.0	0.9	1.9
69	10.5	9.3	19.9	0.9	0.8	1.7
70	9.4	8.4	17.8	0.8	0.7	1.6
71	8.8	8.0	16.8	0.8	0.7	1.5
72	8.8	7.5	16.3	0.8	0.7	1.4
73	8.5	7.4	15.8	0.7	0.6	1.4
74	8.1	7.1	15.2	0.7	0.6	1.3
75	7.5	7.0	14.5	0.7	0.6	1.3
76	7.2	7.5	14.7	0.6	0.6	1.2
77	7.4	7.1	14.5	0.6	0.6	1.2
78	7.6	7.9	15.6	0.6	0.6	1.2
79	7.2	8.5	15.7	0.5	0.6	1.1
80	7.7	8.7	16.4	0.6	0.6	1.2
81	7.9	8.3	16.2	0.6	0.6	1.2
82	8.4	6.8	15.2	0.7	0.5	1.1
83 est	10.0	6.2	16.2	0.8	0.4	1.2
84 est	11.4	5.9	17.3	0.8	0.4	1.2

SOURCE: U.S. Government, Office of Management and Budget, *Federal Outlays for Major Physical Capital Investment* Memorandum, February 1983, pp. 5 and 7.

an H-bomb, coupled with the launch of Sputnik in 1957, stimulated concern that the United States might be losing its technological leadership. In response, real R&D outlays increased more than 200 percent between 1955 and 1960, and fivefold between 1955 and 1964. The compounded growth rate over that nine-year period exceeded 20 percent.

By any measure, R&D outlays remained high for several years. Their share of GNP peaked in 1964 at 2.2 percent. Measured in 1972 dollars, the peak was reached in 1967 at $22.4 billion.

Since then, R&D outlays have fallen, both as a percentage of GNP and in real terms. They reached a low of $14.5 billion in 1975, increased for a few years to $16.4 billion in 1980, then fell again to $15.2 billion in 1982. As a percentage of GNP, the decline was quite rapid in the 1960s, somewhat slower in the early 1970s, finally reaching 1.2 percent in 1976. R&D outlays have hovered in that range ever since—at about half the 1964 rate.

Total R&D outlays fell only slightly faster from 1980 to 1982 than their average rate of decline from 1967 to 1980. However, beginning in 1982, a substantial increase is projected through 1984. R&D as a percent of GNP remains basically unchanged. This is because the cycle in R&D outlays is projected to be similar to that in GNP.

The projected increase in R&D is entirely in defense. As a percentage of GNP, defense R&D spending is projected to rise to .8 percent in 1983 and 1984. In real terms, this is an increase from $7.2 billion to $11.4 billion, or a 58 percent increase over the five-year period ending in 1984.

I noted above the difficulties in dividing R&D outlays into categories according to their likely effects on economic growth. Nevertheless, it is tempting to claim that the defense outlays are unrelated to economic growth, and that the nondefense outlays are directly related to the economy. But we all know that defense research supports work on some basic scientific and technological issues that will eventually turn out to be of commercial interest, and that some of the nondefense research focuses on social programs that have little direct relation to economic growth. However, despite these qualifications, nondefense research is more likely to be related to economic growth. Indeed, the support of economic growth is one of the purposes of nondefense research while it is only an incidental effect of military research.

The basic purposes of both defense and nondefense R&D outlays are described by OMB in Special Analysis K.

The Federal Government funds R&D activities to serve two broad purposes:

- To meet specific Federal Government needs—where the principal user of the R&D is the government itself—for example, to ensure a strong national defense,

- To meet broad national needs—where the Federal Government supports R&D that the private sector lacks incentive to invest in adequately, in the national interest—to help assure the strength of the economy and the quality of life for all people. . . . (K-1)

If economic growth was a major objective of the Reagan administration, one would expect an increase in nondefense R&D spending. Instead, table 1 shows a substantial decline in nondefense R&D spending from $8.7 billion in 1980 to $6.8 billion in 1982. This decline is projected to continue until a level of $5.9 billion is reached in 1984. This represents a cut of 32 percent over the four-year period, and a 22 percent cut over the 1980-82 period that has already been completed. Nondefense R&D outlays will be about $5.9 billion ($1972)—about half of what they were in 1966.

As a percentage of GNP, the decline is even more dramatic. From a peak of 1.1 percent of GNP in 1966, nondefense R&D fell quickly to .7 percent in 1970, and then to .6 percent in 1973, a percentage that was roughly maintained through 1981. Then expenditures declined sharply, culminating in a projected figure of .4 percent for 1983 and 1984.

Figure 1 dramatizes what a departure the Reagan administration is from previous administrations. Under President Reagan, there has been a substantial decline in the average levels of real nondefense R&D spending provided by every administration since Kennedy-Johnson.

However, if we examine the annual data in table 1, we see that the changes in spending that gave rise to these dramatic differences between the administrations began even before several of the administrations took office. The trends were strongly continued in the fiscal year shared by two administrations, a year whose budget I have assumed in table 1 to be dominated by the outgoing administration. Thus we must question the extent to which the variations shown in the table represent changes in policy enacted by the different administrations, or a continuation of underlying political forces that were already causing the changes before the elections—indeed, may have determined them.

Components of Nondefense R&D Spending

Although aggregate nondefense R&D spending is declining, some of its components have been increased, and part of the justification given for their increase is to support economic growth. For example, NSF received a $200 million increase, the Federal Aviation Administration in the Department of Transportation received a $160 million increase, and NIH received a $70

FIGURE 1

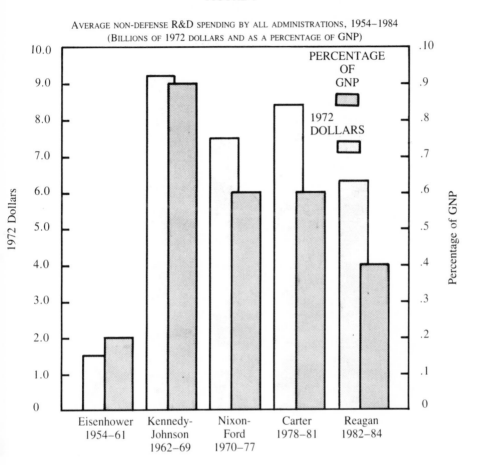

AVERAGE NON-DEFENSE R&D SPENDING BY ALL ADMINISTRATIONS, 1954–1984
(BILLIONS OF 1972 DOLLARS AND AS A PERCENTAGE OF GNP)

million increase. There were no major increases in any other program, regardless of the relationship between that program and economic growth.

Trying to assess the true motive behind some of these policy changes is extremely difficult. Just as defense-related R&D outlays can be partly justified by their effects on economic production for households, so outlays for economic or technological leadership can be justified by their likely effects on defense.

Indeed, language in the summary in Analysis K of administration policies suggests that the defense motivation is the dominant one.

The 1984 budget continues to reflect the established policies of the Administration in funding R&D but further strengthens support in areas of major Federal responsibility. It provides for:

- Major increases across all R&D programs of the Department of Defense;

- A significant increase in government-wide support of basic research with emphasis on support of research in the physical sciences and engineering. Advances in these fields are key to future national defense and the long-term competitiveness of the U.S. economy, particularly in high technology industries. . . . (Analysis K, pp. 1,2)

Within the NSF budget, increases in the purest forms of basic research are justified not by their long-run effects on human well-being, but by their effect on international competitiveness. Specifically, the 1984 budget would

- Provide special emphasis on disciplines such as mathematics, materials science, astronomy, and electrical, computer and chemical engineering. Research in these disciplines has the potential to make important contributions to the long term competitiveness of the U.S. economy, particularly in high technology dependent industries. (Analysis K, pp. 18–19)

Thus, although we can give this administration credit for its concern about science, and for its recognition that science is vital to our future well-being, we need not conclude that the administration chose to support scientific research in order to promote economic growth and wellbeing. A consistent strategy of this kind would require increased outlays for R&D in several other areas as well, some of which are noted below. But in these areas, budgets have been reduced. A more likely motivation for the pattern of R&D increases we see is the administration's resolve to support defense-related projects and to maintain U.S. technological superiority in related fields.

In Special Analysis K, the description of the Energy Department's R&D budget shows in microcosm the strategies affecting R&D in the budget as a whole. Energy Department research includes (1) a national defense program (nuclear weapons), (2) a general science program (high energy physics and nuclear sciences), and (3) an energy program "focused on long-term R&D." The national defense program has a proposed increase from $1.7 to $1.9 billion, and the general science program an increase from $553 million to $643 million. The energy program has a proposed cut from $2.4 billion to $2.2 billion. Included in the energy program are proposed cuts for the fossil, solar, and conservation programs from $707 million to $302 million. Without knowledge of the technological merits of the programs that were cut, we cannot know if the cuts can be justified on the grounds of efficiency. But a likely interpretation of this pattern of cuts and increases is the administration's pro-defense, rather than pro-growth emphasis.

In fairness, it should be noted that the administration justified these cuts not because it disapproved of the functions, but because it felt that these are areas appropriate for private-sector research, not public. Thus the pro-defense orientation is complemented by a strategy of shrinking the public sector and replacing it with private activities.

In Analysis K, we can find many examples of cuts in future-oriented programs for which no explanation is given. For example, we find a decrease in requested outlays for research for the Forest Service, whose purpose is "to provide knowledge needed to manage and protect forest and related rangeland resources to gain maximum economic and social benefits from their use"; a decrease for R&D for the National Oceanic and Atmospheric Administration, among whose purposes it is to find "better ways to conserve, protect and manage the nation's fishery resources"; a decrease for the Department of the Interior in applied mining and geological research; a decrease in the Department of Transportation's research in areas other than the Federal Aviation Agency; and a decrease of 14 percent in R&D for the Environmental Protection Agency. There is a modest apparent increase in food research, but even this is at a rate less than inflation.

The pattern of R&D outlays leads inexorably to the conclusion that the administration did not pursue economic growth through its budget policy. One wonders, with Olson, whether the massive tax cuts were also enacted primarily to meet political rather than economic objectives.

Federal Investment

Although neoclassical growth models are generally specified so that an increase in investment cannot affect the long-term growth rate but can only temporarily reallocate consumption from the present to the future, the possibilities for reallocation are significant enough that policy discussions of economic growth often emphasize investment. Of course, this is partly because investment is thought to be more amenable to policy influence than are the other determinants of growth.

However, it is important to remember how slightly changes in investment affect the growth rate, even in the short term. For example, consider the effects on growth of a 10 percent increase in the rate of investment. Remember that a 10 percent increase in investment would be substantial by historical standards, given the relative constancy of investment as a share of GNP over the last ninety years.[11] A 10 percent increase in the rate of investment would lead in the long run to a 10 percent increase in the capital/output ratio.[12] If the elasticity of output with respect to capital is about 30 percent, then output would be 4.5 percent higher at the new long-run equilibrium than it would have been had the increase in investment not taken place.[13] Of course, the 10 percent increase in net investment would represent an additional claim on GNP of about one percentage point. Thus of the 4.5 percent increase in GNP, roughly 3.5 percentage points would be available for increased consumption.

If we allow 20 years for the adjustment to the new equilibrium, we find that the growth rate of consumption would have been increased by less than 0.2 percentage points over that period. This is a rather meager effect from what appeared to be a substantial increase in investment. The meagerness of this effect is one reason why it is commonly thought that government can do little to influence economic growth by changing the rate of investment.

Government does a substantial amount of investment itself. In the 1984 budget, OMB estimates that $170.9 billion of federal outlays in 1982 should be classified as investment.[14] This investment is clearly subject to policy influences. The data on federal investment are reported in Special Analysis D, which is entitled, "Investment, Operating and Other Federal Outlays." This analysis classifies outlays several ways. One is a six-way classification according to the nature of the outlay: (1) lending and financial investments; (2) construction and rehabilitation of physical assets; (3) acquisition of major equipment; (4) conduct of research and development; (5) conduct of education and training; and (6) other, a category including data collection and inventory accumulation. A second breakdown is a three-way classification into defense, nondefense, and off-budget outlays; a third classification is into grants-in-aid, loans, and direct federal programs. The second of these classification

11. Paul A. David and John L. Scadding, "Private Savings: Ultrarationality, Aggregation, and Denison's Law," *Journal of Political Economy* 82 (2), part 1, pp. 225–50.

12. This is the fundamental equation of equilibrium in neoclassical growth theory, namely, that in equilibrium, the ratio of the capital stock to the rate of output must equal the ratio of the saving rate to the growth rate. See Robert M. Solow, "A Contribution to the Theory of Economic Growth," *Quarterly Journal of Economics* 70 (1) (February 1956), pp. 65–94.

13. At equilibrium, then, we must satisfy the two equations that $1.0 + \% \triangle K = 1.1$ ($1.0 + \% \triangle Y$) and that $\% \triangle Y = .3\% \triangle K$. An increase in Y of 4.5 percent and an increase in K of 15 percent satisfies these two equations.

14. U.S. Office of Management and Budget, "Special Analysis D: Investment, Operating and Other Federal Outlays," in *Budget of the United States Government, Fiscal Year 1984, Special Analyses*, p. D-23, table D-1.

TABLE 2

SUMMARY OF FEDERAL BUDGET OUTLAYS FOR INVESTMENT
(*Millions of current dollars*)

	1982 estimate	1983 estimate	1984 estimate
National defense			
Construction and rehabilitation	3,558	4,728	5,560
Acquisition of major equipment and other physical assets	44,664	56,544	70,199
Conduct of research and development	19,809	24,673	29,277
Other investment-type programs	666	745	1,077
Subtotal	68,697	86,690	106,113
Civil			
Loans and financial investments	11,932	8,021	2,125
Construction and rehabilitation	27,066	27,333	30,567
Acquisition of major equipment	1,398	1,640	803
Conduct of research and development	14,850	14,032	13,909
Conduct of education and training	21,570	20,748	19,203
Commodity inventories and other physical assets	3,787	4,052	2,193
Other investment-type programs	3,279	3,509	3,369
Subtotal	83,882	79,335	72,169
Addendum			
Off-budget federal entities (civil):			
Loans	14,333	14,262	5,947
Other investment-type programs	3,989	1,809	2,961
Subtotal	18,322	16,071	8,908
TOTAL	170,901	182,096	187,190

SOURCE: Special Analysis D, table D-4.

schemes can be seen in table 2, which is taken from table D-4 in Special Analysis D.

Table 2 shows the substantial size of federal investment. It also shows an enormous growth in defense investment over the 1982–1984 period, and a major shrinkage in nondefense investment, confirming our previous hypothesis that the budget strategy of this administration is pro-defense, not pro-growth. Indeed, table 2 shows that between 1983 and 1984, every category of civil investment is scheduled to fall except for the construction and rehabilitation of physical assets. This category is scheduled to rise by $3.2

billion, a figure that is entirely attributable to the increased spending on highways mentioned above.

Admittedly, many of the categories in table 2 do not represent investments that would pass a market test of profitability; therefore, reducing them should not have a major effect on economic growth. Nevertheless, it is surprising to find a decline proposed in every category except highways.

I will now discuss each category separately and note the difficulties involved in estimating their effects on growth.

Loans and financial investments. The decline in loans and financial investments is largely due to the experience in agriculture, an area where increased lending takes place when market prices are low, not when the administration feels that increased loans are in order. Thus, this decline has nothing to do with a strategy of reducing investment. Non-agricultural lending is discussed in the next section.

Construction and rehabilitation. Construction and rehabilitation of physical assets is the largest category of civil investment in table 2. It includes a wide variety of investments from the most needed public infrastructure to the worst of pork barrel abuses. It also includes the construction of office buildings and other facilities where the decision to build rather than rent can strongly influence variation in budget outlays over time and, therefore, also influence the variation in federal investment outlays. But this variation need not strongly affect total national investment because buildings that are not constructed by the federal government for itself will be constructed instead by the private sector. Here, private and federal investment are perfect substitutes for each other.

In the 1950s and 1960s, a series of studies on the rates of return to public investment showed that many investments were of questionable value. This led OMB in 1972 to adopt Circular A-104, which requires that all proposed investments must pass a cost-benefit test that incorporates the use of stipulated public discount rates. Circular A-104 requires a rate of 7 percent for buildings, and 10 percent for most other forms of investment.[15]

In principle, the use of this cost-benefit test should direct investment toward those projects with the greatest returns and away from the wasteful projects. In practice, however, it has simply changed the nature of the debate

---

15. For a discussion of physical investment issues, see: CBO, *The Federal Buildings Program: Authorization and Budgetary Alternatives*, June 1983, and U.S. Department of Commerce, *A Study of Public Works Investment in the United States* (Washington: Government Printing Office, 1980).

over profitability.[16] For example, critics of the Corps of Engineers argue that the benefits of certain investments are commonly overstated in the cost-benefit studies. Presumably, new *ex post* studies of profitability would run into many of the same difficulties that cause the *ex ante* studies to disagree, namely, how to place a value on certain benefits for which there is no market. For this reason, it is hard to conclude that a decline in construction expenditures would have a very negative effect on economic growth.

Education and training. The remaining sizable category of investment outlays is education and training. Here the problem is the blurring of the investment-consumption distinction. For example, education clearly represents an investment in human capital. But some kinds of education outlays— for instance, education for the handicapped—are motivated more by their ability to enhance the lives of individuals than by the likelihood that they will enhance future national output. Medical care services for handicapped people are not dissimilar in this regard, yet they are classified by OMB and by BEA as consumption. The similarity of these two outlays, despite their difference in classification, warns us of the somewhat arbitrary nature of the consumption vs. investment categories. Indeed, Eisner and Nebhut classify one-half of all medical care outlays as investment.[17]

Employment and training programs are another example. They are classified as investment although they have also been justified as having an important role in maintaining the current income of low-income families. While some employment and training programs have been shown to have a rate of return that is competitive with other investments, some have been shown not to.[18] Public Service Employment, in particular, is often indistinguishable from other forms of public employment. Where the service provided by such employment is not itself an investment-type activity, there is little justification for classifying such employment as investment while regular public-sector employment is classified as consumption. The experience received by workers on public service jobs may indeed be a form of investment, but it is little different from the experience being received by government

---

16. See Joseph L. Cawall, Robert H. Haveman, and Joseph V. Karaganis, "Where Complicated Facts Threaten Court Reviews: Litigation over Navigation Projects," *Journal of Policy Analysis and Management* 2 (3) (1983), pp. 418–431.

17. Eisner and Nebhut, op. cit.

18. For a review of the differences in returns to various CETA programs, see Laurie J. Bassie, *CETA: Is It a Cost Effective Method for Increasing the Earnings of Disadvantaged Workers?* (Washington, D.C.: The Urban Institute, 1982). For a review of existing studies, see Mark Bendick, "Employment, Training, and Economic Development," in John L. Palmer and Isabel V. Sawhill (eds.), *The Reagan Experiment* (Washington, D.C.: The Urban Institute Press, 1983), pp. 247–70.

workers in non-PSE jobs, or, for that matter, from the experience being received by workers in the private sector.

Studies of the returns to employment and training programs generally indicate that these programs are of value. However, as with the other investment categories described above, the programs encompassed in this category differ greatly from each other. Therefore, it is difficult to generalize from the extensive body of studies about the overall rate of return to these outlays.[19]

There are several difficulties inherent in evaluating education and training programs. First, the return to a program that prepares workers of marginal skills for employment depends critically on the national unemployment rate. If unemployment is high, marginal workers are likely to be unemployed even after having received training. Evaluations of such a program would then indicate that it was a failure even though the program might have intrinsic merit if the aggregate unemployment rate was lower. Many of the evaluations of employment and training programs done in recent years suffer from this defect because unemployment rates have been unusually high since the mid-1970s. Of course, in a sense, the evaluations are not tainted by this defect. Programs that provide skills for marginal workers are not needed if there is no shortage of educated workers. The evaluations tell us exactly that. It is the interpretation of these results that is in error, and, in particular, the tendency to use the estimates of program profitability that apply when the unemployment rate is high to periods when it is not.

A second barrier to evaluation is a tendency to overestimate the national value of employment and training programs by using estimates of their value to individuals who participate in them. For example, consider the value of a program that teaches job search skills in a recession, when there are many excess workers. If the program simply helps certain workers to find the few jobs that are available, it will be of value to those workers. But from a national perspective, it has no value unless it increases the total level of employment.

To a certain extent, all employment and training programs share these characteristics. By virtue of being in the program and in contact with instructors and counselors, students hear of job openings more readily than they otherwise would. Furthermore, where credentialism exists, even the substantive skills that the workers acquire may be of no national value although they may add to the nation's stock of human capital and increase the income of the workers who acquire them. The size of this distortion factor cannot be measured, but it clearly biases upward estimates of the returns to employment

---

19. See Bassie, op. cit.

and training programs. More unfortunately, it biases the returns to different programs in different ways. That is, programs that provide only job search skills are most likely to be affected by this bias, while programs providing skills that are in short supply are least likely to be affected.

Despite the difficulties in evaluation, it seems clear that the longer and more intensive programs tend to have a higher rate of return than those which are shorter and less intensive. An excellent example is Job Corps.[20] This is a program for low-income youths, who board at the training centers and stay in the program for many months at a time. In contrast, some of the CETA training programs last only a few weeks. Indeed, these programs were designed to reach as many unemployed people as possible—to give them hope and keep them in the labor market. Early evaluations suggest that these shorter programs have a lesser return.

The supported work experiments are additional examples of longer-term successful programs. These programs gave extensive training to several groups of hard-to-employ workers. Even for groups who had experienced chronic employment difficulties, the experiments showed that an extensive training program could lead to a far better employment record, and, in particular, to enough added employment to pay for the costs of the program.

The Reagan budgets have cut funds for education and training. Of course, state and local governments are already providing most of the funding for education. The federal cuts are consistent with the strategies of returning certain functions to the state and local sector or to the private sector, and of reducing the size of government. They are not consistent with any strategy of encouraging economic growth.

Private Saving and Investment

The federal budget can also affect private saving decisions and, through them, the rate of economic growth. Certain outlays substitute for private saving, and increasing them would presumably cause saving to fall. Other outlays may complement saving, and increasing them could cause saving to rise. In this section, I discuss the two major classes of budget outlays thought to affect private saving: social security and federal loan programs.

---

20. Charles Mallar et al., *Evaluation of the Economic Impact of the Job Corps Program: Second Follow-up Report* (Princeton, N.J.: Mathematica Policy Research, 1980).

Social Security

An unfunded social security system provides a way for the current work-ing generation to support the current retired generation through direct transfer payments. As Samuelson showed in his famous consumption-loan paper, this provides a way for all individuals to save when young and to dis-save when old without requiring that the society accumulate any capital.[21] Thus the unfunded U.S. social security system could, in principle, provide a substantial threat to capital accumulation.

How big is the threat? Martin Feldstein has estimated that private saving has been reduced by as much as 38 percent because of the social security system now in place.[22] Some earlier estimates had noted the possibility of a complementary relationship between social security and private saving. This relationship would occur if expanding the system would permit retirees to cross a threshold that would enable them to live away from their children when old. Clearly, in this case, the level of private saving could increase in response to expanding the social security system.

This administration is most strongly influenced by those who believe that social security is a substitute for private saving: Martin Feldstein is the chairman of the Council of Economic Advisers. Therefore, one might expect that the administration would be making a major attempt to influence private saving by its proposals to improve the financing of the social security system.

However, these proposals largely adhere to the recommendations of a bipartisan commission, assembled to study the issue in as nonpolitical a fashion as possible. This commission called for a substantial package of tax increases and benefit reductions, and this is largely the package that the administration requested in its 1984 budget. If these proposals are not adopted, the promised benefits and the proposed tax rates would be inconsistent with the principle of a self-financing system.

If we use annual data, the new social security proposals call for quite modest changes. The president's budget claims that $12.2 billion would be saved by these proposals in fiscal 1984, and $67.2 billion over the next four years.[23] About two-thirds of these savings would be in the form of increased taxes and about one-third in reduced benefits.

21. Paul Samuelson, "A Pure Consumption-Loan Model of Interest with or Without the Social Contrivance of Money," *Journal of Political Economy* (1958).

22. Martin Feldstein, "Social Security, Induced Retirement, and Aggregate Accumula-tion," *Journal of Political Economy* 82 (September-October 1974), pp. 905–25.

23. U.S. Office of Management and Budget, *Budget of the United States Government, Fiscal Year 1984*, chapter 3, p. 33.

But the effect of social security on saving depends not only on current taxes and benefits, but on current expectations of future taxes and retirement benefits as well. Therefore, it is wrong to measure how changes in the system affect saving by measuring how they affect outlays in the current year alone. Since the long-run effects of the proposed changes are quite large compared to the short-run ones, it could be argued that the former are more important to citizens making saving decisions in the present.

But a closer look at the expectations issue raises questions about this effect. By a line of reasoning similar to that which is used in macroeconomics to support the "policy-ineffectiveness" hypothesis, one could conclude that the enacted changes in the social security taxes and benefits did not come as a surprise to the public. The future gap that would have developed between outlays and receipts if no changes were made had received a lot of publicity and criticism. The savvy observer of public affairs might have expected that the principle of a self-financing system would prevail, and that it was quite obvious that something was going to be done to close the financing gap. Thus, when proposals to close the gap were actually made, they did not come as a surprise to savers and, therefore, the changes did not signal them to change their behavior.

Of course, this line of reasoning leads to the extreme position that the political actors themselves have no independent influence on policy. According to this broader view, it is because the public wanted saving rates to be increased that the Reagan administration was elected. In this case, why would we give credit to an administration for influencing the public's saving decisions if the administration was elected simply to carry out the public's wishes?

In general, I do not subscribe to this nihilistic view of policy. However, this extreme position makes more sense in the case of the social security system than it does in the area of short-run macroeconomic stabilization. The policy ineffectiveness argument assumes the existence of perfect information and of a perfectly responsive political apparatus. These assumptions are much less appealing in the short run than in the long run, and much less appealing where they require the public to understand the workings of complicated macroeconomic systems than where they require the public to grasp the simple principle of a self-financing system.

On far different grounds, Eisner has argued that the social security system need have no effect on saving.[24] He contends that when social security taxes are changed, automatic macroeconomic responses cause other taxes to be

---

24. Robert Eisner, "Social Security, Saving and Macroeconomics," *Journal of Macroeconomics* 5 (1) (Winter 1983), pp. 1–9.

changed in offsetting ways. For example, in one particular macroeconomic model he shows that, in equilibrium, an increase in perceived social security wealth would be offset dollar for dollar by a reduction in publicly held government securities, which are also a form of wealth. The net effect of this change on any of the important variables in the system would be zero. However, in Eisner's model, the total level of wealth can be affected by policies of easy money and tight fiscal policy. This means that any effect that the social security system could be shown to have on private saving could be offset by shifts in macroeconomic policy. Eisner gives a plausible example in which these responses are automatic. Certainly, for a program as large as social security, the issue of these macroeconomic responses should not be ignored.

In sum, it would be difficult to establish that the proposed changes in the size of the social security system will affect saving. Any effect that could be isolated would surely be small, and, as Eisner suggests, easy to offset with other policies.

Federal Lending Activities

Another area of controversy is how federal lending activities affect saving. Some of these activities are removed from the budget and are carried out by off-budget agencies. Presumably, this is to reflect the fact that these agencies are more similar to financial intermediaries than they are to spending agencies. They borrow from the public by issuing debt, and they relend to the public on preferential terms. These loans do not affect any activities that are measured in the national income accounts.

It is an open question whether these lending activities have any effect at all on saving.[25] One can imagine an equilibrium in which the banks, who would otherwise lend directly to individual borrowers, instead buy securities from the government, who relends the borrowed funds to the same borrowers who would otherwise have gone to the banks. In this case, the lending activity would simply be a redundant form of financial intermediation with no real effects. Changes in its level could not affect saving.

As an example of this, Manski and Wise have found in a recent study that the policy of lending to students who attend traditional colleges and

---

25. See, for example, David Small and M. Kay Plantes, "The Choice of Instrument and Policy Rules for Federal Credit Agencies," unpublished, University of Wisconsin, Jan. 1983.

universities has little effect on their decision to go to college.[26] Possibly it could even affect their decision to spend and consume while attending college and, therefore, it could affect saving in a negative way. But since it has little effect on their decision to attend college, it has little effect on national investment.

On the other hand, one could make the argument that federal home loans to GIs after World War II on terms that were unavailable from banks opened a new market for private lenders. By showing how credit worthy these borrowers were, at least in an economy that maintained its prosperity, the federal lenders caused overall housing investment to rise. They did this without incurring large financial losses, the threat of which had kept private lenders out of the market.

On balance, however, the Reagan administration's policy of cutting such lending is more likely to have a negative effect on saving, if it has any effect at all.

Conclusion

If the Reagan administration had wished to use budgetary spending decisions to enhance economic growth, it would have proposed increases in those areas thought to stimulate growth rates. These areas certainly include R&D, physical facilities, the environment, and human capital formation. The absence of increases in these activities—except when they are related to defense—indicates that economic growth was not a major objective of the administration when it set its budget policy. Indeed, because outlays in these critical investment areas have, in general, been reduced, I must conclude that the prospects for economic growth have been hurt. However, because it is so difficult to measure the returns to these activities, this conclusion must remain tentative.

---

26. Charles F. Manski and David Wise, *College Choice in America* (Cambridge: Harvard University Press, 1983).

ALTERNATIVE MEASURES OF FEDERAL INVESTMENT OUTLAYS

Charles L. Schultze

The first two tables in this section provide two alternative measures of the federal government's outlays for investment in both human and physical resources to promote economic growth. All the estimates exclude defense outlays.

Table 1, the most comprehensive measure, reproduces the Office of Management and Budget (OMB) estimates of constant-dollar investment in physical resources and civilian research and development (R&D), including federal grants-in-aid to state and local governments for those purposes. This table also includes federal spending on education and training, excluding expenditures for public service employment.[1]

Over the two decades prior to 1981, the sum of real federal expenditures in physical capital and R&D remained amazingly constant whereas investment in human resources increased rapidly. Since the late 1960s, however, federal investment including education and training had been declining as a percentage of GNP. On the basis of the January 1983 budget document, all three categories of public capital formation will have been cut sharply between 1981 and 1984, in absolute terms and, even more, as a percentage of GNP.

Private business investment projects normally have to meet some test of profitability; there is at least a presumption that a project is likely to have a marginal product greater than the cost of capital. But no market test is imposed on public investment; the mere fact that a particular budget outlay is defined as an "investment" type expenditure carries no presumption that it adds to economic growth. If we accept the Harberger convention that, at the margin,

---

1. In some of the earlier years, identification of public service employment outlays was difficult, and minor errors may have crept in.

TABLE 1

FEDERAL SPENDING ON PHYSICAL INVESTMENT, CIVILIAN R&D, AND EDUCATION AND
TRAINING: *BROAD DEFINITION*
(Billions of 1972 dollars, selected fiscal years)

	1964/65	1968/69	1973/74	1978/79	1981	1984[a]
Physical Investment	11.3	10.8	11.9	15.3	14.0	12.1
R&D	9.8	9.8	7.3	8.2	8.2	5.7
SUBTOTAL	21.1	20.6	19.2	23.5	22.2	17.8
(% of GNP)	(2.4)	(2.0)	(1.5)	(1.6)	(1.5)	(1.2)
Education and Training	2.1	7.7	6.8	9.1	9.0	6.3
TOTAL	23.2	28.3	26.0	32.6	31.2	24.2
(% of GNP)	(2.6)	(2.7)	(2.1)	(2.3)	(2.1)	(1.6)

NOTES: *Physical Investment*, OMB tabulation of "major physical capital investment," both
direct and grants-in-aid (from Special Analysis D) deflated to 1972 dollars by OMB.
Research and Development, federal civilian research and development, tabulated and
deflated by OMB. *Education and Training*, federal budget expenditures for the functional categories "elementary and secondary education," "higher education," and
"training, employment, and labor services" less expenditures for various types of
public service employment. These data were deflated by the OMB deflator for grants-
in-aid other than transfers.
a.   Reagan administration's FY 1984 budget request.

federal investments are funded by federal borrowing, then, in periods of high
employment, failure of a federal investment project to yield the opportunity
cost of private capital implies that such projects actually reduce potential
GNP.

A number of economic studies have called into question, on an opportunity cost basis, the merits of several federal investment types of programs,
including many water resource projects. Other federal investment outlays may
have quite high social merits but contribute nothing to the growth of measured
potential output. Pollution control investments are a case in point; for purposes
of a production function for GNP they should be excluded, just as they are
for private capital.

Could the sharp reductions in federal outlays for investment be defended
as consistent with a growth-oriented budget policy on grounds that they were
concentrated in the categories of federal investment in which returns were
below the opportunity cost of capital? The only way to answer that question
precisely would be to have marginal yield estimates for every federal investment project, an obvious impossibility. A rough-and-ready alternative
was attempted in which whole categories of federal "investment" were excluded from the total on one of two criteria: (1) where a strong consensus
exists among economists that the yield of a large number of projects in the

category fell below the cost of capital; (2) where the outlay, however desirable on other grounds, does not contribute to the growth of measured GNP.

Using these criteria, the following categories of federal investment programs were excluded: water and power facilities; pollution control investment; community and regional development outlays; and the conduct of R&D by the National Institute of Health (NIH) and the National Aeronautics and Space Administration (NASA). Obviously although some outlays in these categories would meet the test of yielding the opportunity cost of capital or contribute to the measured GNP, the bulk probably would not. Moreover, erring in the other direction, outlays for mass-transit capital grants were left in, and it is doubtful that they pay their way in national benefits.

TABLE 2

FEDERAL SPENDING ON PHYSICAL INVESTMENT, CIVILIAN R&D, AND EDUCATION AND TRAINING: NARROW DEFINITION FEDERAL EXPENDITURES, 1964–1984
(Billions of 1972 dollars, selected fiscal years)

	1964/65	*1968/69*	*1973/74*	*1978/79*	*1981*	*1984*[a]
1. Physical Investment	8.8	7.6	7.5	6.9	7.3	7.7
2. R&D	2.2	3.0	3.1	4.2	4.2	3.3
3. SUBTOTAL	11.0	10.6	10.6	11.1	11.5	11.0
4. Education and Training	2.1	7.7	6.8	9.1	9.0	6.3
5. TOTAL	13.2	18.3	17.5	20.2	20.5	17.3
6. Civilian Budget (less interest)	84.9	109.1	148.0	201.3	215.9	215.3
7. TOTAL (line 5) as % of Civilian Budget	16	17	12	10	9	8

Percentage of constant-dollar GNP, selected fiscal years

	1964/65	*1968/69*	*1973/74*	*1978/79*	*1981*	*1984*[a]
1. Physical Investment	1.0	0.7	0.6	0.5	0.5	0.5
2. R&D	0.3	0.3	0.3	0.3	0.3	0.2
3. SUBTOTAL	1.3	1.0	0.9	0.8	0.8	0.7
4. Education and Training	0.2	0.7	0.5	0.6	0.6	0.4
5. TOTAL	1.5	1.7	1.4	1.4	1.4	1.1
6. Civilian Budget (less interest)	9.7	10.3	11.9	13.9	14.3	14.2

NOTE: *Physical Investment*: Table 1 amount, *less* investment in (i) water and power facilities (ii) pollution control and (iii) community and regional development. The three exclusions were deflated by the overall OMB physical investment deflator. *Research and Development*: Table 1 amount, *less* expenditures for the conduct of research and development by NIH and NASA. The exclusions were deflated by the overall R&D deflator. These estimates leave in the total a small amount for the construction of R&D facilities by NIH and NASA.

a. Reagan administration's FY 1984 budget request.

The resulting, more narrowly defined, totals for federal investment are shown in table 2 and the magnitude of the excluded outlays in table 3. These tables show that most of the Reagan administration's reductions in federal spending on physical investment and R&D did indeed come in programs whose contribution to measured GNP growth is questionable. After the exclusions described above the sum of physical investment and R&D was held roughly constant, although this, of course, still results in a slight decline of these outlays as a fraction of GNP. Spending on human resource investment was cut back sharply. Total investment outlays, even on the narrow definition, fell.

A final caveat is in order. Many of the federal programs for investment in physical resources and for education and training are carried out in the form of grants-in-aid to state and local governments. To a varying extent in each program these grants-in-aid are subject to substitution effects. With grants-in-aid available, state and local governments may spend less from their own revenues on the programs to which the grants-in-aid are directed and divert the funds so saved to other public purposes or to tax reduction. A dollar of federal grants-in-aid designated for an investment purpose does not necessarily add a dollar to total public investment.

TABLE 3

FEDERAL INVESTMENT AND R&D OUTLAYS *EXCLUDED* FROM TABLE 2
(*Billions of 1972 dollars, selected fiscal years*)

	1964/65	1968/69	1973/74	1978/79	1981	1984[a]
Physical Investment	2.5	3.2	4.4	8.4	6.7	4.5
R&D	7.6	6.8	4.2	4.0	4.0	2.4
TOTAL	11.1	10.0	8.6	12.4	10.7	6.9

a. Reagan administration's FY 1984 budget request.

THE LONG-TERM EFFECTS OF CURRENT MACROECONOMIC POLICIES

Lawrence H. Summers

When Ronald Reagan ran for the presidency of the United States, he asked voters this question: Are you better off today than you were four years ago? In the interval between the 1976 and 1980 elections, the unemployment rate had declined from 8.0 percent to 7.5 percent, but the inflation rate had jumped from 3.7 to 13.1 percent. Given Reagan's defeat of Carter, the American people apparently thought they were worse off. Under the macroeconomic policies followed during Reagan's term in office, unemployment is expected to return, by the time of the 1984 election, to approximately the rate that prevailed in 1980, while inflation will have declined about eight percentage points.[1]

Although this simple comparison can hardly provide a serious basis for an evaluation of the long-term macroeconomic policies pursued during the past few years, the comparison does serve to underscore an important point. The American public views inflation as far more costly than is suggested by the models with which economists tend to work. Whether or not professional economists approve the result, or even understand the reasons for it, Ronald Reagan was elected president with a mandate to end a pattern of rising inflation rates and to reduce the absolute level of inflation. It is against this backdrop that the impact of Reagan's policies must be evaluated.

The Reagan program, as described in countless campaign statements and codified in the administration's March 1981 budget submissions to Congress, had four main elements:

---

1. These estimates are derived from Congressional Budget Office (CBO), "Baseline Budget Projections for Fiscal Years, 1985-1989," February 1984.

179

1. Major tax reductions relative to preexisting law

2. A major reallocation of federal spending priorities away from civilian spending toward national defense, along with a sharp reduction in total spending relative to GNP

3. Support of the Federal Reserve in the pursuit of a noninflationary policy of stable money growth

4. An unshackling of the private economy through deregulation.

The argument was advanced that this policy package would usher in an unparalleled approach of noninflationary, rapid real growth. Many observers at the time greeted this rosy scenario with incredulity, and history has proved the skeptics right. Whatever the absolute merits of the policy packaged dubbed "Reaganomics," it has clearly fallen far short of the promises of its proponents. At this point, analysis requires use of a more reasonable standard—comparison with the possible outcomes if other policies had been pursued.

As things have turned out, deregulation has been of no macroeconomic significance and of little microeconomic significance. Monetary policy has been noninflationary, but hardly steady or stable. Tax cuts relative to a Carter administration benchmark have been enormous, but spending cuts have not kept pace, resulting in large, seemingly permanent, budget deficits.

Hence, Reaganomics, as it has panned out, appears to have three main elements, listed here in declining order of importance: First, a policy of drastic disinflation has been followed, with resulting sharp declines in both inflation and output. Second, the mix of "demand" policy instruments has been altered in a semipermanent way toward looser fiscal and tighter monetary policies. Third, the tax and transfer system has been reformed in an effort to give greater incentives to productive economic activity.

At the outset, I should acknowledge that the first and much of the second element of what I am calling the Reagan economic policies were implemented at the Federal Reserve rather than in the White House. As many observers have pointed out, the Fed's chairman, Paul Volcker, was a Carter appointee, and the shift towards disinflationary policies began in October 1979, more than sixteen months before the Reagan administration took office. Nevertheless, I shall not try to allocate credit or blame between the federal government and the Reagan administration, but to consider the policy package that has been followed as a whole.

My task in this paper is to examine the long-term effects of the macroeconomic policies that have been followed in the past three years. To that end, I shall not dwell on the recent record of recession and disinflation, but will instead concentrate on the future. The first section of this paper examines the likely effect of the recent recession on inflation and output. A judgment about the ultimate long-term effects of a sharp recession on inflation and output is presumably central to an evaluation of the desirability of using a recession as a device for fighting inflation. The second section examines the long-range impact of sustained budget deficits on the composition of economic activity. Tautologically, in the economists' long run, where full employment must prevail, deficits must crowd out other forms of spending. Some crude estimates of the effect of crowding out by sector are presented. The third section examines the supply-side effects of the tax increases that have been introduced. I argue that these effects are likely to be significant but have to date been dwarfed by the effects of the recession. The fourth section offers some concluding observations.

The Long-term Effects of Sharp Disinflation

The United States is now emerging from the most severe economic downturn of the post-World War II period. In 1982 the unemployment rate reached double-digit levels, far surpassing its previous peak of 8.9 percent during the 1975 recession. At the same time, capacity utilization fell to its lowest level since collection of the data began. Virtually every economic statistic associated with production of goods and services declined further than in any previous recession. The recent downturn is also unmatched in its duration. At the end of 1982, the real gross national product (GNP) was below its 1979 level. Most forecasters do not expect unemployment to decline even to 7 percent prior to 1986. The cumulative GNP gap incurred so far since 1979 has been $900 billion in current dollars. The projected gap out to 1987 is another $500 billion.[2]

Table 1 presents a profile of the recent downturn. Two features of the table warrant discussion. First, the rate of inflation declined sharply from 13.5 percent in 1980 to 3.2 percent over the first two quarters of 1983 (as measured by the Consumer Price Index). Even using the GNP deflator, the inflation rate has declined by 5.5 percentage points over the same interval. Declines of comparable size have also occurred in a variety of indices of wage inflation.[3] Second, despite the recession, real consumption has increased

---

2. This calculation assumes that potential GNP is reached at 6 percent unemployment.

3. For a discussion, see George Perry, "What Have We Learned about Disinflation?" (Washington, D.C.: The Brookings Institution, 1983); *Brookings Papers on Economic Activity*, 1983:2 (Washington, D.C.: The Brookings Institution), pp. 587–602. Adjusted hourly earnings rose at a 3.9 percent rate in 1983 compared to 9.6 percent in 1980.

TABLE 1

RECENT ECONOMIC INDICATORS
*(Percentage change from previous period at seasonally adjusted annual rates,
unless otherwise noted)*

	1980	1981	1982	1983
Real GNP	−0.3	2.6	−1.9	3.3
Final sales	0.5	1.8	−0.7	2.8
Consumption	0.5	2.7	1.4	4.2
Business fixed investment	−2.4	5.2	−4.7	1.1
Residential investment	−20.4	−5.2	−15.4	39.6
Government purchases	2.2	0.8	1.8	0.5
Inventory change				
(billions of 1972 dollars)	−4.4	8.5	−9.4	−2.4
Net exports				
(billions of 1972 dollars)	50.3	43.0	28.9	11.7
Industrial production	−3.6	2.7	−8.2	6.6
Capacity utilization (percentage)	90.4	80.2	72.1	75.4
Payroll employment (millions)	7.2	91.2	89.6	90.0
Civilian unemployment rate (percentage)	13.5	7.6	9.7	9.6
Inflation rate				
CPI-U	9.8	10.4	6.1	3.2
GNP deflator (fixed weight)	7.0	9.5	6.4	4.3

SOURCE: This table is reproduced with modifications from Congressional Budget Office, Economic and Budget Outlook, January 1984.

NOTE: Percentage change is measured from previous period at seasonally adjusted annual rates, unless otherwise noted.

quite steadily, rising in every quarter of 1982. The burden of the recession fell largely on investment and net exports. While investment showed strength, net exports continued to be very weak during the 1983 recovery.

These two observations lead naturally to the two questions on which this section focuses. First, is a sharp, protracted downturn likely to achieve durable progress against inflation? Second, what are the long-term costs to the economy of a sharp recession?

How Durable Is Our Progress Against Inflation?

To answer this question, it is useful to consider a simple stylized model of the inflation process. I assume that inflation evolves according to the equation:

$$\dot{P}_{t-} \dot{P}_{t-1} = aGAP_t + b(GAP_t - GAP_{t-1}) + (Z_t - cZ_{t-1}). \quad (1)$$

Equation (1) is a slightly augmented Phillips curve holding that the change in the role of inflation has three determinants: the size of the GNP gap, its rate of change, and supply shocks. The parameter c measures the extent to which supply shocks are propagated through the wage process.[4] Research on the American economy tends to suggest that c is close to unity, and so supply shocks do not permanently influence the inflation rate.

A large literature,[5] much of it in the *Brookings Papers on Economic Activity*, has been directed at estimating parameters corresponding to a and b econometrically. Although no clear consensus exists, a middle-of-the-road estimate is that it takes about five point years of GNP gap to reduce the inflation rate by 1 percent, and that a and b are of roughly equal size (i.e., equal to -0.2). Unfortunately, the evidence is very weak on the relative size of these "level" and "rate of change" effects. This issue is critical. For example, if $a = 0$, recessions will yield no permanent dividends in terms of disinflation. Any gains realized as the economy declines will be lost as the economy recovers.

With these assumptions, the equation for the evolution of inflation becomes:

$$\dot{P}_t - \dot{P}_{t-1} = -0.4 \, GAP_t + 0.2 \, GAP_{t-1} + Z_t - Z_{t-1}. \qquad (2)$$

It follows immediately that if there are no supply shocks, half of a given period GNP gap can be made up on that period without causing inflation to accelerate. Given a current GNP gap of about 6 percent and a potential growth rate of about 2.5 percent, this equation implies that (assuming no supply-shock effects) inflation will not accelerate even if the economy grows at 5.5 percent over the next year and at 4.0 percent in the following year.[6] Of course the assumption of no supply-shock effects is critical to this result.

Note, however, that the rate of economic growth consistent with no acceleration in inflation depends only on the ratio a/b and is independent of the size of these coefficients. To produce a more pessimistic inflation outlook than the one suggested here, we would have to assume that the "rate of

---

4. See, for example, Jeffrey Sachs, "Wages, Profits and Macroeconomic Adjustment," *Brookings Papers on Economic Activity*, 1979: 2, pp. 269–332.

5. See references in Perry, "What Have We Learned About Disinflation?"

6. If Z_t and Z_{t-1} are zero (no supply shocks), nonaccelerating inflation ($p_t = p_{t-1}$) implies that $GAP_t = \frac{1}{2}GAP_{t-1}$. In other words, half the gap can be made up without increasing the rate of inflation. If GAP = 6 percent, then GNP can grow at 5.5 percent without increasing inflation if the potential (high-employment) rate of GNP growth is 2.5 percent ($0.5 \times 6\% + 2.5\%$). In the following year, the GAP is 3 percent, implying ($0.5 \times 3\% + 2.5\% = 4.0\%$) as the growth rate of GNP associated with a constant rate of inflation.

change" effect of output on prices exceeded the "level" effect. Alternatively, we could argue that this calculation has assumed too large a GNP gap. The GNP gap considered here is consistent with a NAIRU (nonaccelerating inflation rate of unemployment) of a little over 6 percent. Given the favorable demographic developments over the past several years, this assumption seems reasonable. The principal qualifications to the relatively optimistic calculation in the preceding paragraph involve the possibility of adverse supply shocks.

Predicting the path of raw material prices is notoriously difficult, and any prediction is likely to be falsified by the time this is printed. It is important to note, however, that favorable developments in the oil and food markets have reduced the rate of inflation in the past year by at least 1 percent. This means that Z_{t-1} in (2) is negative, implying that even with normal luck, we will suffer an adverse supply-shock effect because the good luck of the past will not have continued. In addition, raw materials prices have probably been reduced by the combination of world recession and high real interest rates. These factors will diminish as time passes.

Another factor pointing in the same direction is the recent behavior of the exchange rate. The real value of the dollar relative to a trade-weighted basket of foreign currencies is now about 30 percent above its long-term average level. This situation, and the associated disarray in the trade sector of our economy, is unlikely to persist indefinitely. The rate at which it unwinds will have an important effect on the path of inflation over the next few years. As a rough rule of thumb, a 1 percent decline in the exchange rate raises the U.S. price level by at least 0.1 percent and perhaps by as much as 0.25 percent, depending on the price index and lag length considered.[7]

This means that wrapped up in the exchange rate are between three and eight percentage points' worth of supply-shock inflation that we will have to suffer at some point. Comparison of real interest rates here and abroad suggests that the market expects the decline in the dollar to be negligible, implying only very small inflationary impacts over the next several years. Many observers, especially those sensitive to political considerations here and abroad, seem to expect a more precipitous drop-off. But the foreign exchange futures markets clearly do not share this view.[8]

This discussion has assumed the existence of a stable relationship between inflation and its determinants. Much modern work in macroeconomics

---

7. For a discussion of the relationships between exchange rates and inflation, see Rudiger Dornbusch and Stanley Fischer, "Monetary and Fiscal Policies in the Open Economy," Massachusetts Institute of Technology, mimeographed.

8. For a discussion of this question, see O. J. Blanchard and L. H. Summers, "Why Are World Real Interest Rates So High?" mimeographed.

suggests that the parameters of the Phillips curve type of relationships are likely to be functions of the policy environment. The crucial idea for economic policy is that a government that is credibly committed to disinflation can disinflate at much less cost than is implied by equation (2). A number of recent studies by Perry, Gordon, and Earle and Kneisner[9] have attempted to test this idea by examining how well Phillips curves of various types have held up over the past several years. Typically they have found no strong evidence that inflation as measured using wages or prices has subsided more rapidly than might have been expected given the severity of the recession and the sharp appreciation recently observed in the exchange rate.

These results are not, however, consistent with the hypothesis that recent experience will tend to hold down inflation in the future by making it clear that government will not always follow policies of accommodation. But no evidence now exists to support this idea. To the extent that this hypothesis is true, it supports an even more optimistic outlook on inflation than the one implicit in the previous discussion.

In sum, there can be little doubt that real progress has been made against inflation and that, barring bad luck, much of the gain will be permanent. In particular, it is noteworthy that the rate of wage inflation, which had exceeded 6 percent in every year since 1968, had fallen below 4 percent by the end of 1983. A reasonable estimate is that the disinflationary policy and the associated recession have reduced the long-term rate of inflation by about 5 percent. Substantial acceleration of inflation appears unlikely even on quite rapid recovery paths. But this progress against inflation has been achieved at a great cost—the recent recession. We now turn to the question of the long-term costs of the recession.

The Long-term Costs of the Recession

The costs of the recent recession and its associated protracted period of economic stagnation are all too apparent. Much less clear is the shadow the recession casts over future economic activity. Perhaps the most straightforward long-term cost of the recession is a permanently lower capital stock as a result of reduced investment during the recession. Although this cost is often added to the output loss that occurs during a recession, such a procedure involves double counting. If, and this is a rather big if, the economy is at an optimal level of capital intensity, the present value of the returns in the form of future output from a one-dollar investment is just one dollar. Hence,

---

9. This work is reviewed in Perry, "What We Have Learned About Disinflation?"

measuring the value of all the output lost during a recession captures the present value of lost future output. If, because of some imperfection, capital is too scarce, the social loss from forgoing one dollar of investment will exceed one dollar. In that case, the recession can be said to impose long-term costs beyond its contemporaneous burden.

Gauging the appropriate shadow price to put on forgone investment is difficult. The traditional argument for a shadow price greater than one was premised on the wedge between the social and private returns to investment, resulting from taxes on capital income. With the sharp reductions in effective tax rates brought about by the 1981 tax reforms, this argument loses much of its force. A shadow price of two on new investment would surely be an upper-bound estimate. Lost plant and equipment investment attributable to the recession can be generously estimated at 4 percent of GNP. These figures imply an upper-bound estimate of 4 percent GNP for the lost future output resulting from the recession.

The case of forgone human capital investment is more complex. There are several mechanisms through which recessions are alleged to retard human capital accumulation. The first is simply the lost experience of the work force that results from reduced employment levels during the recession. Cross-sectional evidence points to the existence of a steep wage-experience profile. Whether this profile can be extrapolated to gauge the effects of unemployment spells on productivity is unclear. If the experience-wage profile reflects only human capital accumulation, such an extrapolation is valid. If, however, it also reflects the effects of screening or implicit contracting, such an extrapolation is not valid. Several studies using data on teenagers have directly examined the issue of whether unemployment leaves scars. Perhaps the most careful study, by David Ellwood,[10] finds weak evidence of scars. But Ellwood reports that, other things being equal, local labor market conditions during a person's teenage years have no effect on that person's subsequent employment patterns or wages. It does not appear that the long-term costs of having a less experienced work force are high. Moreover, it is likely that in slack times workers who remain on the job have increased opportunities for training.

A second way in which a serious recession may cast a shadow is by slowing or halting the process of worker upgrading. This argument was advanced by Arthur Okun and Lester Thurow[11] as a reason for supporting a

---

10. David Ellwood, "Teenage Unemployment: Permanent Scars or Temporary Blemishes," and Richard Freeman and David Wise, eds., *The Youth Labor Market Problem: Its Nature, Causes and Consequences* (University of Chicago Press) 1982.

11. See Arthur Okun, "Upward Mobility in a High Pressure Economy," *Brookings Papers on Economic Activity*, 1973:1 pp. 207–252 and L. C. Thurow, *Generating Inequality: Mechanisms of Distribution in the U.S. Economy* (New York: Basic Books, 1975).

high-pressure economy. It holds that the number of workers who get to enter the primary sector depends on economic conditions. Once in the primary sector, workers are able to remain there and to be far more productive than they could have been in the secondary sector. This argument must confront the question of whether a recession imposes a permanent cost or whether it simply penalizes one cohort at the expense of a future cohort. There must be some limit on the potential size of the primary sector.

An issue closely related to human capital accumulation is persistence in labor supply. In a recent paper, Kim Clark and I[12] contrasted two alternative views of labor supply. One view that has come into vogue with the new classical macroeconomics holds that intertemporal substitution plays a primary role in labor supply decisions. In other words, workers schedule work when it is most attractive. An alternative view holds that persistence plays a dominant role in determining labor supply. It stresses effects involving habit formation and the acquisition of home- or job-specific human capital.

These two views have very different implications for the long-term impact of a recession. According to the "intertemporal substitution" view, a recession may actually increase subsequent output, as workers schedule themselves back into the labor force. According to the "persistence" view, a recession reduces subsequent labor force participation and therefore potential output. Clark and I examined several types of evidence including the World War II experience and the experience in local labor markets. We found that persistence effects predominate and are quite strong. Across local labor markets, for example, there is a strong association between the "permanent" unemployment rate and the labor force participation rate. This suggests that the recession may have a long-term adverse impact on output by reducing labor force participation.

The final way in which a recession may affect subsequent potential output is through its impact on productivity. The argument is frequently made that a sharp decline in sales forces businesses to reduce their break-even points by cutting out waste. Similarly, workers come to value their jobs more highly and, as a consequence, work harder. Alternatively, it is argued that progress and innovation come more rapidly when markets are large and growing than when they are contracting. Aggregate time series are not long enough to make it worthwhile to seriously attempt to disentangle these issues. However, recent research by Hulten and Schwab[13] sheds light on the issue. They find that

12. Kim Clark and Lawrence Summers, "Labor Force Participation: Timing and Persistence," *Review of Economic Studies*, Special Issue, vol. XLIX(5), no.159, 1982, pp. 825–844.

13. Charles R. Hulten and Robert M. Schwab, "Regional Productivity Growth in U.S. Manufacturing: 1951–78," *American Economic Review*, March 1984, pp. 153–163.

there are only minor differences in long-term growth of total factor productivity across regions in the United States despite the very different cyclical conditions that have prevailed. This suggests that these effects are offsetting or small, or both.

European experience, particularly the recent rapid growth of productivity in Britain, is sometimes cited as evidence of a productivity-enhancing effect of recessions. This conclusion depends on a subtle issue of interpretation. Does productivity depend on the level or the rate of change effects? It seems likely that relatively inefficient workers and capital are the first to be taken out of production during recessions and the first to be rehired as the economy recovers. If this is so, recessionary gains in productivity will be lost when an economy returns to full employment.

On balance, then, the disinflationary binge of the past few years has caused much pain and will cause more, but is likely to have few lingering effects on real economic performance. Progress in reducing inflation is likely to be much more durable. Whether our investment in reducing inflation was a wise one is a question answerable only by looking at alternatives. This task lies outside the scope of this paper.

The New Policy Mix

An inadvertent legacy of the Reagan economic program has been a large, seemingly permanent, structural federal budget deficit. The bottom section of table 2 makes it clear that if 1981 economic policies had been maintained, no significant structural deficits would have arisen. Under current policy, however, the outlook is for large and growing structural deficits. The structural deficit is projected to rise from 3.0 percent of GNP in 1984 by about 0.5 percent a year to 5.5 percent of GNP in 1989. No structural deficits as large as 3.0 percent for even a single year have occurred in the past three decades. The current outlook is clearly unsustainable. The national debt is projected to rise rapidly as a share of GNP from 35.4 percent in 1983 to 49.4 percent in 1989.

Table 2 also provides an explanation of how the Reagan economic program, as enacted by the Congress, has led to this situation. Relative to a baseline determined by policies in effect at the end of the Carter administration, there have been only minimal cuts in total federal outlays exclusive of interest payments. In 1984, cutbacks in civilian spending exceed increased defense outlays by only 0.6 percent of GNP. As the Reagan defense buildup continues, this difference will dwindle to only 0.1 percent of GNP by 1989.

TABLE 2

CAUSES OF THE REAGAN DEFICITS
(*Percentage of GNP*)

	1984	*1985*	*1986*	*1987*	*1988*	*1989*
1981 policy deficit	3.1	2.1	1.5	.8	.3	− .2
Tax reductions	2.6	3.0	3.5	3.9	4.1	4.4
Defense spending increase	.7	.9	1.0	1.2	1.3	1.4
Nondefense spending cuts	− 1.3	− 1.5	− 1.7	− 1.6	− 1.5	− 1.5
Interest cost effects	.2	.5	.8	1.1	1.4	1.9
Current projected deficit	5.3	5.0	5.1	5.4	5.6	6.0
Structural deficits						
1981 policy	.8	.4	.2	− .3	− .4	− .8
Current policy	3.0	3.3	3.8	4.3	4.9	5.5

SOURCE: The estimates are derived from table D-1 of the Congressional Budget Office, "Baseline Budget Projection for Fiscal Years 1985–1989," February 1984. The 1981 policy defense spending assumption involves 3 percent real growth from 1981 on. The structural deficit is defined as the deficit that would occur if the unemployment rate were 6.0 percent.

Policy actions directed at limiting civilian spending have been almost entirely offset by increases in defense spending.

It is obvious that the primary causes of the large deficits now in prospect are the Reagan tax cuts and the extra interest costs incurred in their financing. In 1989, for example, the combined effects of the 1981 and 1982 tax legislation will be to reduce revenues by 4.4 percent of GNP. Extra interest costs, which are due almost entirely to the debt accumulation caused by revenue reductions in previous years, totaled 1.9 percent of GNP. These two factors more than account for the entire projected deficit. The growing role of interest expenses in table 2 deserves emphasis. Simply paying the extra interest costs incurred as a result of the tax cut in 1989 would require a tax increase of close to 2 percent of GNP. This is equivalent to more than a 20 percent surcharge on individual income taxes.

In sum, there is no mystery about how the large budget deficits have materialized. The Reagan administration reoriented but did not substantially change the level of federal spending. It legislated massive tax cuts that led to direct increases in deficits, and further indirect increases as interest expenses rose on the mounting debt.

Before turning to an analysis of the economic effect of budget deficits, it is crucial to stress one point overlooked in most discussions. Running deficits is not a true alternative to increasing taxes or reducing spending. In present value terms, the government must balance its budget. Greater deficits today require future tax increases or spending cutbacks to meet interest payments on increased indebtedness. Indeed, if, as is true at present, the real interest rate exceeds the economy's growth rate, deficits will lead to increases in future tax rates greater than those that would be required to eliminate the deficits now. Rational economic analysis cannot proceed by contrasting the costs of deficits with those of alternative fiscal actions. Rather, it must examine the effects of deficits, recognizing that the costs of financing spending cannot be avoided no matter what policies are pursued. The choice is not between tax increases and deficits, but between tax increases and deficits followed by tax increases.

Economic Effects of Deficits

Traditional Keynesian economic models hold that, other things being equal, budget deficits should increase output through the familiar income-expenditure mechanism. Such multiplier analysis of the effects of deficits takes a short-run view in assuming that the economy's resources are not fully employed and that monetary policy is passive. It is clear that neither assumption is warranted in examining the effects of protracted structural budget deficits. In the medium term, the level of output will hover around its capacity level. In the shorter term, the Federal Reserve can determine the level of output in face of any given fiscal policy by altering monetary policy.

The important questions about fiscal policy thus do not relate to its impact on the level of GNP, but to its effect on the composition of GNP. If the level of GNP is held constant, it is tautologous that increases in deficits must crowd out something. A natural way to round up the suspects is to use the national income-accounting identity to write the equation:

$$D = G^f - T^f = PS + (T^s - G^s) + NFI - I. \qquad (3)$$

where D represents the federal deficit, PS is private savings, $G^s - T^s$ is the deficit of nonfederal governments, NFI is net foreign investment, and I is domestic investment. In the absence of official reserves transactions, NFI will simply be the negative of the current account balance. Equation (3) demonstrates that with income held constant, increases in federal deficits must raise private savings, raise state and local surpluses, draw funds in from abroad by crowding out net exports, reduce investment, or have some combination of these effects.

Although the last effect is emphasized in simple textbook expositions and the first effect is stressed by classical macroeconomists, there do not

seem to be any widely accepted estimates of the magnitude of these effects.[14]
Later I attempt to reduce uncertainty by reporting some crude reduced form
estimates of the effects of deficits on the composition of GNP, and by looking
at some published simulations of the DRI econometric model.

The reduced form approach was implemented by estimating equations
of the form:

$$\frac{Z_{it}}{GNP_t} = a_i + b_i \frac{D_t}{GNP_t} + C_{it}Cycle_1 + C_{2t}Cycle_2 + U. \qquad (4)$$

where Z_{it}, i = 1, . . . ,4, represent the components of GNP on the right-
hand side of (3) and $Cycle^1$ and $Cycle^2$ are variables intended to control for
cyclical conditions. The coefficient b_i measures the extent to which deficits
affect each national income component. All estimated equations were cor-
rected for first-order serial correlations. In alternative specifications, capacity
utilization, its lagged value, and real GNP growth rates were used as proxies
for cyclical conditions. Equations were estimated using both the standard
deficit and an inflation-adjusted deficit, which accounts for inflation's erosion
of the real value of the outstanding debt. The sample period was 1949–1982,
except in the case of the net foreign investment equation, which was estimated
over the 1973–1982 period to allow for the effects of the shift to floating
exchange rates. Results are shown in table 3. (These specifications and a
number of other variants will be discussed more fully in a forthcoming paper.)

The results differ somewhat across equations, but several reasonably
robust conclusions emerge. Budget deficits call forth increased private savings. Such savings rise by roughly thirty cents for each dollar of federal
deficits. A somewhat larger estimate is obtained with inflation-corrected measures, and a smaller estimate is obtained with the standard measures. The
extra savings may reflect provision for the future tax liabilities associated
with deficits, a positive response of savings to the higher real interest rates
associated with deficits, or the crowding out of consumer durable expenditure
by increased real interest rates. The data clearly refute both the extreme
Ricardian equivalence view and the polar assumption that deficits call forth
no extra private savings. The estimate also suggests some substitutability
between federal and state and local saving. A one-dollar increase in the federal
deficit appears to increase state and local savings by about five cents. This
may reflect substitution on either the tax or spending side.

---

14. The so-called Ricardian equivalence theorem holds that deficits call forth extra savings
dollar for dollar because consumers recognize their need, or that of their heirs, to provide for
the resulting future tax burdens. Most economists regard as untenable the assumption that people
increase their savings in response to taxes that might be levied on their children or grandchildren.

TABLE 3

THE EFFECTS OF FEDERAL DEFICITS ON THE COMPOSITION OF GNP

	Standard Deficit Concept		Inflation-adjusted Deficit Concept	
	GNP Growth	Capacity Utilization	GNP Growth	Capacity Utilization
Net private savings	.204	.233	.440	.464
	(.108)	(.126)	(.099)	(.098)
State and local savings	.058	.051	.062	.018
	(.030)	(.040)	(.025)	(.031)
Net foreign investment (1973–1982)	.270	.684	.256	.236
	1.061	(.749)	(.175)	(.112)
Net investment	−.624	−.602	−.380	−.423
	(.086)	(.117)	(.074)	(.086)
Net nonresidential investment	−.235	−.129	−.172	−.099
	(.067)	(.049)	(.061)	(.031)

NOTE: Estimates refer to b_i in equation (4). Numbers in parentheses are standard errors. Except where noted, estimates refer to the sample period 1949–1982. All equations were estimated with correction for first-order autocorrelation.

The results also suggest that increased deficits crowd out net exports by attracting foreign capital inflows. Theory suggests that this result should occur much more rapidly with floating than with fixed exchange rates, so estimates for the 1973–1982 interval are probably most relevant. They suggest that each dollar of deficits calls forth about twenty-five cents in increased net foreign investment, and so crowds out an approximately equal amount of net exports. In an extreme model of a small country with perfect international capital mobility, such crowding out would occur dollar for dollar. However, the United States bulks large on the world capital market, capital is not perfectly mobile, and foreign monetary authorities act to prevent exchange rate fluctuations that might lead to domestic inflation.

Finally, the estimates suggest that each dollar of federal deficits crowds out about forty cents of net investment. The average estimate in the table is somewhat greater than this but neglects the effects of deficits on foreign capital inflows, which have only become important in the past decade. The estimates in the final row of the table indicate that a little less than half the crowded-out investment is plants and equipment, with the remainder being inventories and housing. While crowding out of investment is clearly important, the impression left in some popular discussions that deficits crowd out business fixed investment dollar for dollar is clearly misleading.

The limitations of these crude reduced forms are all too apparent. An alternative perspective can be gleaned by examining some recent DRI simulations of the effects of a deficit reform package. The deficit reform package that DRI considered reduced the federal deficit as a share of GNP by 3.5 percent of GNP on average over the 1986–1989 period through a balanced combination of defense and civilian spending cuts and tax increases. DRI also estimated the effects of this package on the components of GNP.

Table 4 reports the results. They tend to corroborate the estimates just presented. About one-third of the effects of deficit reduction are offset by increases in private saving. A little less than a third are offset by increased state and local surpluses and reduced net foreign investment. Just over a third of deficit reductions flow into increased net investment. It is encouraging that these large econometric model estimates are so close to the estimates obtained from the reduced forms. While each methodology has its problems for an exercise of this sort, the errors should be relatively independent.

These estimates suggest that prospective federal deficits of 5 percent of GNP will reduce net investment by about 2 percent of GNP, and net exports by about 1 percent of GNP. Net business fixed investment will decline about 1 percent of GNP, about one-third of its average share over the past several decades. Such declines in investment have implications for growth. Based on standard growth accounting assumptions, deficits will reduce the growth rate of potential GNP by between 0.1 and 0.2 percent per year. If the structural changes caused by deficits, particularly the loss of U.S. competitiveness, have some consequences, the damage may be greater.

Against what benefits should these effects of deficits be compared? As already emphasized, deficits should not be compared with tax increases or spending cuts, because they defer, but do not obviate the need for, these

TABLE 4

DRI ECONOMETRIC MODEL ESTIMATES OF THE EFFECT OF A REDUCED DEFICIT ON THE COMPOSITION OF THE GNP
(Percentage of GNP)

	Baseline	*Reduced Deficit*	*Difference*	*Share*
Federal deficit	5.9	2.4	3.5	100
Net private saving	7.0	5.8	1.2	34
State and local saving	1.5	1.2	.3	9
Net foreign investment	2.0	1.3	.7	20
Net investment	4.6	5.9	1.3	37

SOURCE: Data Resources Incorporated Review; November 1983, and author's calculation.

actions. The correct question is whether there are advantages to deferring other fiscal actions at the present time. One rationale for deficits is "tax smoothing." If expenditures are transitorily high, as in a war, financing them with deficits reduces the total tax burden by allowing for a smoother path of marginal tax rates than would otherwise be possible. But there is little reason to think expenditures are transitorily high at present. Moreover, no evidence exists that the benefits of tax smoothing are large.

Another possibility is that deficits are serving a useful function in stabilizing the economy. As emphasized already, the effects of deficits on the level of economic activity are uncertain and depend critically on monetary policy. It is hard to see what beneficial effects a protracted deficit can have over an interval when the economy is expected to be operating at a level close to full employment. Nor would actions to reduce deficits have a destabilizing effect if accompanied by an appropriately accommodating monetary policy. Indeed, N. Gregory Mankiw and I recently estimated that even with the money stock held constant, personal tax increases would be unlikely to reduce aggregate demand.[15]

A final rationalization for high budget deficits comes from what might be called the dietary theory of public expenditure. In this view, deficits exert discipline by holding down the demand of public spending by denying sustenance to the public sector. Whether this is desirable is ultimately a value judgment, but the deficit strategy has had some effect. Civilian spending outside the major middle-income entitlement programs has been cut dramatically. What is more important, calls for new initiatives toward day care and national health insurance and proposals to alleviate poverty have slipped off the national agenda. Whether this effect is permanent is problematic. Indeed, if deficits lead to the passage of a value-added tax, they could well prove to be counterproductive in terms of holding down the size of the public sector.

In summary, the Reagan economic program has left us a semipermanent legacy of high budget deficits. These deficits will call forth some extra private savings but will nonetheless significantly reduce investment and net exports. Ultimately, they will lead to tax increases or spending cuts to cover the interest payments or amortization of the accumulated national debt. Little good seems to be coming of the high deficits.

---

15. N. Gregory Mankiw and Lawrence H. Summers, "Are Tax Increases Necessarily Expansionary?" draft, 1984.

The Supply-Side Program

The major aim of current policies, at least at the time of their inception, was to stimulate aggregate supply by offering increased incentives to work, save, and invest. As I stressed in the introduction, the supply-side program has clearly been a failure, relative to what was promised, but it may ultimately have a limited desirable effect. Many observers have been quick to seize on recent economic events as evidence that tax cuts have only minimal effects on economic behavior. This inference is not warranted.

For the past several years, output has been demand constrained. Workers have not been able to work as much as they would like at prevailing wages, and firms have not been able to sell as much as they would wish at prevailing prices. This is a consequence of the wage and price rigidity characteristic of a Keynesian economy. It means that we have no opportunity to observe points on workers' or firms' supply curves. As a consequence, we have not yet had a chance to estimate the supply responses to the recent tax changes, but there are reasons to think these responses will be significant.

The simplest and most basic response to a reduction in marginal tax rates was expected to be an increase in labor supply. As Jerry Hausman and others have observed,[16] a tax cut in a progressive tax system is likely to give rise to larger substitution effects than income effects. Consider the extreme example of a cut in the top-bracket rate for a person just inside the top bracket. There will be a substitution effect toward more labor supply but no income effect. It follows that even if the uncompensated elasticity of labor supply is zero, tax cuts in a progressive system will increase labor supply. In a demand-constrained economy, these effects will not show up in employment, which is determined by product demand. It is noteworthy, however, that during the recent recession labor force participation held up much more strongly than would have been the case under its normal cyclical pattern.

The large empirical literature on taxation and labor supply has concentrated almost entirely on decisions about hours of work and retirement, but there are other important dimensions to labor supply. Perhaps the most important of these is the trade-off between on-the-job amenities and productivity. Reduction in marginal tax rates will tend to induce workers to substitute away from on-the-job leisure and other perquisites, and toward more arduous, less pleasant forms of labor. At this point, we have almost no evidence on the extent of this effect, although part of the decline in the productivity growth

---

16. Jerry A. Hausman, "Labor Supply," in Henry J. Aaron and Joseph A. Pechman, eds., *How Taxes Affect Economic Behavior* (Washington, D.C.: The Brookings Institution, 1981), pp. 27–83.

rate in the 1970s is often attributed to a reduction in effective labor input. Nor do we have evidence about the effects of taxes on the entrepreneurial energy of managers. If taxes induce managers to work less hard, the consequences for productivity could be quite serious.

The crucial point to understand here is that effects of this type are unlikely to occur immediately in response to tax changes. Institutions adapt slowly to changing conditions, and people reallocate themselves among institutions only gradually. And, most important, these sorts of changes will not occur when supply curves are not binding constraints.

The second major aim of the supply-side program was to spur savings and investment. As the previous section emphasized, private investment must (aside from capital inflows from abroad) be financed from national savings— the sum of private and public savings. Tax cuts that are unmatched by expenditure reductions reduce public savings, other things being equal, reducing private investment. These effects are ignored in this discussion, which focuses on the effects of recent tax reforms assuming no change in budget deficits.

Measures directed at encouraging personal savings were a major element in the supply-side tax package. It was hoped that reductions in marginal tax rates would encourage personal savings by raising real after-tax rates of return. In addition, the 1981 tax act provided for extending Individual Retirement Account (IRA) provisions to all taxpayers. It was also hoped that the reductions in corporate tax burdens would spur savings by raising available rates of return.

The performance of personal savings has not, at least on cursory examination, borne out supply-side hopes. The behavior of the personal savings rate has attracted particular attention. During the second quarter of 1983 it declined to 3.9 percent, close to its historic low. In general, it has run below historically normal levels during the recession, but this statistic is less discouraging than it may seem at first. The personal savings rate is a number in search of a meaning. It fails to include as savings the increments to wealth enjoyed by consumers when the value of the assets they hold appreciates. If the $700 billion increase in wealth enjoyed by consumers over the past year were treated as savings, the personal savings rate would have exceeded 20 percent. Furthermore, the personal savings rate is badly distorted by the use of nominal rather than real accounting. All interest payments received by the household sector are treated as income, even though a sizable fraction of them are in fact repayments of principal, when nominal interest rates include an inflation premium. This means that the savings rate is overstated. During the current period of disinflation, the magnitude of this overstatement has declined substantially. Finally, it should be emphasized that a reduction in savings is a natural response of many people to a transitory decline in their incomes.

For these reasons, evidence on the recent behavior of the savings rate does not provide a basis for evaluating the effects of recent tax policies or savings behavior. Note that the types of tax policies that have been put in place are likely to work only gradually. Consider, for example, IRAs, which permit individuals to save up to $2,000 each year tax free until retirement. The initial effect of such a measure is likely to be very small. For most families it will have no marginal impact, as wealth will simply be transferred from taxable to tax-free forms. However, this process cannot continue indefinitely. Eventually, most families will run out of taxable wealth and the incentive will start to have a marginal effect.

In sum, we have little more basis now for judging the long-term effects on savings of tax policies than we had in 1981. The likely response of savings to changes in the real after-tax rate of return is, ultimately, an empirical question. My own reading of the evidence suggests that savings are likely to respond substantially to increases in real after-tax rates of return. But the question is difficult.

Although attention tends to be focused on personal savings, the lion's share of private savings in the United States is done by corporations through retained earnings. The recession and the associated decline in corporate profitability have greatly reduced business savings, contributing to the very low savings rate of the past several years. The corporate tax cuts enacted in 1981 also should encourage business savings as the economy recovers.

The final major objective of the tax cuts was to spur investment in plants and equipment. This issue is addressed in detail in Don Fullerton and Yolanda Henderson's paper in this volume. I want to note here only that the motivation for the tax cuts was almost certainly macro- rather than microeconomic. The goal was to raise the size of the American capital stock so as to increase output, not to try to better achieve microeconomic efficiency conditions. Indeed, microeconomic efficiency conditions can be derived only with a huge set of assumptions about the homogeneity and malleability of capital. Policymakers will consider their policies to have been successful if business investment expands significantly over the next decade. Because investment is currently determined by output-constrained firms, we do not yet have an opportunity to judge the efficacy of recent investment incentives.

The message of this section is simple. The level of aggregate demand has determined economic activity for the past several years and will continue to do so for the next several years. Until the economy once again approaches full employment, we will have little basis for judging the ultimate effects of recent tax measures on aggregate supply. We will have to rely on the same combination of knowledge, faith, and hunch that have provided the basis for previous discussions of these issues.

Conclusions

A basic principle of econometrics holds that the precision with which a relationship can be estimated depends on the variance of the exogenous variables. From this limited point of view, recent economic policies have been a treasure trove. Policy variables and the economy have been pushed beyond previous limits. This paper has tried to lay out some of the key elements necessary for evaluation of these policies. However, a theme throughout has been the difficulty of trying to reach early judgments about economic policies directed at the long run. At this stage, analysts are simply not in a position to render verdicts.

REAGANOMICS AND GROWTH: THE MESSAGE IN THE MODELS

Alan S. Blinder

A Framework for Growth Policy

The Reagan administration came to Washington vowing to raise the nation's rate of economic growth, and soon enacted a program to this end. How effective is this program, viewed from a variety of time perspectives? In particular, what do large macro-econometric models tell us about the likely effects of the Reagan economic program on growth in each of these time frames?

In this paper, I attempt to answer these questions by contrasting the simulation outcomes of three widely used models, with and without the Reagan fiscal program. My point of departure is a standard production function, in which output depends on technology and on inputs of labor and capital. The production function points out that the most natural approaches to spurring economic growth are very different in the short, medium, and long runs. Thus, within the limitations of the models, I estimate the results of Reagan's policies at various points over this decade.

In the remainder of this section, I summarize what the production function suggests as the most appropriate way to spur growth in the short, medium, and long runs, note how the models handle these economic behaviors, and discuss an important basic critique of economic models. In section two, I

For their help in using and understanding the models discussed in this paper, I am deeply indebted to Albert Ando, Flint Brayton, Paul Kupieck, Eileen Mauskopf, and Rick Simes (MIT-Penn-SSRC model); John Green and Howard Howe (Wharton model); and Eric Dressler, Russell Robins, and Matthew Salomon (Data Resources model). I also thank Albert Ando, Frank de Leeuw, Stephen Goldfeld, John Helliwell, Dale Jorgenson, Isabel Sawhill, and participants at the Urban Institute Conference on *The Legacy of Reaganomics: Prospects for Long-term Growth*, Washington, D.C., September 1983, for helpful comments on earlier drafts.

discuss an important basic critique of economic models. In section two, I define Reaganomics and discuss the bases for the REAGAN and NO REAGAN simulations. Section three presents the simulation results. In section four, I return to the critique of economic models, and examine whether the models make systematic errors in the ways suggested by the critique.

The Short Run

A production function specifies the maximum amount of output that can be produced by any set of specified inputs, given the state of technical knowledge. A production function tells us that, if we want to raise the growth rate of output, we must raise the growth rates of utilized factor inputs or spur technological progress.

For the short run, the critical word is *utilized*. If some resources are underutilized, then the fastest and surest route to better growth is to raise utilization rates by expansionary monetary and/or fiscal policies. Since analysis of stabilization policy is precisely the purpose for which large macro-econometric models were designed, we might expect them to be relatively good tools for assessing the effects of Reaganomics on growth in the short run—say, up to three years.

However, the critique of econometric policy evaluation made by Robert Lucas[1] has cast doubt on the validity of using the models for this purpose. Lucas argued, quite persuasively, that policy changes which affect expectations can cause shifts in allegedly "structural" econometric equations that use observable variables as proxies for unobserved expectations. Thus, these models would be prone to systematic errors.

Economists in different walks of life have reacted very differently to the Lucas critique. Economists in government and industry, whose business it is to analyze stabilization policy, have more or less ignored the critique and proceeded with business as usual, albeit perhaps a bit self-consciously. The practice of econometric policy evaluation at the Congressional Budget Office or at Data Resources is not noticeably different today than it was several years ago. In sharp contrast, academic economists, who can afford the luxury of not answering questions not of their own choosing, have wholeheartedly embraced the critique and rejected the models. Rare is the academic today who pays them any mind.

Both attitudes are curious. On one hand, since the Lucas critique is undoubtedly correct on conceptual grounds, those who earn a living from

---

1. Robert E. Lucas, Jr., "Econometric Policy Evaluation: A Critique," in K. Brunner and A. H. Meltzer, eds., *The Phillips Curve and Labor Markets* (Amsterdam: North Holland, 1976).

econometric models might have done more to address these shortcomings. On the other hand, since the empirical importance of the critique has yet to be established, it is surprising that so many academic economists discarded the models with such alacrity.

In this paper, I try to stake out the unpopulated middle ground. Since no one has made a persuasive empirical case that the critique is quantitatively important,[2] I use the models to estimate the effects of the Reagan program, fully aware that they might be disregarding strong expectational effects. Then I look to see if the models make large errors in the places where Lucas-type reasoning suggests that they should.[3]

The Medium Run

The production function suggests that the way to stimulate growth in the medium run is to stimulate the growth rates of factor supplies. If there is an intellectually respectable supply-side economics, this is it. The personal income tax cuts were allegedly designed to raise the supply of labor. The corporate income tax cuts and saving incentives were allegedly designed to raise the supply of capital.

We cannot expect such policies to raise the growth rates of labor and capital permanently. The growth rate of labor supply must ultimately equal the growth rate of population. Lower marginal tax rates on earnings may (or may not) increase the level of per capita labor supply by increasing hours of work or labor force participation rates. But tax cuts surely cannot increase the steady state growth rate unless, in defiance of the laws of arithmetic, tax rates are lowered year after year. Similarly, growth theory teaches us that the growth rate of capital must ultimately equal the sum of the growth rates of population and each worker's increased efficiency due to technical progress.[4] Tax incentives may lead to a period of capital deepening (accumulating capital goods faster than labor grows), and hence to a temporarily high growth rate of potential GNP; but this cannot go on forever.

Where business behavior is concerned, the econometric models contain empirical representations of most of the linkages suggested by supply-side economics. This study makes use of three different models of the U.S.

---

2. Albert Ando and Arthur Kennickell, "'Failure' of Keynesian Economics and 'Direct' Effects of Money Supply: A Fact or a Fiction?" (mimeographed), March 1983, have in fact argued that the critique has not been quantitatively important for the MIT-Penn-SSRC model.

3. Otto Eckstein, *Core Inflation* (Englewood Cliffs, N.J.: Prentice-Hall, 1981), takes a similar approach.

4. Robert M. Solow, "A Contribution to the Theory of Economic Growth," *Quarterly Journal of Economics*, vol. 32 (1956), pp. 65–94.

economy—the Data Resources quarterly macro model (DRI), the Wharton annual model (WEFA), and the MIT-Penn-SSRC quarterly model (MPS). In each of them, more generous depreciation allowances and/or higher investment tax credits lower the user cost of capital, raise investment, and spur growth of the capital stock. Hence, subject to the reservations implied by the Lucas critique, the models should provide an appropriate vehicle for assessing the effects of Reaganomics on medium-run growth through increasing factor supplies.

Where individual behavior is concerned, the models are less promising— but so are the policies. Only the DRI model has a labor supply schedule that is sensitive to the after-tax real wage. (The elasticity is about 0.05.) In principle, it would be nice to see wages appearing as arguments of labor supply functions. In practice, however, empirical wage elasticities are so low[5]—especially for permanent wage increases[6]—that we probably lose little by assuming that they are zero. Similarly, none of the models allows any of the special savings incentives (such as liberalization of Keogh accounts and IRAs) to affect personal saving, but the literature on the interest-elasticity of saving gives little reason to think that this is a grave omission.[7]

I conclude that, if Lucas-critique problems are not too severe, the models may do a satisfactory job of assessing the effects of Reaganomics on growth in the medium term (say, three to six years). But doubts linger about the price elasticities of labor supply and saving.

The Long Run

The biggest problems—both for formulating and assessing policy—come in the long run. As we know from growth theory, the only way to raise the steady-state growth rate is to speed up technical progress. This is much easier to say than to do. A supreme optimist might expect some of the Reagan policy changes to have this effect. But none of the econometric models allows for such a possibility. Apart from cyclical influences and (in some cases)

---

5. See, for example, Jerry A. Hausman, "Taxes and Labor Supply," NBER Working Paper 1102 (March 1983).

6. See Robert E. Lucas, Jr., and Leonard A. Rapping, "Real Wages, Employment, and Inflation," *Journal of Political Economy*, vol. 77 (September/October 1969), pp. 721–754; Joseph G. Altonji, "The Intertemporal Substitution Model of Labour Market Fluctuations: An Empirical Analysis," *Review of Economic Studies*, vol. 49 (1982), pp. 783–824.

7. For a recent survey of studies of this question, see Thorvaldur Gylfason, "Interest Rates, Inflation, and the Aggregate Consumption Function," *The Review of Economics and Statistics*, vol. 63, (May 1981), pp. 233–245, which was too early to include the interesting results of Gerald A. Carlino, "Interest Rate Effects and Intertemporal Consumption," *Journal of Monetary Economics*, vol. 9 (1982), pp. 233–234.

energy prices, total factor productivity follows an exogenously determined time trend in the models. So the models, by their nature, must answer ''zero'' to the question: ''What is the effect of Reaganomics on the steady-state growth rate?''

Personally, I find zero a believable answer. But it is unfortunate that the models assume zero, rather than estimate it, because technical progress provides the only lever by which policymakers could conceivably have a major effect on long-term growth. Some simple calculations illustrate this point.

Suppose investment incentives are phenomenally effective and raise the share of investment in GNP by 3 percentage points for a full decade. With a capital-output ratio around 3, this would add 1 percentage point to the growth rate of the capital stock leading, after ten years, to a capital stock 10.5 percent higher. With a share of capital in output of 30 percent, the level of real GNP would wind up 3.15 percent higher. That would be a spectacular achievement. But, if we take a 25-year perspective, it amounts to adding only 0.12 percent to the GNP growth rate.[8]

Labor supply incentives cannot be expected to do more. Most economists would be astonished if the Reagan personal tax cuts raised labor supply by as much as 5 percent. If labor's share is 70 percent, this would add 1.15 percentage points to the annual growth rate of GNP over a three year period, an impressive gain. But over a twenty-five year period, the rise in the growth rate would amount to just 0.14 percentage point.

Nothing but arithmetic is required to substantiate my claim that supply-side policies will have negligible effects on long-term growth rates. Since these policies naturally affect the levels of factor supplies, not the rate at which those factors grow, they must fade into insignificance as the time horizon lengthens.

Because the models inherently have nothing to say about the determinants of growth in the very long run, and because they often have unreasonable long-run properties—not having been designed for such purposes—I restrict my long-term analysis to a period of seven to nine years, beginning in 1981 and ending in either 1987 (for the MPS model) or 1989 (for the other two). This time horizon is a cowardly compromise. It is probably longer than the longest period over which a sensible person would place any credence in what the models say; but it is probably shorter than the time perspective that motivates this volume.

---

8. Lawrence H. Summers, ''Tax Policy and Corporate Investment,'' in *The Supply-Side Effects of Economic Policy*, Proceedings of 1980 Economic Policy Conference (St. Louis, Missouri: Center for the Study of American Business, 1981), provides a similar assessment, based on similar reasoning.

Defining Reaganomics

Part of the discipline imposed by an econometric model is that the analyst must define the policy to be studied in quantitative terms. If the models are to tell us how Reaganomics affects growth, we must first tell the models exactly what Reaganomics is.

I begin this section by listing the Reagan policy changes that potentially influence the rate of economic growth, noting which ones can be handled by the models and which ones cannot. Then I explain in detail the differences between the model simulations with and without the Reagan fiscal program. Finally, I address the vexing issue of how to handle monetary policy.

The Reagan Program and Growth

The Reagan administration disavowed short-run stabilization policy and focused, at least in its rhetoric, on increasing growth in the medium and long runs.

(1) To raise labor supply, the administration advocated the three-stage reduction in marginal tax rates proposed some years earlier by Senator Roth and Congressman Kemp. This was enacted as a 5 percent reduction in all bracket rates in October 1981, and 10 percent reductions in July 1982 and July 1983, amounting to a total reduction of 23 percent. The idea was that lower marginal tax rates on earnings would encourage labor supply. If substitution effects on labor supply outweigh income effects, this can be viewed as a pro-growth policy.

In the models, income tax reductions have the standard demand-side effect: they increase consumer spending. The alleged supply-side effect on hours of labor supplied plays little role. However, increased demand resulting from higher consumer spending does stimulate higher labor force participation.[9]

(2) To speed capital formation, the tax rate on capital income was cut in several ways.

(a) Lower personal income tax rates automatically reduced the taxation of income from property, especially in the upper income brackets where the top rate was lowered from 70 to 50 percent in 1981. As just observed, this tax cut has standard demand-side effects in the models, but little in the way of supply-side effects.

---

9. In fact, the labor force participation rate does not rise in the WEFA model. Here and elsewhere, to avoid tedium, I generalize about the models even when one differs from the others in a minor way. Important differences among models will always be noted.

(b) The Accelerated Cost Recovery System (ACRS) sharply reduced the effective rates of taxation on the earnings from new investments. In concert with the investment tax credit, it actually implies negative tax rates on some types of investments.[10] To those who do not worry about deadweight losses from distorting taxes, the ACRS certainly must appear to be a pro-growth policy; and the models do not fret over such things.

In the models, the ACRS is handled straightforwardly by shortening service lives for tax purposes and/or by speeding up depreciation schedules. These changes reduce the user cost of capital, leading to both demand-side (investment spending is part of aggregate demand) and supply-side (the capital stock is augmented) effects.

(c) A number of special incentives for saving, such as liberalization of Keogh plans and IRAs and the infamous "All-Savers' Certificates," were added by the administration, with help from an enthusiastic Congress. Whether or not these incentives really are pro-growth depends on the extent to which they add new savings or simply substitute for savings that would have occurred anyway.

In the short run, anyone can avail himself of the tax benefits of IRAs and/or Keoghs simply by moving existing taxable funds into tax-exempt accounts. The "incentives" are pure revenue giveaways.[11] In the longer run, we must distinguish between people who would save more than the legal maximums for IRAs and Keoghs anyway, and those who would not. For the former group, the "incentives" continue to be lump sum transfers. For the latter group, making interest tax exempt does tilt relative prices in favor of saving. If substitution effects outweigh income effects, these people will save more.

With so many slips twixt the IRA cup and the savings lip, many economists are skeptical that these putative saving incentives provide much of an incentive to save. In addition, there is the old fashioned (but nonetheless important) question of whether more saving translates into more investment or simply into less demand and less output. In any case, the models do not allow for any of these special incentives; so nothing more will be said about them except to note that recent savings rates have been exceptionally low, not high.[12]

---

10. See U.S. President, *Economic Report of the President, 1982* (Washington, D.C.: U.S. Government Printing Office, 1982), and the paper by Fullerton and Henderson in this volume.

11. In the case of the All-Savers' Certificates, this is the whole story because they were permitted for only one year and restricted, by the market, to high-income people, who presumably have substantial assets.

12. In the first half of 1983, the personal saving rate was only 4.9 percent.

(d) The process of disinflation itself—a major thrust of the Reagan program—lowers the tax rates on business investment in plant and equipment because our tax system is not indexed. Most prominently, the real value of depreciation allowances rises automatically as inflation falls. Lower inflation also leads to lower (tax deductible) nominal interest costs; but this is apparently not enough to offset the depreciation effect.[13] All the models capture these effects, though sometimes in a rough way, through the user cost formula.

(3) The remaining aspects of the Reagan program pertain to the Solow-Denison productivity residual,[14] rather than to factor supplies, and are mainly anti-growth.

(a) Outside the defense area, government spending on R&D has been cut.[15]

(b) Many of the cuts in social spending can be classified as reductions in subsidies to human capital formation.

(c) Deregulation might have stimulated growth.[16] But while the Reagan administration has talked a lot about deregulation, it has done little.

(d) Recessions are bad for productivity. It is is perhaps problematic to consider a recession as part of the Reagan program, but it is hard to know how the underlying inflation rate was supposed to be reduced without one. In any case, the recession did come and did have its usual damaging effects on productivity.

Of these five aspects of Reaganomics, only recessions are dealt with by the models. The level of productivity returns to trend after a slump, so the ill effects are transitory. The models tacitly assume that the other four aspects have no effects on growth.

(4) One last aspect of the supply-side agenda should be mentioned in this context. What I call the "Feldstein twist" is a policy mix that combines strong tax incentives for business fixed investment with tight money and high real interest rates.[17] The idea is that the high interest rates will crowd out housing, thereby freeing funds for business investment, which is stimulated by tax breaks. Though the president never declared war on housing, the Feldstein twist was a major component of the Reagan program.

---

13. Fullerton and Henderson explain this phenomenon in detail and provide some evidence.

14. That part of the increase in productivity due not to increases in capital or labor but to technical change—scientific and engineering advances, industrial improvements, management expertise, and training of labor.

15. For details, see Nichols' paper in this volume.

16. Gregory B. Christainsen and Robert H. Haveman, "Regulation, Productivity Growth, and 'Supply-Side' Economics." (Paper prepared for Urban Institute Conference on Changing Domestic Priorities, Washington, D.C., June 13–14, 1983), provide some estimates.

17. See Martin Feldstein, "Tax Rules and the Mismanagement of Monetary Policy," *The American Economic Review, Papers and Proceedings*, vol. 70 (May 1980), pp. 183–190.

Why a policy of reallocating capital in this way should be considered "pro-growth" escapes me. It makes sense only if, for example, services produced by the housing stock are of less social importance than video games produced in factories.[18]

The 'Reagan' and 'No Reagan' Simulations

Each of the three models was simulated under two different fiscal policies and the same monetary policy. These policies are defined precisely below. The simulations covered the period 1981–1989 for the DRI and WEFA models and 1981–1987 for the MPS model.

Fiscal Policies

The REAGAN simulation uses historical fiscal policies from 1981 through early 1983 and, with a few exceptions, uses a common set of forecasts for future policy variables. The NO REAGAN simulation represents my educated guess about what fiscal policy would have been had Reagan not been elected. Thus within the limits imposed by the differing structures of the three models, the differences between the REAGAN and NO REAGAN fiscal policies were the same in each model. However, I made no effort to homogenize the forecasts of other exogenous variables, so each model produces a rather different baseline solution. For this reason, I do not report the results of any particular simulation, but only the differences between the REAGAN and NO REAGAN simulations for each model.

The expenditure side of the budget was relatively straightforward (see table 1). For the REAGAN simulation, the budget generally follows history for 1981 and 1982; for 1983–1988, I used the June 1983 WEFA forecast of exogenous variables. For the NO REAGAN simulation, I used the WEFA forecast made in October 1980. Whenever WEFA projected spending variables in nominal terms, I used their forecasted price deflators to create corresponding forecasts of real spending variables.

Defense purchases grow in an irregular pattern, but at an average rate of 5.1 percent in real terms between 1981 and 1989 in the REAGAN budget versus only 3.1 percent in the NO REAGAN budget. This reflects WEFA's June 1983 assumption that the president will have to compromise somewhat with Congress, and their October 1980 assumption that there was going to

---

18. A possible argument is that the Feldstein twist simply counters tax distortions that favor investment in housing. However, Fullerton and Henderson show that this distortion is not as large as commonly supposed. And there are obviously more direct ways to attack such distortions.

TABLE 1

BUDGET POLICIES IN REAGAN AND NO REAGAN SIMULATIONS
(Billions of 1972 dollars)

	1983	1985	1987	1989
Defense Purchases				
REAGAN	84.1	94.2	102.0	109.8
NO REAGAN	82.2	88.0	91.8	94.8
Difference	+ 1.9	+ 6.2	+ 10.2	+ 15.0
Nondefense Purchases				
REAGAN	34.8	31.7	33.1	35.1
NO REAGAN	36.6	37.4	39.0	41.1
Difference	− 1.8	− 5.7	− 5.9	− 6.0
Transfers to Persons				
(except unemployment				
benefits)				
REAGAN	142.9	147.8	156.6	166.3
NO REAGAN	146.3	156.8	168.0	180.2
Difference	− 3.4	− 9.0	− 11.4	− 13.9
Grants-in-Aid				
REAGAN	40.6	40.0	40.1	44.5
NO REAGAN	44.8	48.4	50.3	54.3
Difference	− 4.2	− 8.4	− 10.2	− 9.8

be a military buildup regardless of who was elected. By 1989, defense purchases are 15 percent higher in the REAGAN simulation.

Real nondefense purchases decline at a rate of 0.5 percent between 1981
and 1989 in the REAGAN simulation but rise at a 1.5 percent rate in the NO
REAGAN simulation. By 1989, nondefense purchases are 15 percent lower
under Reagan. But military purchases are much larger, so total federal purchases are higher in the Reagan budget.

Most of the Reagan budget cuts show up in transfers to persons and in
grants-in-aid to states and localities.

I used WEFA forecasts of October 1980 and June 1983 that real *transfers
to persons* (except for unemployment benefits) would have grown at a 3.5
percent rate without Reagan but at only 2.5 percent with Reagan. (Unemployment benefits are endogenous in all the models and follow the same
equation in the two simulations.) By 1989, real transfers are 8 percent lower
in the REAGAN budget, which just about offsets the higher defense spending.

Cuts are much deeper in *grants-in-aid*, which influence state and local
government spending (an endogenous variable). Grants grow in real terms at
a 2.2 percent rate in the NO REAGAN budget, but are essentially unchanged

between 1981 and 1989 in the REAGAN budget. By 1989, real grants are 18 percent lower in the REAGAN simulation.

As table 1 shows, the Reagan budget policy is mildly contractionary on the spending side despite the sizable military buildup. But the differences between the REAGAN and NO REAGAN budgets are not large.

Taxes are where the action is in Reaganomics. Unfortunately, tax policies are much harder to handle because the three models have very different personal and corporate tax equations. Rather than try to explain the details of implementation, I will limit myself to the basic ideas.

Tax rates in the REAGAN budget follow history for 1981 and 1982 and current forecasts thereafter. Specifically, the third stage of Kemp-Roth happens in the middle of 1983, indexing starts in 1985, and no contingency tax increase is assumed. On the corporate side, the provisions that have been in effect since the 1982 tax act are treated as if they applied from 1981 on. Actually, under the 1981 tax act, depreciation was scheduled to become even more generous starting in 1985.[19] But this was ignored in the simulations on the supposition that these future provisions had no effect on investment behavior in 1981 and 1982.

Actually, neither WEFA nor DRI believes that the budget deficits will be as large as the simulations show, so each includes some kind of substantial tax increase in their current forecasts. However, since my objective was not to predict the future but to characterize the Reagan tax program, I took these tax increases out in defining the REAGAN simulation. It seems obvious that tax cuts were coming regardless of who was elected in 1980, so the NO REAGAN simulation also includes small tax cuts.

On the personal side, a small reduction (about 4 percent) in bracket tax rates is assumed to occur in 1981, and thereafter tax brackets, but not exemptions, are assumed to be indexed. This is intended to reflect Congress's historical habit of periodically cutting tax rates in order to counter bracket creep.[20] The simulation simply makes this happen smoothly, rather than in discrete jumps.

For the NO REAGAN simulation, I assumed continuation of the 1980 corporation tax law. This is certainly not a prediction of what would have happened. Bipartisan support for the Conable-Jones bill which would have reduced service lives to 10, 5, and 3 years for specified types of investments,

---

19. For details on the provisions of the Economic Recovery Tax Act (1981) and the Tax Equity and Fiscal Responsibility Act (1983), see the paper by Fullerton and Henderson in this volume.

20. See Emil M. Sunley, Jr., and Joseph A. Pechman, "Inflation Adjustment for the Individual Income Tax," in Henry J. Aaron, ed., *Inflation and the Income Tax* (Washington, D.C.: The Brookings Institution, 1976).

was widespread in 1980. Had Carter been reelected, this bill might well have become law. But to make Conable-Jones part of the NO REAGAN policy is tantamount to excluding corporate tax cuts from the definition of Reaganomics, which seems absurd. Note, however, that effective corporate taxes do fall (relative to their 1980 levels) in the NO REAGAN simulation because declining inflation raises the real value of depreciation allowances.

In summary, the tax component of Reaganomics is defined as follows:

(1) The large (23 percent) Kemp-Roth tax rate reduction in 1981–1983 plus indexing starting in 1985, instead of a small (4 percent) rate cut in 1981 with immediate indexing. The delay in indexing makes the Kemp-Roth tax cuts much smaller than they appear against a no-cut baseline.

(2) The substantial corporate tax cuts that remained after the Tax Equity and Fiscal Responsibility Act (TEFRA).

Specifying Monetary Policy

Because fiscal multipliers depend on the assumed behavior of the monetary authority, each model's estimate of the effects of Reaganomics will depend on what is assumed about monetary policy. But what is a reasonable assumption to make about Federal Reserve behavior since 1981 (and into the future)? More specifically, what difference, if any, did the Reagan fiscal policy make to monetary policy?

The fact that tight money pursued through monetarist operating procedures was an integral part of the Reagan program suggests making deceleration of money growth part of the working definition of Reaganomics. However, there are at least two difficulties with this view.

The first is that money growth rates did not in fact decelerate. M1[21] grew 6.6 percent in the 12 months ending December 1980, 6.5 percent in the 12 months ending December 1981, and 8.7 percent in the 12 months ending December 1982. The corresponding growth rates for M2 were 8.9, 10.0, and 9.4 percent respectively. So what deceleration should we use? The fact is that monetary policy was tight because velocity[22] fell, not because money growth declined.

---

21. M1 defines the money supply narrowly. It includes demand deposits at all commercial banks (other than government and interbank deposits) plus currency in circulation. M2 is a broader definition. It includes time and savings deposits.

22. Velocity is the ratio of nominal GNP to the money stock.

The second problem is the fact that the Federal Reserve was already pursuing a tight monetary policy, and was at least putatively committed to monetarism, well before the 1980 election. This raises the possibility that monetary policy would have been just as tight whether or not Reagan had been elected.

My personal judgment is that Reaganomics did make monetary policy tighter than it otherwise would have been, but in rather subtle ways. First, the Reagan administration cheered on the Fed's policy of tight money cum monetarism, whereas another administration might have pressured the Fed to ease up. Second, I believe that fears of wildly expansionary fiscal policies made the Fed panic and stick with monetarism too long in the face of declining velocity. However, these ideas are highly speculative. Therefore, I decided to hold monetary policy constant in comparing the REAGAN and NO REAGAN fiscal policies.

But this decision merely changes the question to: How should *constant monetary policy* be defined? Given the Fed's monetarist stance, fixed growth of the money supply would appear to be the natural definition. However, the erratic behavior of the money demand function during the early 1980s makes it hard to impute any meaning to such a policy. Nonetheless, each model does include demand functions for the components of money which (apart from add factors) are presumed to remain stable. So the models can be simulated *as if* a stable money demand function existed.

Why would we want to do such a thing? Only because the alternatives are so unappetizing.

(1) We could define unchanged monetary policy to mean that the time path of interest rates (either nominal or real) is the same in the two simulations. But this would be saying that the Reagan fiscal policy had no effect on interest rates, which seems an absurd position.

(2) We could define unchanged monetary policy to mean that the path of nominal GNP is the same regardless of fiscal policy. But this would come close to saying that the Fed completely offset the macro effects of the Reagan fiscal program (leaving only allocative effects), which also sounds unappealing.

(3) We could define unchanged monetary policy to mean that the path of bank reserves is unaffected by fiscal policy. This differs only slightly from holding money constant, but does imply that Reaganomics led to slightly faster money growth, which is probably the opposite of the truth.

Given these unappealing alternatives, in the end I opted for holding the time path of the money supply (M2 definition) constant in comparing the REAGAN and NO REAGAN fiscal policies.[23] But there is a cost. The question I can use the models to answer is: "What would have been the effect of the Reagan fiscal policy if the Fed held the growth path of M2 constant, and there was a stable demand function for M2?" This perhaps gives new meaning to the word "counterfactual."

Simulation Results

This section reports the results of simulating the Reagan economic program on the WEFA, DRI, and MPS models. Because the three models produce three different baseline forecasts, I report only the differences between the REAGAN and NO REAGAN simulations—that is, the multiplier effects of Reaganomics. Before looking at the numbers, however, it is worth considering what we expect the models to say.

Simple Theoretical Expectations

Each of these models is decidedly Keynesian, even though money certainly matters and some of the linkages stressed by supply-side economics are present.

In these models, GNP is demand-determined in the short run, obtained by adding together consumer spending, investment, government purchases, and net exports. The price level is largely predetermined and adjusts with a lag, so markets often do not clear. Inflation depends on costs and on the degree of slack in labor and/or product markets, not (directly) on the rate of change in the money supply. The effects of fiscal and monetary policies do not depend on whether or not the policies are anticipated. And neither labor supply nor saving is very responsive to marginal tax rates.

We can think of each model as having three central ingredients:

- **Aggregate Demand:** A rather complicated IS-LM system[24] that determines real GNP, and via which monetary and fiscal policy work;

---

23. The actual time path of M2 differs somewhat across the three models. But, for any single model, it is the same in the REAGAN and NO REAGAN simulations.

24. In the Hicks-Hansen diagram, the IS curve shows the combinations of interest rates and income that equate savings and investment. The LM curve shows the combinations of interest rates and income that equate supply and demand for money.

- **Aggregate Supply:** A production function through which capital deepening increases labor productivity and potential GNP;

- **Price Adjustment:** A Phillips curve,[25] which is quite flat in the short run, that determines wage and price inflation from the amount of slack in the economy.

Figure 1 illustrates how the Reagan program works in such a model. The personal tax cuts, which are offset to only a minor degree by the reductions in transfer payments, raise consumer spending. The business tax cuts raise investment spending. And the defense buildup, partly offset by cutbacks in nondefense purchases, raises government purchases. With consumption, investment, and government spending all rising, the IS curve shifts out along a stationary LM curve because M2 is fixed in the simulations. Therefore, output and interest rates both rise.

FIGURE 1

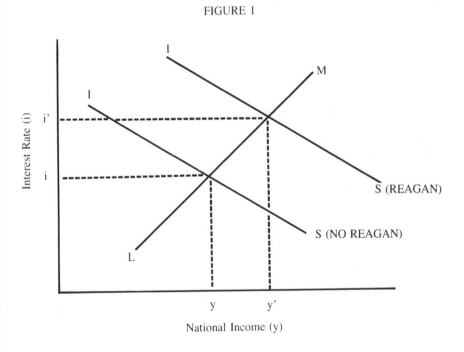

National Income (y)

---

25. A Phillips curve depicts the tradeoff between unemployment and wage-price rises.

The size of the rise in interest rates, the first of three critical ingredients that govern the degree of crowding out,[26] depends on the slope of the LM curve. The second critical ingredient in crowding out is the sensitivity of interest rates to aggregate demand. On both of these issues there are large quantitative disagreements among the models. But, with business taxes down and interest rates up, the Feldstein twist presumably should take place to some extent in all models.

On the supply side, labor supply changes little and the capital stock is fixed in the short run. So aggregate supply is essentially fixed in the short run, and the stimulus to demand makes markets more taut, causing inflation. Just how far prices rise is the third critical determinant of the degree of crowding out; and the models disagree here, too. In the longer run, capital deepening augments aggregate supply and dampens inflationary pressures, as hoped for by supply-siders.

With this conceptualization of the Reagan program as background, let us now turn to what the models say.

Output, Prices, and Unemployment

Figure 2 shows the simulation results for the major macroeconomic aggregates: output, the price level, and unemployment. It is immediately apparent that the WEFA and DRI models agree fairly well,[27] while the MPS results are dramatically different.

Which model's results are surprising? Where prices are concerned, the MPS model confirms simple theoretical expectations, while the other two deny that the Reagan fiscal package is inflationary. But where output is concerned, the DRI and WEFA models behave as expected, while the MPS model says that crowding out ultimately exceeds 100 percent. Let us examine these differences more closely.

In all the models, the expansionary effects of the Reagan policy on output start small and then build. According to the DRI and WEFA models, real GNP is eventually about 2 percent higher because of the policy. In the MPS model, the expansionary effects of the policy come more quickly and dissipate sooner, reaching a peak of 2.1 percent of GNP in 1983:4. By mid-1985, crowding out is complete and GNP is almost the same in the REAGAN and NO REAGAN simulations. Thereafter, however, GNP continues to fall; and

---

26. Crowding-out refers to the fall in private consumption or investment as the result of deficit spending.

27. The unemployment results differ because employment is almost unit elastic with respect to output in the WEFA model whereas the DRI models adheres, more or less, to Okun's law.

FIGURE 2

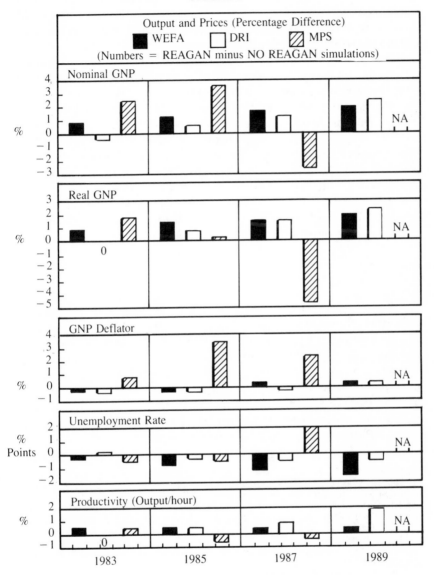

by 1987, when the MPS simulation ends, real output is a stunning 5 percent lower because of the Reagan policies.[28]

The results shown in figure 2 pose two questions. The first is why does expansionary fiscal policy not produce more inflation in the DRI and WEFA models? That is, why does all the nominal GNP growth go into real output, rather than into prices?

The answers are quite different in the two models. In the WEFA model, the Phillips curve is a step function which is completely flat within the range of the simulation. So no expansionary policy would be inflationary. The DRI model does have a Phillips curve, but the productivity improvement due to capital deepening is so large that unit labor costs are held constant even though wages rise. The MPS model has a sloping Phillips curve and a much smaller productivity effect, so the Reagan policies do cause inflation.

The second question posed by figure 2 is why crowding out is so much more severe in the MPS model than in either of the other two. To answer this, we must investigate the behavior of interest rates and investment.

Interest Rates, Investment, and Capital

Figures 3 and 4 show that there are substantial disagreements among the models where interest rates and investment are concerned.

Interest rates rise much more in the WEFA model than in the DRI model, and much more in the MPS model than in the WEFA model (figure 3). The differences are dramatic. For example, the Reagan policies push 1985 long-term rates up about 200 basis points in the MPS simulation, about 70 basis points in the WEFA simulation, but only 7 basis points in the DRI simulation. In fact, the short-run LM curve in the DRI model is virtually flat; after two years of Reaganomics, interest rates are unchanged.[29]

---

28. Unlike the other two models, the MPS model responds to aggregate demand shocks in a highly cyclical manner when the money supply is fixed. The cycles it produces are either explosive or barely damped. In this simulation, 1987 happens to be a low point in a cycle. The negative effects in later years would, I believe, be smaller. The MPS results make obvious something that is also true of the other two models: by the end of the simulations, the models still have not settled down to a steady state at the natural rate. Thus the increases in real output shown in figure 2 are a mixture of *demand side* effects (from the fiscal stimulus) and *supply side* effects (mostly from capital deepening).

29. In doing multiplier runs with money fixed, the proprietors of the DRI model typically exogenize a subset of financial variables that are—both in principle and in the model—endogenous. I did not follow this practice. If I had, the rise in interest rates would have been even smaller, and the expansionary effects of the Reagan program a bit bigger. However, the differences are not large, and they certainly do not explain why I obtained such a flat LM curve with the DRI model.

FIGURE 3

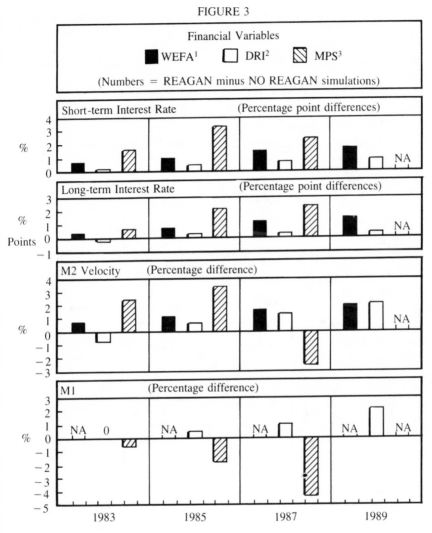

Financial Variables

■ WEFA[1]   □ DRI[2]   ▧ MPS[3]

(Numbers = REAGAN minus NO REAGAN simulations)

[1] Large negotiable CDs.
[2] Three-month Treasury bills.
[3] Moody's corporate bond rate.

Naturally we expect a bigger investment stimulus in the DRI model than in the WEFA model, and the data shown in figure 4 match that expectation. By 1985, Reaganomics raises real business fixed investment by 6.8 percent according to the DRI model, but by only 3.7 percent according to WEFA.

FIGURE 4

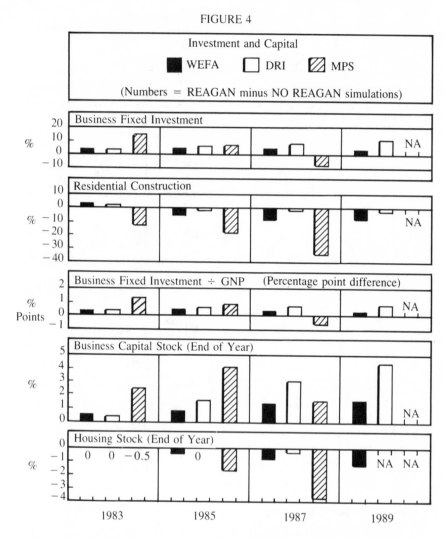

By 1989, the difference is 10.1 percent in DRI versus only 3.3 percent in WEFA. Business fixed investment as a share of GNP is higher by about 0.2 or 0.3 percentage point through most of the Wharton simulation; but in the DRI simulation the increase gets as high as 0.8 percentage point. The ultimate effects of such differences on the capital stock are quite noticeable. By 1989, the Reagan tax cuts raise the capital stock by 4.5 percent according to DRI, but by only 1.7 percent according to WEFA. With a 30 percent share of capital in output, this discrepancy is enough to account for almost a 1 percent difference in the level of potential GNP.

Another striking difference arises in the Feldstein twist. In the Wharton simulation, the nation must sacrifice some of its housing stock to build more business capital. For example, by 1989 total (residential plus nonresidential) investment is barely higher in the REAGAN simulation; but the composition is very different. However, sacrificing homebuilding to spur industrial capital formation is not necessary in the DRI model. The housing stock hardly declines.

We can summarize the characteristics of the MPS results as follows:

- Interest rates rise much more than in either of the other two models, and much more quickly.

- Investment spending is far more sensitive to the cost of capital in the MPS model, so the estimated stimulus to investment from the tax cut is also greater, and felt sooner, than in the other models.

- On balance, the investment boom kicked off by Reaganomics is biggest in the MPS model in the short run, despite higher interest rates. In 1983, for example, business fixed investment is up by 13 percent and its share in GNP is higher by 1.1 percentage points.

- Over a longer period, the higher interest elasticities in the MPS model take over. By mid-1986, Reaganomics has depressed, rather than stimulated, business investment, according to the MPS model.

- Investment in housing suffers from the outset of the Reagan program, and is down a whopping 33 percent by 1987.

I have already partially explained why interest rates rise so much, and do so much damage, in the MPS model. The LM curve is the steepest and the IS curve is the flattest of the three models. But two additional elements bear mention.

First, the MPS model reacts rather violently to a policy of stimulating the economy while holding M2 constant. Most of what is in M2 but not in M1 (hereafter, M2-minus-M1) bears interest at market-determined rates, so interest rate differentials between M2-minus-M1 and other assets (such as Treasury bills) hardly change. As a result, the demand for M2-minus-M1 is almost totally insensitive to the level of interest rates. When the Reagan program raises income, it raises the demand for M2-minus-M1. Rising interest rates do not deter this demand. So, with a fixed supply of M2, demand for M1 must fall. As figure 3 shows, M1 is down throughout the simulation, and the decline reaches 4.4 percent by 1987. The model accomplishes the required reduction in M1 demand by pushing up short-term interest rates sharply.[30]

To see whether the induced decline in M1 was dominating the results, I simulated the Reagan program on the MPS model holding M1, rather than M2, constant. As expected, interest rates rose less, but still much more than in either of the other two models. As a consequence, crowding out was substantially less severe, but still far more severe than in either of the other two models. In particular, crowding out remained ultimately greater than 100 percent. Thus the results with fixed M1 were qualitatively similar to, but quantitatively less severe than, the results with fixed M2.

The second special aspect of the MPS model concerns the effect of Reaganomics on the stock market. In the MPS model, rising interest rates have a damaging effect on the stock market, and stock market wealth affects consumption. According to the model, after an initial boom the Reagan program causes a long slide in the stock market; by 1987 nominal stock prices are down 22 percent. As a consequence, the stimulus to consumer spending is less than in the other models. In fact, according to the MPS simulations, the Reagan program actually reduces consumer spending after mid-1985, despite lower taxes. In the other two models, Reaganomics stimulates consumer spending strongly throughout the simulations.

However, none of this is enough to explain crowding out in excess of 100 percent, which is logically impossible in IS-LM analysis. The answer to this puzzle lies in the lag structure and in the aforementioned cyclical nature of the MPS model. The initial stimulus to the IS curve from Reaganomics quickly pushes short-term rates up and the stock market down. With a lag, higher interest rates and lower stock prices will reduce aggregate demand, ending the upward pressure on interest rates, and therefore reducing crowding out. Within the period of the simulation, we do see a slackening of interest rate pressures: the effect of Reaganomics on interest rates peaks in 1986:3 and then begins to recede. But because of lags, the subsequent effects on spending do not occur until after 1987.

The Budget Deficit

The effect of Reaganomics on the federal budget deficit has garnered much attention recently. With large differences across models in the behavior

---

30. I thank Albert Ando for explaining this aspect of the model to me. The model's behavior merely reflects the off-discussed point that paying market interest rates on money makes the LM curve nearly vertical. Somehow, the DRI and WEFA models have avoided (or evaded?) this problem. In fact, figure 4 shows that M1 actually rises slightly under Reaganomics in the DRI model. There is no M1 variable in the WEFA model.

of real output, inflation, and interest rates, we expect to find large differences in this area as well. And we do (figure 5).[31]

On the spending side, the DRI and WEFA models agree moderately well; but the MPS results are radically different and claim that the Reagan program raises, not lowers, total spending. The main reason is interest payments, which soar in the MPS simulation of the Reagan program.

On the revenue side, differences are moderate through 1985. Then the models diverge largely because of their different assessments of the strength of the economy. For example, this accounts for the huge revenue shortfall in the MPS simulation.

Putting the two sides together, we see that the models basically agree in estimating the effect of Reaganomics on the 1983 budget as a $25-$35 billion deficit. But by 1987, the differences among the models are enormous. Reaganomics adds $37 billion to the deficit according to DRI, $78 billion according to Wharton, and a whopping $211 billion according to MPS.

Summary

The Reagan economic program was controversial from its inception. As in the nursery rhyme, its supporters said it would be very, very good; its critics said it would be horrid. Each view can find support in these results.

Proponents of Reaganomics claimed the program would cause a boom in capital formation and in labor supply, thereby speeding real growth without worsening inflation, which was supposed to be held in check by tight money. The DRI model produces a scenario very much like this. According to DRI, after nine years the Reagan program will give the U.S. economy almost 5 percent more capital, over 2 percent more GNP, and no higher prices than it otherwise would have had. That sounds awfully good. However, even in this rosy view, the addition to the economy's annual growth rate over the decade is quite small—about 0.2 percentage point.

Opponents of Reaganomics said that the stimulus to aggregate demand would be inflationary, and that the mix of gaping deficits and tight money would drive up interest rates and damage investment. Some Wall Streeters even claimed that the fiscal multiplier was negative, though I think academics were always skeptical of this proposition. The MPS model produces a scenario that gives aid and comfort to the enemies of Reaganomics. According to the model, interest rates rise severely and, after seven years of Reaganomics, the

---

31. In addition, the models disagree about how the economy affects the budget, and this is an additional source of discrepancies in estimating the budgetary effects of Reaganomics.

FIGURE 5

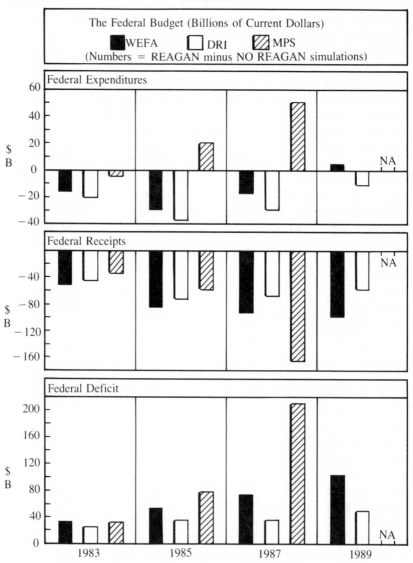

The Federal Budget (Billions of Current Dollars)

WEFA   □ DRI   ▨ MPS

(Numbers = REAGAN minus NO REAGAN simulations)

country winds up with a price level 2 percent higher and real GNP 5 percent lower. That sounds awfully bad.

Can we decide which model is correct? Unfortunately, I think not. One of the major sources of disagreement revolves around the LM curve, and virtually all econometric modelers agree that the good old reliable demand function for money has misbehaved—perhaps even disappeared—in recent years. We know that long-term interest rates rose by more than 200 basis points between January 1981 and January 1982, which makes the DRI results look a bit dubious. But little of the Reagan program had taken effect by then. It was probably the Fed's tight monetary policy, which is not very well described by targeting on M2, that pushed interest rates up. Or perhaps it was expectations of future deficits (more on this below).

On balance, I find the MPS results on interest rates more believable. However, the sensitivity of aggregate demand to real interest rates is thought to be excessive in the MPS model, and part of this sensitivity stems from a notoriously unreliable stock market equation.[32] So there is reason to be skeptical of the extreme degree of crowding out that the model produces. Unfortunately, the interest elasticity of aggregate demand has proven, after decades of econometric research, to be an elusive parameter to pin down. No honest economist can claim with any confidence to know its value.

In the final assessment, it appears that we can decide which model is "correct" only by imposing prior judgments about interest elasticities. However, there is one important area of agreement among the models. Even the most optimistic assessment of the effect of Reaganomics on real growth (by the DRI model) says that the effect is small. Why resist the obvious conclusion?

Expectations and Econometric Policy Evaluation

Expectations are treated rather cavalierly in all large-scale econometric models. In the three models considered here, the expected rate of inflation is essentially adaptive and expectations about most other variables are ignored. If these ad hoc assumptions are far from the truth, the models might misstate the effects of the Reagan program. Indeed, partisans of Reaganomics argued in 1981 that the models should be ignored for precisely this reason.

There is no doubt that the WEFA, DRI, and MPS models are vulnerable to the Lucas critique. Thus in using them to estimate the effects of a change in policy, I have committed Lucas's cardinal sin. But is the critique quantitatively important in this instance? Although there is no way to know for sure, theory can be used to suggest places where important expectational

---

32. However, the New York Stock Exchange composite index did fall 18 percent in nominal terms between January 1981 and July 1982.

effects might lead the models astray, and then we can look to see if the models actually err in the predicted direction.

Intertemporal Substitution

The 1981 personal tax cuts were phased in. When changes in marginal tax rates are phased in, opportunities for intertemporal substitution arise because individuals have good reason to believe that relative prices will change in a predictable direction. Let's consider possible effects in three areas.

Labor Supply. With lower tax rates on earnings scheduled for future years, most workers in 1981–1983 could reasonably expect a greater return on their work effort in the near future. If intertemporal substitution is important, this should have led to a temporary reduction in labor supply. Did it happen?

A true believer (which I am not) can find some supporting evidence in the models. Of the three models, only the DRI model presumes that a lower marginal tax rate should stimulate a larger labor supply, and that model has overpredicted the labor force for the past two years. The other two models assume no wage effect on labor supply, and each underpredicted the labor force somewhat. However, the WEFA model has been underpredicting the labor force since 1976, so we should hesitate before attributing the error to intertemporal substitution.

Permanent Income Hypothesis (PIH). The PIH suggests that the phasing in of the personal tax cuts might have set up a different sort of intertemporal effect. Consumers in 1981–1983 had reason to expect lower taxes, and hence higher incomes, in the near future. If they behaved according to the PIH, they would have raised their spending in anticipation of this higher income, so consumer spending would have been unusually high during this period. Did it happen?

Apparently not. The MPS and DRI models make their errors (which are not enormous in any case) in different places, but in most quarters through early 1983, consumption is lower than the models predict, not higher. The WEFA model does underpredict spending, but the fault seems to lie in a problematic equation for one particular spending component (furniture).

Business Investment. Under the Economic Recovery Tax Act (August 1981), there was also an intertemporal substitution effect built into the business tax cuts. The 1981 tax act liberalized depreciation allowances, but promised even more generous allowances beginning in 1985 and 1986. In principle, this should have induced some businesses to postpone investment. Did it happen?

Since the incentive to postpone ended with the passage of TEFRA in August 1982, the crucial quarters seem to be 1981:1 through 1982:3. Did the models overpredict investment spending in that period? No. The DRI model did overpredict spending on producers' durables, but underpredicted spending on structures, leaving the total not far off. The MPS equations underpredict investment by small amounts and the WEFA equations underpredict it by large amounts.

Disinflation and Credibility

A quite different source of expectational effects pertains to the disinflation program. If the Reagan program convinced market participants that Washington was, at last, serious about disinflation, then the expected rate of inflation might have fallen faster than the adaptive proxies used in the models.

Such an event would cause several equations in the models to malfunction, but the most prominent one seems to be the Phillips curve. In principle, the Phillips curve explains wage changes by unemployment and expected inflation. In practice, a distributed lag on past inflation is often used in place of the latter. If expected inflation falls faster than the distributed lag proxy, then the Phillips curve should systematically overpredict wage inflation. Did it happen?

None of the models makes very large errors in predicting wage inflation in 1981 and 1982, but overprediction is the norm. The WEFA equation overpredicts wage inflation moderately in 1981, but underpredicts it slightly in 1982. The MPS and DRI equations both exhibit consecutive overpredictions in 1981–1983, which might be evidence for the aforementioned expectational effects,[33] but very few of these residuals are large.

Deficits and Crowding Out

Reference has been made to the Wall Street view that allegedly expansionary fiscal policies that lead to larger deficits will reduce real GNP, that is, that the fiscal policy multiplier is negative. The best intellectual case that can be made for this seemingly outlandish proposition is based on expectational effects, and goes as follows.[34]

---

33. Wayne Vroman, *Wage Inflation* (Washington, D.C.: The Urban Institute Press, 1983), finds similar residuals for a period that ends somewhat earlier.

34. This argument is by now part of the oral tradition. It is clearly stated in print by Stephen J. Turnovsky and Marcus H. Miller, "The Effects of Government Expenditure on the Term Structure of Interest Rates," Journal of Money, Credit, and Banking, vol. 16, no. 1 (February 1984), pp. 16–33.

Policies that promise large future deficits set up expectations of high future short-term interest rates. If long-term rates are an average of expected future short rates, then long rates will rise in anticipation of future deficits. But since long rates, not short rates, govern investment decisions, investment will suffer. If this argument is true, it should leave its mark on the slope of the yield curve, which should become steeper. Can we find evidence in the models for this effect?

This question is hard to answer in the DRI model, which does not get the long-term rate from a term structure equation. Instead, it has a separate equation (presumably the solution of a supply = demand equation) that determines interest rates for each financial asset. However, long-term rates were much higher in 1981 and 1982 than the model predicted. So an effect of expected future deficits is certainly possible. Sinai and Rathjens[35] report far smaller residuals with an equation augmented to include a proxy for expected future deficits.

However, the other models, which do use a term structure approach, give quite different results. The WEFA equation underpredicts the long-term rate in 1981, but overpredicts it in 1982. The MPS equation actually overpredicts long-term rates in most quarters, in stark contrast to the expectational argument.

Conclusion

I have pointed to five plausible expectational mechanisms which, if quantitatively important, would have affected the economy in ways that are not captured by the models, thus causing systematic errors. Three of them— the Phillips curve, the permanent income hypothesis, and intertemporal effects of taxation on investment—are the original examples used by Lucas to illustrate his fundamental critique of the use of econometric models.

On balance, my investigation does not suggest that the Lucas critique is of great empirical importance. The expectational arguments based on Lucas-type reasoning predict that certain econometric residuals should have particular signs. Once we recall that such predictions ought to be correct 50 percent of the time purely by chance, the results look quite underwhelming.

Therefore, despite the conceptual validity of the Lucas critique, I suggest that the exercises with large-scale econometric models that are at the heart of this paper are not nonsense. In fact, compared with the currently fashionable

---

35. Allen Sinai and Peter Rathjens, "Deficits, Interest Rates, and the Economy," *Data Resources Economic Studies*, Series 113 (Lexington, Mass.: Data Resources, June 1983).

alternatives (such as reduced forms and vector autoregressions), old fashioned econometric policy evaluation looks pretty good.

Of course, this is victory by default. Large scale econometric models surely have their problems. As this paper illustrates, the models often disagree severely among themselves, leaving nonpartisan users somewhat in the dark. In addition, their structures are unwieldy and often pay little attention to economic theory—which may explain why their long-run properties are sometimes odd. These and other problems have been known for years.

But Mark Anthony's dichotomy is not appropriate. We may not wish to praise the models, but we need not bury them.

IDEOLOGY AND ECONOMIC GROWTH

Mancur Olson

At a conference on economic growth and the Reagan administration, it is natural to ask about the relationship between the ideological complexion of governments and the rate of economic growth. It is immediately obvious from the pronouncements of the Reagan administration that it espouses a conservative and probusiness ideology, and that this ideology probably plays a larger role in its deliberations than any standard ideology has played in other administrations in this country in recent years. Thus it is a good time to ask what impact the ideological coloration of the Reagan administration, and the varying ideologies of other administrations or governments, have on economic growth. And what impact will the eventual departure of the Reagan administration, and its possible replacement by an administration of contrasting ideology, have on the future rate of economic growth?

Because the same ideologies that provide the framework for political debate in the United States are influential in other developed democracies, we can also ask what impact each of the familiar ideologies has had on the rate of growth in comparable foreign countries. We will obviously be able to get a broader range of evidence about any correlation between ideology of governments and the rate of economic growth if we can make comparisons across comparable countries with governments of different ideologies as well as comparisons over time in a single country with successive administrations with different ideologies.

I am deeply thankful to Amy Abramowitz, Natalie McPherson, and Murray Ross for research assistance, and to the International Institute of Management in Berlin, the National Science Foundation, and the Sloan Foundation for indispensable support for my research.

229

One difficulty in answering the question of how ideology is related to economic growth is that the prevailing ideologies, whether left-wing or right-wing, are vague, multifaceted, and occasionally even inconsistent. There is also the problem that an administration may not succeed in obtaining, or perhaps in practice may not even choose, policies that are valued by its ideology. In any study of causation we would, of course, prefer that the variables were precisely defined, tangible, and accurately measured. If an economist were to study, say, the extent to which prices diverged from marginal costs in different periods or countries, there would be difficulties enough, but in the realm of ideology, alas, there is not even this degree of conceptual clarity.

Nonetheless, for the limited purposes of the present paper, the elastic character of the familiar ideologies is not such a serious problem. The aspiration here is not to measure the degree to which given movements along the ideological spectrum might add to or subtract from economic growth, but only to determine what, if any, *strong* relationship each of the familiar ideologies has to the general level of economic performance. Despite the vagueness of the ideologies, there is normally a consensus about whether any given government has this or that ideology. There is, for example, no dispute about whether the Reagan administration and Thatcher government are decidedly on the right side of the political spectrum, or about whether the U.S. government shifted to the left when Franklin Roosevelt replaced Herbert Hoover as president.

Thus all that is necessary for present purposes is to identify the right with the argument that the growth of government intervention in the economy in modern times impairs economic performance and individual freedom and the belief that overgenerous welfare-state programs designed to aid low-income people have seriously impaired the incentives to work and save in society. The left for the purpose at hand may be identified by its concern that there be a compassionate and generous public provision for those people for whom the market does not provide an adequate income and by a readiness to use the instrumentalities of democratic government and the intelligence of planners to improve the society. The debate between the two sets of views that have just been described has been the overwhelming preoccupation of many politicians and journalists in the United States and in other advanced democracies, and also a principal concern of many of the best-known economists.

Why Not Look at the Facts?

The first, and perhaps the most important, conclusion of this paper is that it is surprising how little systematic study has been given to the question of how well each ideology succeeds or fails in explaining either the overall level of economic performance or the standard of living of the poorest classes in different countries or historical periods. Given the overriding preoccupation with the familiar ideological debate, and the number of economists and other social scientists as well as politicians and journalists who participate in this debate, we might hope that this matter had been the subject of hundreds of careful empirical tests. Many of the propositions in the familiar ideologies are empirically testable. If the right, or classical liberal, side of the argument is correct, we ought systematically to find that those societies in which the role of the government is the smallest and the redistribution of income in the direction of low-income people is the least were growing the most rapidly and had the highest per capita incomes. Conversely, if the left, or the democratic socialistic, side of the argument is correct, we ought to find the most impressive economic performance and the highest standard of living (at least for the poor) in the societies in which the role of government is larger and the redistribution of income to low-income people most generous. One can also test the familiar ideologies by looking at changes across historical periods, because in different historical periods the role of government and the extent of income redistribution have been different.

There are many impressive empirical studies of the aggregate consumption function, of the demand for money, of the relationship between capital accumulation and technological change and economic growth, and of many other economic concepts and ideas. The empirical studies of the aforementioned topic are so numerous that even a cursory search of the literature generates a large number of skillful studies. But my preliminary inquiry has turned up very few studies of the impact of the familiar ideologies, or the role of the government, or the extent of income redistribution to the poor on the rate of economic growth or the standards of living of the lower socioeconomic classes in different periods or countries. Milton Friedman and Anna Schwartz have produced two imposing empirical books in support of their conviction that changes in the stock of money are the principal determinants of the level of nominal income. But where has Milton Friedman or any other advocate of the classical liberal ideology published similarly awesome empirical studies of the baneful effects of big government and overgenerous welfare-state programs? And what economists or other social scientists on the left have published comparable studies showing that economic progress, or even progress for the poorer classes, comes mainly from left-wing administrations or governments? Conversations with many economists and social scientists of diverse specializations and predilections reveal that many other researchers are similarly ignorant of studies of the kind at issue.

Comparing the Developed Democracies Since World War II

One of the apparently few people to look at the evidence on this central debate of modern democratic societies is David Smith. In an article in the *National Westminster Bank Quarterly Review* published in 1975, he examined the percentages of the national income (or, more precisely, "national disposable income") which were used or handled by government in different developed democracies, and looked for a relationship between this variable and the rate of economic growth in the society. What Smith found, as I see it, was only a weak and questionable association. This weak and questionable association was a negative one, with those societies in which government had the larger role having a somewhat slower rate of growth. Smith himself seemed to regard the relationship as reasonably strong (and most of his values meet conventional levels of statistical significance). But a glance at Smith's tables (see tables 1 and 2) makes it clear that, if Japan—a very special country in many ways—is omitted from the statistical test, the relationship all but disappears. Japan has a much smaller public sector and a much faster rate of growth than the other major developed democracies, and it alone was responsible for most of the relationship between the role of government and growth.

One of the relatively small number of other studies of this issue that I am aware of is an article by Samuel Brittan, a leading economic journalist with the *Financial Times* of London and one of the most influential advocates of monetarism and free markets in the United Kingdom. When Brittan was a visiting professor at the University of Chicago in 1978 he published an article in *The Journal of Law and Economics* on the "British Disease," the slow economic growth of the United Kingdom. In this article Brittan argued, no doubt to the surprise of most of those who share his general approach, that we apparently cannot explain the surprisingly poor performance of the British economy in terms of the role of the state or the extent of income redistribution to low-income people. When you compare the United Kingdom with its European neighbors, Brittan pointed out, it is not really different from other West European countries in the proportion of the nation's resources that are consumed or handled by government. The role of the government—the percentage of the national income consumed and handled by government—has, in fact been lower in the United Kingdom than in Holland, all three Scandinavian countries, West Germany, and France, but these other countries have enjoyed a better postwar economic performance than the United Kingdom. This observation alone would seem to make it unlikely that the role of government in Britain is the main explanation for its poor economic performance.

But Samuel Brittan brought forth even more persuasive evidence when he looked at the historical pattern in his country. The British economy, he pointed

TABLE 1

THE ECONOMIC STRUCTURE OF NINETEEN INDUSTRIAL NATIONS
(Percentage)

	National Disposable Income			
	Proportion Spent on Public Current Expenditure (excluding transfer payments) Increase in Percentage		*Proportion Spent on Public Current Expenditure (including transfer payments) Increase in Percentage*	
	1972	*1961–1972*	*1972*	*1961–1972*
United Kingdom	20.7	+2.7	41.9	+7.9
Australia	14.9	+3.4	32.7	+4.6
Austria	16.1	+2.3	41.5	+4.8
Belgium	16.5	+3.1	39.4	+8.2
Canada	22.4	+4.4	40.9	+9.9
Denmark	23.8	+8.9	49.1	+19.8
Finland	18.6	+4.6	42.4	+8.8
France	14.0	+0.7	43.1	+3.3
West Germany	20.4	+4.9	44.8	+4.4
Ireland	16.7	+4.5	35.3	+9.4
Italy	16.0	+3.2	37.6	+6.1
Japan	10.4	+0.8	25.9	+1.9
Netherlands	18.3	+3.1	52.0	NA
New Zealand	17.2	+2.7	NA	NA
Norway	19.4		56.5	NA
Spain	12.3	+3.1	21.5	+7.8
Sweden	25.6	+8.1	45.3	+15.4
Switzerland	12.9	+0.8	30.3	NA
U.S.A.	23.2	+2.3	35.0	+3.7

SOURCE: David G. Smith, ''Public Consumption and Economic Performance,'' OECD, *National Accounts,* 1961–72.

NA = Not applicable.

out, began to fall behind the rates of growth of comparable European economies in the last two decades of the nineteenth century. This was the very time when Great Britain and the British Empire had the closest thing to an ideal laissez-faire government that the world has ever seen. The relatively slow British growth continued through the interwar period and became all the more noticeable in the post-World War II period, when Britain was often under democratic socialistic governments and when the welfare state came into being. The poor British performance has also, I would point out, become still worse under the resolutely conservative and monetarist government of Margaret Thatcher. So Britain has grown relatively slowly under laissez-faire governments, moderate conservative governments, and labor or democratic socialistic governments alike.

TABLE 2

THE ECONOMIC PERFORMANCE OF NINETEEN INDUSTRIALIZED NATIONS
(*Percentage*)

	Annual Growth Rate of Real GDP[a], 1961–1972	Annual Growth Rate of Real GDP Per Capita, 1961–1972	Inflation: Annual Rate of Increase in GDP Deflator, 1961–1972
United Kingdom	2.5	2.0	5.0
Australia	5.4	3.4	3.7
Austria	5.0	4.4	4.0
Belgium	4.8	4.3	4.1
Canada	5.5	3.8	3.3
Denmark	4.7	4.0	6.3
Finland	4.9	4.5	5.8
France	5.8	4.7	4.8
West Germany	4.5	3.6	4.0
Ireland	4.0	3.4	6.9
Italy	4.8	4.1	5.0
Japan	10.1	8.9	4.6
Netherlands	5.6	4.4	6.4
New Zealand	NA	NA	NA
Norway	NA	NA	NA
Spain	6.9	5.7	6.6
Sweden	3.7	3.0	5.0
Switzerland	4.1	2.8	5.3
U.S.A.	4.4	3.2	3.1

SOURCE: Smith, "Public Consumption and Economic Performance." Smith's sources were IMF, *International Financial Statistics*, and OECD, *National Accounts*, 1961–1972.
a.   GDP = gross domestic product.
NA = Not applicable.

Thus a beginning glance, at least, at the empirical literature on the main developed democracies does not suggest that the role of government has an obvious and strong relationship to the rate of economic growth or the level of income. There may be a relationship, and I believe that there is one, but it is probably not the strong or compelling relationship that one might expect from the preoccupation in modern societies with the role of the government and the welfare state.

The Historical Evidence

Let us now take a historical perspective and ask in what historical periods economic growth has been most impressive, and then note what the role of government and the extent of income redistribution have been in each period.

If we go back to the nineteenth century, we find (as I have already noted) that in Great Britain, and to a considerable extent in the United States, and to a lesser extent on the Continent of Europe, there were policies that approached laissez-faire and free trade. Great Britain and its empire had laissez-faire in domestic policy and free trade. The United States had something approaching laissez-faire internally, but it certainly did not have free trade, and neither did most of the countries of the Continent. The nineteenth century was a period in which the world as a whole came closer to laissez-faire and free trade than it has, probably, at any other time. According to most estimates of late-nineteenth century national income and product accounts, government expenditures in major Western nations were often less than 10 percent, and in some cases no more than 5 percent, of the gross national product (GNP).[1] In the late-nineteenth century in at least some of these countries, the real value of the GNP was probably increasing a bit faster than were government expenditures.[2] The percentage of the working population in government is a conceptually less satisfactory measure of the relative role of the government, but it is calculated from data that are probably more accurate, and we know that for Great Britain and the United States at the turn of the century, government employment at all levels of government was around 5 percent of the total work force.[3]

The nineteenth century was also a period of unprecedented economic advance. Taken by itself, this piece of evidence would support the conservative or classical liberal argument that we should limit the role of the state and be wary that redistribution to lower income people might have an adverse effect on the incentives to work and save.

The period between World Wars I and II was very different. Although the main period of growth of the welfare state did not occur until after World War II, the interwar period still had an incomparably higher level of protectionism and economic nationalism than was the case before World War I. The most striking features of the economic history of the interwar period were protectionism and high tariffs; even the British Empire abandoned free trade. Now, as we know, the interwar period was, in general, one of poor economic performance and, above all, the period of the Great Depression.

---

1. See, for example, table I in Sam Peltzman, "The Growth of Government," *Journal of Law and Economics*, vol. 23 (October 1980), p. 210. See also Phyllis Deane and W.A. Cole, *British Economic Growth, 1688–1959* (Cambridge: Cambridge University Press, 1967), pp. 175, 257, and 333.

2. Peltzman, "The Growth of Government," p. 210.

3. Moses Abramovitz and Vera Eliasberg, *The Growth of Public Employment in Great Britain* (Princeton: Princeton University Press, 1957), table 10, and Simon Kuznets, *Economic Growth of Nations* (Cambridge, Mass.: Harvard University Press, 1971).

Admittedly, different things happened in different countries, and I am perhaps being too aggregative and casual in talking about the interwar period in general. So let us switch for a moment to one country, the United States. Developments here were perhaps a little simpler and easier to describe than in other countries and at the same time also instructive from the point of view of the issue we are considering now.

In the United States in the 1920s the administrations of Harding, Coolidge, and Hoover were, of course, conservative and probusiness. Not only were these presidents conservative Republicans, but also they wanted to keep the role of the American government at a minimal level. At the same time, there were extremely high levels of protection, with the Fordney-Macumber tariffs of 1922 and then the colossally protective Hawley-Smoot tariff passed just as the Great Depression set in, 1929–30.

The American economy did fairly well under Harding and Coolidge and in the first months of President Hoover's administration. Then came the greatest depression that the United States—indeed, the world—had ever seen. So a substantial period of conservative and probusiness (though protectionist) government ended in a catastrophic depression. This deepest of all depressions was not really cured, though it was somewhat ameliorated, under the New Deal administration of Franklin Roosevelt; it was only with World War II that the American economy really recovered.

Now let us turn the post-World War II period, more precisely to the period from the end of World War II until about 1970. Two facts about this period of economic history stand out above all others: (1) In all the major developed democracies, the welfare state reached its full development and came to handle a significant proportion of the national income. (2) All the major developed democracies grew more rapidly than they had ever grown before. Some, like Germany and Japan, and for a time Italy, grew with incredible speed, but even the slowest growing, such as Great Britain and the United States, grew more rapidly than they had ever grown before. So the welfare state, on the one hand, and unprecedented rapid economic growth, on the other, came to the major developed economies of the West at essentially the same time. The post-World War II period was the period of greatest increase in the peacetime role of the government, greatest level of income redistribution to the poor, and most rapid economic growth the world has known.

So, we must ask, was there a causal connection between large governments and the welfare state and rapid economic growth? It would seem so, but this observation does not fit with the experience of the nineteenth century or of the 1970s or the present, when the welfare state has become still larger and the economic performance has turned sour. At first the welfare state and big government were accompanied by rapid economic growth, but in the 1970s and the present they have been accompanied by poor economic performance. The historical experience, like the cross-sectional observations on the developed democracies since World War II, does not immediately suggest a strong and obvious relationship between the role of government or the extent of transfers to the poor and the rate of economic advance.

The Need for Research on the Relationship between Ideology and Growth or Poverty

The foregoing argument is intended to suggest that there is a need for much more research than I have so far been able to find on the relationship between the role of government and the extent of income redistribution to low-income groups and the rate of economic progress. If there has been definitive research on this subject of which I am not aware, then the conclusion must be that this research needs to be more widely publicized, both in the economics profession and in the political and journalistic debates.

There is also a need for systematic research on how much the standard of living of the relatively low-income groups in a society is influenced by the size of the government and by the extent of the effort to redistribute income to the lower-income groups in a society. It is clear a priori that government transfers to persons who are so impaired in body or mind that they cannot work at all, who have no private wealth, and who also receive no private transfers must leave the recipients of these transfers better off. So everyone must agree that *some* of those at the bottom of the income scale are helped by welfare-state types of programs, and that generous programs will leave individuals in these categories with a higher standard of living than will less generous programs.

But most welfare-state programs in modern societies are targeted toward persons who obtain part of their incomes by working, saving, or contributing to families with income-earning members, or who would have or could have obtained some income by such methods in the absence of the government programs. In these latter and probably more common cases, it is logically possible that the impact of generous welfare-state programs on both the incentives of the recipients of benefits and on the level of economic performance could leave the beneficiaries of government programs for low-income groups with lower standards of living than they would have enjoyed had these programs been less generous, or even with lower standards of living than they would have enjoyed in the absence of these programs. Thus it cannot be shown on a priori grounds that a larger role for the government or more

generous welfare-state programs will improve the standards of living of low-
income groups.

Most of the people with relatively low incomes in a society that has a
relatively small role for the government and even a modest level of welfare-
state type transfers could have a higher standard of living than do their
counterparts in a society with a large role for government and very expensive
welfare-state programs. The impact of the scale of government and the extent
of programs for low-income groups on the actual standard of living of people
with relatively low incomes is mainly a matter to be determined by empirical
investigation.

Alas, my research assistants and I have so far failed to find any study
that provides compelling evidence on the relationship between the role of
government, the ideology of the government, or the extent of welfare-state
programs, on the one hand, and the actual standard of living of the low-
income groups, on the other. Simon Kuznets and others have done impressive
studies of the size distribution of income, and scattered fragments of evidence
in various studies by the OECD, Kuznets, Lydall, and others leave me with
the highly tentative impression that the association between the role of government and the extent of the welfare-state programs is much more tenuous
than the familiar ideological debates would lead one to expect.[4]

For lack of compelling evidence on the relationship between the role of
the government and the standard of living of the poor or the level of economic
performance, let us return to the most preliminary cross-sectional and historical evidence of the proceding sections of this paper. This preliminary
evidence does not permit any definitive conclusions, except that there is a
need for more thorough research, but it may justify a tentative working
hypothesis that will prove helpful for the rest of the argument: that there is
probably no really strong and unambiguous relationship between the role of
government and the level of economic performance that can be inferred from
either the cross-sectional or historical experience of the developed democracies. Given the almost universal and overwhelming preoccupation with the
role of the government and the extent of income redistribution to low-income
people, we might expect that, if either side of the ideological debate had
gotten the matter right, there ought to be conspicuous evidence of an association one way or the other. But that conspicuous evidence is not there.

---

4. See, for example, Simon Kuznets, *Modern Economic Growth; Rate, Structure, and
Spread* (New Haven: Yale University Press, 1966); OECD Occasional Studies, "Income Dis-
tribution in the OECD Countries," by Malcolm Sawyer, July 1976; Economic and Scientific
Research Foundation, *Trends in Income Distribution: A Comparative Survey* (New Delhi, 1971).

Thus we are justified in assuming, at least until better studies have been done, that something else must be involved besides the matters around which the ideological debates revolve. When we see what else is involved, we will also be better able to understand why the ideological rhetoric of governments provides such an imperfect guide to what they actually do.

The Theory We Need to Analyze the Matter

My candidate for the role of the "something else" is the nature of collective action in society. Let us focus on the role of the organizations and collusions that engage in either lobbying the government or in combining in the marketplace to influence prices and wages, such as professional associations of physicians and lawyers, labor unions, trade associations, farm organizations, and oligopolistic collusions.

The government favors and the monopolistic or monopsonistic prices or wages obtained by combination are, analytically speaking, public or collective goods, in that the benefits automatically go to every firm or individual in some group or category: A tariff or tax loophole favors every firm in some industry or group, and cartelization raises the price or wage for every seller in the relevant market. It follows that any sacrifice an individual makes to support a lobby or cartel for his or her group will benefit others as much as that individual. If the group in question is large, the individual will get only a minuscule share of the benefits of any action he or she takes in the interest of the group. In view of the "external economy" of individual action in the group interest, there is normally less than a group-optimal level of activity, and in large groups there is usually no incentive for an individual to provide any amount of a collective good at all. Collective action to lobby or to cartelize requires, at least for large groups, "selective incentives"—punishments and rewards that are applied to individuals accordingly as they do or do not act in the group interest. Empirical investigations show that large groups that engage in collective action are in fact normally motivated by such selective incentives.

Small groups, such as the small number of large firms in the typical manufacturing industry, may sometimes organize without such selective incentives. This fact, and the greater availability of selective incentives to professional and skilled people, and to established firms and workers as opposed to potential entrants, implies that the capacity for collective action is positively correlated with income and social position.[5]

Collective action, even when possible, is difficult and problematical. Some large groups are not in a position to obtain selective incentives and cannot organize. Groups such as consumers, taxpayers, the unemployed, and the poor are spread out over such wide areas that coercive picket lines are not feasible; these groups are not organized for collective action in any society. Even those groups that are small or have access to selective incentives will usually be able to organize only if they have favorable circumstances and good leadership. Coercion is difficult to organize and likely to be resisted, and it is difficult to find any surplus from which positive rewards for people who act collectively can be obtained. Even the bargaining needed for group optimal action by small groups may be difficult to work out.

It follows that no society will achieve that comprehensive organization of all common-interest groups that would make it possible for the leaders of all groups to bargain with one another until an efficient, core allocation of resources for the society was obtained. As time goes on in stable societies, however, more of those groups that have the potential to organize will have enjoyed the favorable circumstances and good leadership needed to get organized. Since organizations that succeed in obtaining the selective incentives needed to survive rarely disband or collapse, stable societies (which do not destroy organizations through violence or repression) will eventually accumulate more organization for lobbying and cartelization.

Most organizations for lobbying or cartelization have no incentive to strive to make the society in which they exist more efficient or prosperous; the members of the organization will normally get only a minute fraction of society's gains from greater efficiency but will bear the whole cost of any effort to increase social efficiency. Normally these organizations can best serve their memberships by seeking a larger share of the social output for their members by distributional struggle—they will be coalitions concerned about distribution rather than production. If, as is always the case in certain societies such as the United States and the United Kindgom, these organizations are small in relation to the whole society, they will rationally persist in distributional struggle even if the excess burden or loss to society should much exceed the amount won. An organization that represents 1 percent of the income-earning capacity of the country will bear on average only 1 percent of any losses in social efficiency, but will obtain the whole amount redistributed to its membership, so its clients will gain from any redistri-

---

5. See my *Logic of Collective Action* (Cambridge, Mass.: Harvard University Press, 1965, 1971).

bution unless the excess burden is a hundred times or more greater than the amount redistributed.

A society dense with organizations for collective action, then, is like a china shop filled with wrestlers battling over the china and breaking far more than they carry away. A society in which the difficult task of organizing collective action has been achieved in many sectors of the society will be a society full of organizations that have little or no incentive to produce anything of value to the society, but greater incentives to struggle to get more of what society is in any case producing, and to persevere in that struggle even when it greatly reduces the output of the society by many times the amount each group gains in distributional struggle.

The argument just put forth is casual and incomplete, but I have stated it fully and carefully in my book on *The Rise and Decline of Nations* published by Yale University Press in 1982. What has been set out here should, however, be sufficient to call our attention to some testable implications or predictions of the argument that we can compare with reality.

Testable Implications of the Theory

If the organization of collective action is difficult and problematical because selective incentives are required, and if only some groups have access to the necessary selective incentives or ''gimmicks,'' we should expect that it will take a long time for societies to accumulate many organizations for collective action. It will, in other words, take quite some time before many groups will have had the good luck and the leadership needed to organize for collective action. These societies should then be expected to be less efficient and dynamic than otherwise similar societies that have had a shorter time to accumulate organizations for collective action. Accordingly, we have the testable implication or prediction that long-stable societies ought to be doing less well economically than would in general be expected.

There is much evidence that this is indeed the case. The society that has had the longest period of stability and immunity from invasion and institutional destruction is the United Kingdom. And that country has the poorest economic performance of all of the major developed democracies, as the theory predicts.

The theory would also predict that if totalitarian government and defeat in war had destroyed the institutional fabric of society, including its special-interest organizations, then, after a free and stable legal order is established, those societies should grow surprisingly rapidly. They will be relatively innocent of special-interest groups, or, if they have some, they are likely to be relatively "encompassing" and thus less of a problem for economic development. So, those societies that have suffered the institutional destruction that eliminates special-interest groups ought to grow more rapidly than they would otherwise be expected to do.

Of course, the economic miracles of Germany and Japan after World War II are precisely consistent with this implication of my argument. In Italy, the institutional destruction in World War II, though considerable, was less complete than in Germany and Japan. The economic miracle in Italy, though there definitely was one, was correspondingly somewhat shorter than and somewhat less sizable than those in Germany and Japan, and this again is in accord with the theory.

With appropriate elaboration,[6] the aforementioned theory also explains the general pattern of regional growth in the United States since World War II. Consider first the nonsouthern states. For these states, the number of years since they achieved statehood gives an approximate measure of the time they have had to accumulate special-interest organization. If we regress the years since statehood in these states against recent rates of economic growth, we find a strong, statistically significant *negative* relationship. The more recently settled and more westerly states are on the whole growing much more rapidly than the northeastern and older midwestern states that have had a longer time to accumulate special-interest organization.

Although the frontier is conventionally supposed to have closed at the end of the nineteenth century, this pattern could be due to lingering frontier disequilibria—and this makes the pattern in the South all the more interesting. The southeastern states are about as long removed from frontier status as any part of the country, but the defeat and turbulence these states suffered have given them far less time to accumulate distributional coalitions than have the states in the Northeast and older Midwest. But the southern states as a group, and even those of them that have been settled the longest, tend to be growing faster than most of the rest of the country. This phenomenon is consistent with the theory. A wide variety of regressions that measure the length of time a state has had both settlement and stability—and relate them to alternative measures of postwar growth—uniformly support the theory. Furthermore, a variety of statistical tests suggest that none of the familiar alternative explanations of southern and regional growth fit the facts nearly so well. On reflection it turns out that a somewhat less simple version of the foregoing theory that distinguishes between the effects of different types of special-interest groups on regional and national growth is needed to explain the timing

---

6. See "The South Will Fall Again: The South as Leader and Laggard in Economic Growth," *Southern Economic Journal*, vol. 49 (April 1983), pp. 917–932.

of southern growth, but it would take us far afield to go into these complications now.[7]

The Importance of Trade and "Jurisdictional Integration"

If space were unlimited, I would also go into the examples of remarkable economic growth or surprising stagnation in previous centuries. We could, for example, consider Germany after the Zollverein or customs union was established in 1834 and after German unification was completed by 1871. Or the growth of Japan after the Meiji Restoration of 1867–68, or the growth of the United States in the nineteenth century, or the growth of Holland during its Golden Age in the seventeenth century, or the growth of Britain during the Industrial Revolution from about 1760 to about 1840, or the commercial revolutions in England and France in the sixteenth century.

With enough time it would be possible to show that all these cases involve what I call "jurisdictional integration." That is to say, they all involve (1) creation of a wide market within which there was free trade and (2) simultaneous creation of a new, larger jurisdiction or government with a new capital, so that successful lobbying required larger organizations than those that were necessary to influence the parochial jurisdictions that existed before. In all the aforementioned cases, a wide area was created *within* which there was free trade, however high the tariffs around the whole area might be, and there was a new jurisdiction that determined economic policy.

Rapid economic growth always followed the creation of the much larger jurisdiction and the wider market. A detailed examination of the matter shows that this rapid growth was due largely to the fact that the jurisdictional integration undercut the special-interest groups of the day. The special-interest groups of prior centuries were called *guilds*, or, in Japan, *za*. When people were freed from the tariffs and economic restrictions that surrounded each feudal fief or walled city, the guilds or the *za* were undercut. People in each feudal fief or walled city could, after the jurisdictional integration, purchase goods from other parts of the integrated jurisdiction and thereby get better value. These purchases from other jurisdictions would undercut the guilds or *za* that had organized behind the protection.

The "merchant-employer" system, which was the main form of manufacturing of textiles in early modern Europe, nicely illustrates the process. Once jurisdictional integration occurred, textile production shifted to the rural areas of Europe. Although production had to be organized under the cum-

---

7. "The South Will Fall Again. . . . "

bersome merchant-employer system, production in the rural areas was no longer under the control of guilds and therefore was less expensive. After jurisdictional integration abolished the local trade restrictions that had supported the guilds or the *za*, production could shift to rural areas or new areas. Even the Industrial Revolution grew up mainly in new towns or sometimes in suburbs of old towns in which the rules of guilds did not apply.

There is, then, a great deal of evidence, only a small part of which I have been able to offer here, that the creation of wide free-trade areas, or common markets, and the creation of larger jurisdictions for setting economic policy, brought startling changes to the pace of economic performance. There is, moreover, every reason to believe that they brought this more impressive economic performance partly because they undercut the special-interest groups that thrive behind the protectionism, particularly in small jurisdictions.

Why There Is No *Strong* Relationship between Governmental Ideology and Economic Performance

So there is "something else" that explains much more of the variation in economic performance than does the relative role of the government or the extent of income redistribution to the poor: the level of private collective action in a society. When we looked earlier at the proportion of the national income the government was consuming or handling in different countries, we found that this proportion probably had no strong relationship one way or the other to the rate of economic growth or the level of per capita income.

One reason the focus on the role of government alone (which is characteristic of the classical liberal laissez-faire position) is insufficient to explain the variation in growth rates and income levels is that it overlooks a terribly important force that impedes the economic development that markets can bring about: This is the force of cartelization, or combination of firms and individuals in the marketplace that can maintain noncompetitive prices or wages, obstruct the free flow of resources, and slow down the innovation that brings more rapid economic growth. In focusing on the role of government alone, the laissez-faire ideology is guilty of "monodiabolism"—singling out one enemy of the market as though it were the only enemy. Some cartelization can take place without the aid of government, as I claim to have shown with examples from Britain, China, and India in *The Rise and Decline of Nations*.

Another reason the traditional argument about the limits of government or democracy does not explain the variation in economic performance across countries is that it neglects *the way* that government operates. What a government actually does depends largely on the extent of lobbying. A lobby-free democracy will not operate perfectly, but it is likely to operate very much more efficiently than one under the thrall of special-interest groups, especially narrow rather than encompassing special-interest groups. Thus one reason we do not see the strong association between the role of government and the rate of economic growth that we might expect is that there is another factor partially distinct from the role of government: the extent to which government policies are dominated by groups that have an incentive to redistribute rather than to produce. To the extent that governments are dominated by lobbies that have an incentive to seek policies that redistribute income to themselves, the government will have an adverse effect on economic performance incomparably greater than the effect it would have had if it had been free of these lobbies.

Most Redistribution Is to the Nonpoor

There is one other reason, which I do not discuss at all in *The Rise and Decline of Nations*, why the traditional slogans of left and right so inadequately explained the main features of the world around us: The traditional ideologies of left and right focus mainly on the extent to which government policies redistribute from people of high and middle incomes to those of relatively low incomes. This is what the debate between the left and the right is mainly about.

In fact, when we focus on government policies that are designed to aid low-income people, we are looking at only a tiny part of what governments actually do. Most of the redistribution of government is *not* from upper-income and middle-income people to low-income people. Most of the redistribution of income in fact is from middle-income people to other middle-income people, or from the whole society to particular groups of rich people, or from one group to another where the groups are distinguished not by one being poor and the other being rich, but only by the fact that some groups are organized and some are not.

This phenomenon is not accidental. There is no society in which the poorest people are well organized. If you look at contributions to candidates for the House of Representatives or the Senate, you do not find the organizations of welfare mothers or other recipients of public assistance for the poor giving major campaign contributions. You also do not find well-organized or well-financed lobbies working for the poor in other societies. It is big firms, upper-income people, the professions, and blue-collar workers with jobs that are organized. As I argued earlier, this is because small groups of large firms can organize without selective incentives, and because professional, skilled, and established people have better access to selective incentives. Naturally, it is mainly to those groups that have succeeded in organizing that the government redistributes income. In all societies there are compassion and sympathy and, accordingly, some aid to the poorest people. But, as other analysts have shown before, helping the poor is only a small part of what the government does, and most redistribution is not in fact redistribution to the poor.

It is partly because of this greater capacity for collective action of the nonpoor that there is only a weak association between the role or ideology of the government and the living standards of the poor. If the argument here is right, there are no societies in which the size of the government is very large and where the whole energies of a vast government are directed to improving the lot of the poor. A society with exceptional compassion for its poor and a resolve to use big government exclusively for the aid of the poor is an abstract possibility, but the logic of collective action suggests there will be no such societies. Casual empiricism supports this prediction. A complete analysis would, of course, also need to consider the disincentive effects of any generous welfare-state programs and the accompanying adverse effects on the standard of living of low-income groups. The prediction here, however, is that the quantitative effects of such programs on the income of society, and even on the production levels of the poor, will not be extremely large. The reasons for this prediction are set out in the next section.

Efficiency Is Hurt Most by Distorting the Incentives Facing the Most Prosperous and Productive

The redistribution to the poor usually has a smaller impact on the incentive to produce and on production than does the redistribution to the nonpoor. This would be true even if the redistributions were of similar size. The reason is that poor people are, on average, less productive than nonpoor people; they are more likely to be people with handicaps or without marketable skills, or aged people, or female-headed families. Although there are exceptions, most people who are extraordinarily productive and whose productive skills are also currently prized in the society are not, at the same time, poor. It follows that although transfers to poor people also tend to have some adverse effect on incentives, such transfers usually reduce production less than subsidies to the nonpoor do.

Thus when nations subsidize the nonpoor, they channel the time and energies of some of their more productive people into less productive pursuits and thereby reduce social efficiency. Institutional arrangements or policies that misallocate the labor of healthy men in the prime working years are very damaging to the efficiency of a society, yet such institutional arrangements and policies are common. Professional associations and public policies that largely control the practice of law and of medicine are no doubt even more costly to the society, because it is the time of some of the most highly educated and energetic people in the society that is being misallocated; yet few areas of modern society are so rife with cartels, anticompetitive rules, and other redistributions as are the law and medicine. Tax loopholes that induce many people to become tax accountants and lawyers divert some of the most able and aggressive people in the society away from socially productive pursuits, and at the same time twist much of the productive capacity of the whole society into tax-favored activities that have a lower socially marginal product than less favored activities; yet such loopholes are becoming more numerous. Tariffs, tax concessions, and bail-outs to major corporations divert or enfeeble some of the most productive enterprises in the whole economy, yet such tariffs and bail-outs are becoming more common with each passing year.

A nation that redistributes income to its poor buys a civilized and humane society with a minuscule share of the national income and (mainly) a modest reduction in the supply of cleaningwomen. A country that subsidizes workers in their prime working years sacrifices not a dust-free livingroom but the very muscle of the national economy. The society that permits its professions to cartelize and control public policy loses amounts for each professional that make welfare payments seem trivial and cause disorder to the nervous system of the whole society. A people that gives tariffs or tax loopholes or bail-outs to major corporations, whose great scale could normally have been attained only through exceptional productivity, is accumulating deposits of fat in the arteries that lead to its heart.

What Right-Wing Governments Say About Free Markets Is Mainly True, But What They Do for Their Organized Clients Is Especially Harmful

Right-wing governments in democratic countries are more likely to extoll free markets than are left-wing governments. Although this advocacy is not usually tempered by the professional economist's awareness of the important conditions that can generate market failure, it is, on balance, probably useful. A proper understanding of the advantages of markets requires much professional training. Accordingly, the typical noneconomist, even if highly educated, does not adequately appreciate the uses of free markets. Thus the rhetoric in favor of free enterprise that emanates from most right-wing governments not only contains much that is true, but also is made more pertinent because it counteracts the general ignorance of the advantages of markets.

The case for free markets is evidently counterintuitive—it did, after all, escape even the leading writers and thinkers until the past couple of centuries.

Unfortunately, what right-wing governments usually do is quite another matter. Since they usually represent upper-income groups and the business establishment in a society, they will often intervene in the markets that are most important to their clients (e.g., through protectionism, regulation, and tax loopholes). This intervention distorts incentives in precisely those markets in which the social loss from intervention is greatest. This is one reason why there is *not* a stronger correlation between ideologies of an administration and the rate of economic growth.

Similarly, one reason why the poor, at least so far as one can tell, are not regularly better off under left-wing governments is that these governments, despite their rhetoric, devote most of their energies to their organized or paying clients.

If what I have said here is true, the ideologies of the left and right, with their untiring emphasis on the role of government and of redistribution of income to people with lower incomes, are inadequate to guide modern society. These ideologies focus almost exclusively on problems and issues which, though significant, cannot explain the main variations in the fortunes of different societies or the fluctuating progress in different periods. These ideologies also obscure other problems that may even prove fatal to modern society. Worst of all, these ideologies leave the impression that the great trade-off is between equity and efficiency. Although there can occasionally be tension between these goals, as between any others, they are not often in conflict today. The money our society pays to appease people with power goes mainly to those who don't need it.

The Reagan Administration

How does the Reagan administration fit into the framework offered in this paper? Like any administration, the Reagan administration includes many people with a variety of views. It has also a large number of specific policies; by no means can all of them be properly handled by any single generalization. Thus it would not be difficult to find specific individuals in the Reagan administration, or specific policies of the Reagan administration, on which this paper has little, if any, bearing. If we look at the Reagan administration in great detail, we can find several choices about which the present argument offers little or no illumination. But there are also a great many respects in which the Reagan administration fits into the framework offered here with a neatness that is almost uncanny.

One striking example has, wondrously, attracted very little journalistic attention. The Carter administration and its immediate predecessors made great strides in deregulating many industries, such as trucking, airlines, railroads, securities markets, and banking. This deregulation greatly increased the scope of free markets. It would take us far afield to go into the unfolding empirical evidence about the consequences of this deregulation here, but the preliminary indications are that it has greatly increased the efficiency of the American economy.

Most strikingly in the area of trucking, the Reagan administration (at least up to the time this essay is written) has practically stopped this deregulation. It has spoken rhapsodically about the virtues of free enterprise, but in such areas as trucking its actions have ruled out the further use of markets, even in circumstances where this would have been unusually beneficial to the economy.

The reasons why the Reagan administration has stopped deregulation in trucking, at least, are precisely those that this paper would lead one to expect. Inefficient as it is, the system of trucking regulation protects many trucking companies and many members of the Teamsters Union. Many trucking companies supported Ronald Reagan's campaign, as did the Teamsters Union. And, as the argument here would predict, the organized special interests won out over the free-market rhetoric. President Reagan appointed an enemy of deregulation, with links to truckers and the Teamsters Union, to the chairmanship of the Interstate Commerce Commission, and the brakes were then applied to deregulation.

Similarly, where foreign trade is concerned, the Reagan administration has again at best a mixed record of promoting the use of the market. There has been no major multilateral reduction of tariffs or trade barriers, such as occurred in the Kennedy Round of tariff reductions or the Tokyo Round completed in 1978. There does not even appear to have been any serious and sustained effort in the Reagan administration to negotiate general and multilateral reductions in tariffs. Meanwhile, the Reagan administration has obstructed market forces and reduced the efficiency of the American economy by imposing high tariffs on heavy motorcycles, "voluntary" limits on imports of Japanese cars, and restrictions on imports of steel. (Hasty critics of this paper may point here to protectionist proposals from constituencies of the Democratic party. There certainly are such proposals, such as Domestic Content legislation, but it is obvious on reflection that these proposals also support the argument presented in this paper.)

Let us turn now to the crucial and distinctive feature of the economic policy of the Reagan administration—the tax cuts. No doubt a complete historical explanation of the Reagan tax cuts would have to bring in a number of factors, some of them far outside the scope of this paper. The most remarkable aspect of the matter is the president's acceptance, at least at one point, of the idea that the cuts in tax *rates* at issue would so greatly increase incentives to work and to save that production would increase to the point that government tax *collections* would increase. Most economists, both on the right and on the left, never accepted this idea; they agreed that it was not consistent with a wide variety of evidence about the supply of labor and of saving. But the idea of essentially self-financing tax cuts had, and perhaps still has, considerable journalistic and political support.

From the perspective of this paper, which begins with the logic of collective action, this journalistic and political attraction to the idea of self-financing tax cuts can be explained in terms of the "rational ignorance" of the average citizen and patron of the journalistic media. Information about public affairs is itself a public or collective good, just as are the services that lobbies and cartels provide to their clients. It follows that the typical citizen has no incentive to invest much time acquiring information about public affairs. If a typical citizen could, by acquiring better information or analysis of public policy, vote more wisely, society as a whole would share any benefits; the typical citizen would get only a minuscule share of the benefits of his or her investment in information. Of course, the changes that any single voter will change the outcome of an election are vanishingly small in any case. Thus the typical citizen has little or no incentive to spend much time studying public affairs: he or she remains "rationally ignorant." The diversionary or entertainment value of *some* news about public affairs is so great that most citizens acquire this information for the fun of it, and they may also acquire a *modest* amount of information about public affairs because of a sense of civic duty.

But this reasoning doesn't apply to the quantitative evidence about the response of labor and saving to changes in after-tax wages or interest rates, or to the complexities of offsetting income and substitution effects that must also be understood to assess the claim that tax cuts will be self-financing. Complex econometric information and economic theory are not presented even in economic newspapers such as the *Wall Street Journal*. If it were, the editorial board would be better informed, but the *Wall Street Journal* would no longer be a newspaper of wide circulation.

Thus a huge democracy and its communications media can largely ignore information that is essential to rational policymaking, even about issues of surpassing importance. They can do this even when virtually all competent specialists, whether on the right or the left, agree about the evidence. This is a logical consequence of the *rational* ignorance of the man-in-the-street. Rational ignorance also explains the power of lobbies and cartels: if all the citizens had complete information and understanding of all public issues, lobbying would have no effect and cartels would not be tolerated.

The analysis in this paper also helps to explain the *character* of the Reagan tax cuts. Although the available evidence perhaps falls short of being absolutely compelling, there is considerable reason to believe that the best way to reduce the inefficiencies arising from our tax system is by eliminating tax loopholes and taxing essentially all forms of income equally. If the tax code were simple and straightforward, all the legal and accounting talent that is now devoted to the complexities of the tax code could be used instead for the production of goods and services. More important, firms and individuals would no longer distort their patterns of activity to make use of the tax advantages that pertain to certain types of revenue and expenditure, and the economy would surely be more efficient. If the loopholes or special provisions of the tax code were eliminated, the same amount of revenue could also be collected with lower tax rates and a further increase in efficiency. Although I know of no systematic survey on the matter, I hypothesize that most professional economists on both the right and the left would agree that a single, uniform, and loophole-free tax code, accompanied by reductions in tax rates that such reforms would allow, would do much more for the productivity of the economy than the Reagan tax cuts did.

If so, the next question is, Why did the Reagan administration advocate a reduction in tax rates without giving any priority to the closing of tax loopholes? I suspect the reason is that it could not have proposed a uniform and loophole-free tax code without taking on the special-interest lobbies, many of which are part of the Reagan coalition.

So the nation is left with tax cuts of the wrong sort and the wrong size, and thus a huge structural deficit as well. This deficit is also made larger, of course, because of special-interest lobbying that prevents reductions in certain types of public expenditure that serve no useful national purpose.

The theory presented in this paper accordingly leads to the prediction that the Reagan administration's policies will not significantly increase the efficiency of the American economy, and in some respects will reduce the efficiency of our economy. But the theory presented here also suggests that replacement of the Reagan administration by any Democratic administration that is the captive of those special interests traditionally allied with that party will not bring economic efficiency either. If the argument in this paper is correct, the answer cannot be found either by going right or by going left. It will be solved only if enough of the opinion leaders and political leaders in the country rise above the outdated slogans of right and left and arrive at a valid diagnosis of the national malaise. If this valid diagnosis is widely understood, the remedies to cure the disease will also be politically feasible.

REAGANOMICS AND ECONOMIC GROWTH: A SUMMING UP

William D. Nordhaus

This has been a useful conference. Instead of being barraged by *Wall Street Journal* editorials or superficial public opinion polls, we have spent two days seriously analyzing the cornerstone of the Reagan economic agenda: to strengthen the economy and enhance long-term economic growth. How successful have we been, and what is our summary assessment of this aspect of Reaganomics?

I will begin with a cautionary note about measurement. When we talk about "increasing economic growth," we are presumably referring to the appropriate discounted value of a comprehensive consumption measure: something like the Measure of Economic Welfare that Tobin and I discussed a decade ago. This conference may have fallen into the trap of defining growth as growth in measured GNP—a trap in which the Reagan administration is itself ensnared. In fact, we may have become even further mired in the mercantile fallacy by unconsciously defining growth as growth of the capital stock, or even worse, growth of the business fixed capital stock. But monetizing the economy by drawing people from households or schools into factories or trenches—while increasing measured GNP—may not increase an appropriately measured index of economic welfare.

The Short Run

In order to evaluate the Reagan program, it is useful to follow Alan Blinder's distinction between the short run and the long run. The short run corresponds to policies that take as given the path of potential output; the long run examines measures that affect potential output.

This conference paid little attention to the issue of whether the administration's choice of a recession was wise or not for the short run. The costs and benefits of inflation are a subject for another meeting. But, for a given inflation path, we might ask whether output was higher because of the Reagan policies. Have they shifted the Phillips curve—temporarily or permanently?

While no one has presented evidence that the natural rate of unemployment has declined markedly since 1980, some of the results presented here suggest that the Phillips curve has been temporarily "fooled." Blinder found that, except for the MPS model, the "REAGAN" policy resulted in a substantial expansion of output, without a simultaneous rise in price. In the WEFA model, there was essentially no price increase associated with higher output; in the DRI model, higher output was accompanied by lower prices.

There are two possible reasons for this surprising outcome. First concerns the productivity effect in the models. There may be some misspecification (as was seen in the original Brookings-SSRC model) that allows price reduction to come from cyclical productivity increases. A second possible way to fool the Phillips curve is the Patman effect: a lower user cost of capital may actually lower prices. The Patman effect is probably at work in the DRI model. Here, the core rate of inflation is determined by labor costs and the costs of capital; a big reduction in the cost of capital gets fed right through into prices. Thus a reduction in the cost of capital, coming from the 1981 cuts in capital taxes, probably led the DRI model to predict a one-shot reduction in the price level as the cost of capital came down. Hence the 1981 measures raised output and lowered prices. Thus spake DRI.

Another central issue, discussed by Lawrence H. Summers,[1] is whether the Reagan policy mix produced a less costly disinflation because of the credibility effect. The "credibility hypothesis" states that having a tough guy in the White House—perhaps encouraging an even tougher guy at the Fed— causes inflation to decline more quickly and at less economic cost than it would simply on the basis of the given path of unemployment and capacity utilization.

One of the major benefits of recent policy—both in the United States and in Britain—is that we have a clear test of the credibility hypothesis. Several recent studies reached the same conclusion as Summers: The cost of the 1980–83 disinflation was not reduced by the particular mix of monetary and fiscal policy, or by having a credible, preannounced policy. In fact, the cost of disinflation has remained pretty much unchanged since Arthur Okun surveyed these costs in 1976.

---

1. The Summers paper is included in this volume.

The Long Run

Let us turn to the longer-run issues of growth in potential GNP. A pro-growth policy is one that increases the growth of appropriately measured potential output. This increase can come either through growth of inputs or growth in total factor productivity. I will examine these in turn.

Growth of Inputs

The major way to increase growth in inputs is to accumulate durable productive assets more quickly—for example, tangible and human capital, resources, and so forth. The most important and accessible way for a nation to increase its asset growth is to save and invest more. The Reagan record here is mixed.

Private Capital. Fullerton and Henderson found that from 1980 to 1982, the tax treatment of investment led to a 3 percent decline in the overall cost of capital, and a decline in the cost of business fixed capital of somewhat over 10 percent. With no change in the interindustry distortion and a Cobb-Douglas production structure, the overall capital stock would respond by increasing 3 percent over the relevant time horizon, and potential output would increase somewhat less than 1 percent.

It appears that Alan Blinder's results are of the same order of magnitude as the Fullerton-Henderson result. For the WEFA and DRI models (where there is no significant offset from interest rates), he finds that business fixed investment is up by 3 to 5 percent at the end of the 1980s. On the other hand, residential construction is down a couple of percent.

Putting these numbers together, and ignoring any offset from crowding out or from monetary policy, I would estimate that the Reagan-supported measures of 1981 and 1982 would lead to a 3 percent higher private capital stock. Running these numbers out to the end of the decade, and assuming an output elasticity of 0.20 with respect to capital, I calculate that the investment incentive results in a 6 to 10 basis point increase in the potential GNP growth rate.

In the calculations that follow, I have made all calculations in "basis points," or more precisely, in "hundredths of a percentage point added to the annual growth of potential GNP for 1981–90." We must use such small numbers, because, as Ed Denison taught us more than twenty years ago, it is very hard to move the potential GNP growth rate, and adding 10 basis points to the growth rate is doing pretty well.

Unfortunately, as CEA Chairman Feldstein has been telling everyone inside and outside the Reagan administration, the calculation cannot stop there. The Reagan policy, combined with other events, has produced an unprecedented deficit and significantly higher real interest rates than we have seen for decades. This raises the question of whether there is "monetary" or "deficit" or "government debt" crowding out.

Let us return to Alan Blinder's remarks. There is no doubt that monetary policy has been very tight since October 1979. But Ronald Reagan was elected in November 1980, so obviously the tight monetary policy preceded (and therefore in the Granger-Sims sense, caused) Reaganomics. However, the real question—and this is where the relation between monetary policy and Reaganomics becomes tricky—is whether monetary policy would have been less tight under a second Carter term?

My view is that monetary policy has been tighter under Reagan. First, it is clear that the Reagan administration has been cheering on the monetarist activities of the Fed since late 1980 or early 1981. Second, and just as important, I think that some of the monetary tightening was in response to the loosening of fiscal policy in 1981. The Fed was, and is, playing "fiscal chicken"—saying in effect it will not lower real interest rates until the fiscal authorities lower the deficit. Thus the net effect of Reagan policies was a monetary policy that was tighter, longer than it would have been under a second Carter regime. Under Carter II, monetary policy would probably have been loosened earlier—somewhere between late 1981 and October 1982.

How much crowding out of capital could occur as a result of higher deficits? At one extreme, suggested by the DRI-Donald Regan view, there is no crowding out. At the other extreme, we can look to Martin Feldstein's inspiration and at Ben Friedman's analysis.[2] Friedman argues that by the end of the 1980s, we could have an increase in the public debt-GNP ratio of about 20 percent of GNP. A situation of full portfolio crowding out occurs when there is one-to-one displacement of private capital by increase in public debt. This occurs when (1) public and private wealth are perfect substitutes and (2) when wealth is perfectly inelastically supplied. I don't think we could be much more pessimistic than this in looking for crowding out. In the Friedman-Feldstein case, crowding out of capital would lead to a 15 basis point slowdown in economic growth over the 1980s.

So I estimate the limits of crowding as between 0 and 15 basis points subtracted from growth over the 1980s. You can take your choice, but the DRI-Reagan end of the spectrum is probably more realistic. We have not

2. Presented at this conference.

found near dollar-for-dollar substitution of private for public wealth since World War II. And the pool of foreign wealth holders, willing to hold dollar assets, is very large.

Whichever numbers one chooses, it is essential to see that one's view on the crowding out debate drives one's conclusion about whether the effect of Reagan's policies on private capital has been positive or negative.

Public Capital. As far as public capital is concerned, I think the Reagan administration has fallen into the trap of misplaced concreteness. Their view seems to be that capital is only productive if it is private and if you can bomb it. This may explain their interest in bombs and their disinterest in anything except business fixed investment.

Let us take a broader view, examining the effect of Reagan policy on all durable assets, whether private business or not. The most important of these is government investments. Using Charles L. Schultze's generous data (those in his table 1), we find a 0.7 percent decline in the public investment-GNP ratio from 1979 to 1984. Assuming this is replaced by non-investment items, and assuming the same rate of return on public as private capital, an order-of-magnitude effect would be a −6 basis point contribution to growth in potential GNP to 1990. If, on the other hand, we follow Schultze and exclude a number of items in true OMB style, we get a low estimate of −4 percent.

Growth in Total Factor Productivity

Let us now turn to the other means for increasing the growth of potential output—that is, increasing total factor productivity. Here I want to concentrate on advances in knowledge, one of the most important tools for increasing productivity.

As we have learned from Kendrick, Denison, and others, the accumulation and effective use of knowledge is the most precarious part of economic growth. It is also potentially a very powerful factor. If we examine the careful studies of Mansfield, we see very high social rates of return on R&D—on the order of 50 percent per annum.

I was disappointed that this conference spent so little time on R&D. To begin such an analysis, I believe we must separate basic research from applied research and development. If we do that, we see a long downtrend in the share of basic federal research to GNP. It was 0.26 percent of GNP in 1965 and declined to 0.21 percent of GNP in 1981; it then dropped sharply to 0.17 percent of GNP for 1983. Basic research, effectively applied, is *the* essential federal role in assuring continued high-quality economic growth. And it has received short shrift from the Reaganauts.

Now it is true that the overall federal R&D to GNP ratio is turning up, at least in the projections. But as Donald A. Nichols has pointed out, this is solely because of defense R&D. Will defense R&D have the same payoff as civilian R&D? Not bloody likely. Experts in this area think that basic research in defense is a pretty close substitute for basic nondefense federal research. But in applied research, and particularly for development—which is after all the bulk of federal research and development—defense R&D basically buys hardware. Defense R&D may improve the technology of destruction, but it is unlikely to have a big payoff for economic growth.

However, rather than being influenced by the wisdom of experts, let us allow Special Analysis K of the budget to explain exactly what $12 billion of defense R&D is buying the nation. This is what the Reagan administration describes as its major efforts in research and development in the Department of Defense: protection against chemical agents; peacekeeper and Trident II efforts; ballistic missile defense; advanced technology bomber; anti-satellite system; upgrading the M1 tank; Bradley fighting vehicle system; deep strike interdiction version of an existing fighter aircraft; more reliable fighter engines; air-to-air missile; new trainer aircraft for undergraduate pilot training; lightweight antisubmarine torpedo; larger range antisubmarine missile; subsystems to improve detection, tracking, and targeting. You may draw your own conclusions as to whether research in these areas is likely to have significant spillovers for civilian R&D.

There have been studies of the spillover effects of defense R&D. One of the most careful was done by the other DRI (Denver Research Institute). About fifteen years ago, they very carefully sifted through a list of space and defense research projects for innovations that were transferable to private industry. They found nothing better than the high-speed welder.

In the energy area, the R&D bias is just as striking. The Reagan program has increased energy R&D in particle physics and in weapons-testing areas. Big-ticket items include the synchronon, the Fermi accelerator facilities, and the breeder reactor. But there have been significant R&D cuts in fossil fuels, in solar, and in conservation. Whatever the intrinsic wisdom of this reallocation, it is hard to see how it will enhance economic growth.

Finally, I will highlight one more problem in the R&D area that is worrisome: Defense and space today take about 32 percent of our national R&D dollars. And the defense part is growing very rapidly. If you want to worry about crowding out, this is the place to focus. When you increase the dollars for defense R&D, you are bidding away resources from civilian uses. And be reminded that the unemployment rate among Ph.D.'s in science and engineering in 1981 was 0.8 percent, so there is not a lot of slack in that sector.

I summarize the R&D discussion by my entry on table 1. I would put a debit of at least 3 basis points for the cuts in federal R&D—using figures Schultze presented plus a 50 percent rate of return on civilian R&D. If we include a higher rate of return on basis research (following a recent study by Mansfield), we could see a decline as great as 8 basis points.

A final topic, which I won't discuss, is regulation. On the basis of recent work that Robert Litan and I have done, I would add a handful of basis points for the Reagan regulatory reform program.[3]

Summary Assessment

Adding up the numbers in each category we have reviewed, I estimate that the Reagan program has contributed something between minus 0.23 to plus 0.06 percent per annum to potential GNP growth for the 1980s. The best guess appears to be that the Reagan policy has actually hurt the nation's potential growth.

One other lesson of the Reagan policy seems clear to me: Using monetary policy to cause a sharp disinflation has very serious negative side effects. In plain language, it was a disaster. It reduced investment. It raised deficits and

TABLE 1

NET EFFECT OF REAGAN ECONOMIC POLICIES ON LONG-TERM ECONOMIC GROWTH, 1981–1990

(In hundredths of a percentage point per annum)

	Increase in growth rate *("basis points," or hundredths of a percentage point per annum)*	
	Low	High
Private capital		
Investment incentives	+6	+10
Crowding out	−15	0
Public capital	−6	−4
Federal support of R&D	−8	−3
Regulation	0	+3
Total effect of Reagan program on economic growth	−23	+6

SOURCE: From papers presented in this conference as explained in the text.

---

3. See Robert Litan and William Nordhaus, *Reforming Federal Regulation*, Yale Press, 1983.

the public debt. It increased the value of the dollar and hurt traded goods. It spilled over perversely to the rest of the world, because those countries linked to us through relatively open capital markets found their real interest rates moving up and their economic activity declining. Finally, less developed countries are teetering on the edge of bankruptcy as they find their debt service ratios skyrocketing. We have learned that monetary disinflation is very costly.

Dismantling the Welfare State

But this discussion may be missing the whole point of Reagan economic policy. The key to understanding Reaganomics is not the growth-accounting framework, and it is certainly not a demand-oriented macroeconomic model. If we want to understand the Reagan program, we must go back to the 1982 Economic Report of the President. This states that economic prosperity is found only in those countries that make decisions in markets; conversely, countries that rely on state decisionmaking inevitably suffer economic decline. The political figures of the Reagan administration appear to think of economic growth not as winning a basis point here and a basis point there. Rather, their program is designed to change the structure of incentives and to stop the pattern of dependency.

This conference, a Reaganite would say, has been looking at the mote but not the beam of economic growth. We have argued about whether the productivity slowdown has been 2.3 percent according to Denison, or 1.9 percent according to Kendrick. But the Reagan philosopher says, in effect: "Look instead at the triumphs of capitalism. Observe that per capita GNP is $15,000 in capitalist United States, but only $150 in socialist India. You must cut taxes and red tape if you want enterprise to flourish. The West's malaise, from San Francisco to West Berlin, arises from a cycle of dependency. Our historical mission is to reduce this dependency."

I will suggest four areas in which the Reaganites have tried to follow this path consistently and, by their standards, may have had some success.

First, they have completely changed the pattern of social regulation. Economic regulation was never really an important issue to this group of people. Some of them liked it, some of them didn't, but they didn't see it as significantly hampering economic growth. But they did see social regulation as interfering with production, investment, and innovation. They stopped social regulation dead in its tracks. After a proliferation of regulatory agencies and programs, there has not been a major new social regulatory program since 1981.

The second area is social dependency. Some, like Dick Nathan, believe that our social programs have bred a cycle of dependency, a new underclass in our society. The Reagan people appear to think that such a cycle was seen in social security, in AFDC, in unemployment insurance, and in the international arena where other nations became dependent on our foreign aid. Although social pressures prevented "cold turkey" withdrawal from such programs, the administration set out to shrink these programs as much as possible. One result, as Gary Burtless has recently shown, is the recent behavior of the insured unemployment rate, which has mysteriously declined relative to overall unemployment. Has the cycle of reliance on unemployment insurance declined?

A third area is energy, where again the Reagan administration saw state programs as encouraging a harmful dependency on government programs. Many economists would agree that price controls and entitlements bred inefficiencies. Recently, the question of standby price control and allocation systems was raised in conjunction with our international obligations under the IEA. The Reagan people made it clear that they will have nothing to do with that: If there is an oil price emergency, people are going to find oil themselves.

The fourth area is industrial policy and free trade. Here too the Reagan people have tried to stay true to their philosophy of minimizing business's dependence on government financial or trade assistance. They resisted a savings and loan or WPPSS bailout. Some significant backtracking on steel, autos, and milk has occurred, but these were politically rather than ideologically accepted.

How seriously should we take this broader view of Western economies caught in a giant web of dependency and sloth? Can we see a resurgence of initiative and innovation in the brave new libertarian resurgence? By my reading, the Reagan view is neither absurd nor convincing. But there is no evidence at hand to convince us of its practical importance. The Reagan administration's dismantling of the welfare state is a shot in the dark whose only casualties so far are the economy and the poor.

ABOUT THE AUTHORS

Alan S. Blinder is Gordon S. Rentschler Professor of Economics at Princeton University. His research specialties include inventories, monetary and fiscal policy, the distribution of income, and pensions. Professor Blinder is the author of *Economic Policy and the Great Stagflation; Toward an Economic Theory of Income Distribution,* numerous articles in scholarly journals and conference volumes, and regular newspaper columns on economic affairs. He is also coauthor of a best-selling introductory economics textbook.

Don Fullerton is an assistant professor at Princeton University, a research associate at the National Bureau of Economic Research, and this year a national fellow at the Hoover Institution of Stanford University. He is the 1979 winner of the Outstanding Dissertation Award of the National Tax Association-Tax Institute of America and is coeditor of *The Taxation of Income From Capital: A Comparative Study of the U.S., U.K., Sweden, and West Germany.*

Robert H. Haveman is John Bascom Professor of Economics at the University of Wisconsin-Madison and research associate at the Institute for Research on Poverty. He specializes in the economics of poverty and income distribution, benefit-cost analysis, and the incentive effects of government taxes and transfers. He has published several journal articles on these topics and is a coauthor of *The Economic Impacts of Tax-Transfer Policy: Regional and Distributional Effects* (1977); *Earnings Capacity, Poverty, and Inequality* (1978); and a coeditor of *Microeconomic Simulation Models for Public Policy Analysis* (1980), all published by Academic Press.

Yolanda Kodrzycki Henderson is assistant professor of economics at Amherst College. Professor Henderson's research focuses on the taxation of income from capital and strategies for achieving long-term growth. Her published work includes contributions to policy-oriented studies at the

Congressional Budget Office as well as development of general equilibrium models to evaluate tax reform measures.

Charles R. Hulten is a research associate at The Urban Institute. His current research interests include tax policy and the analysis of productivity trends. He has edited *Depreciation, Inflation, and the Taxation of Income from Capital* and has published numerous articles in scholarly journals. Prior to joining The Urban Institute, he taught at Johns Hopkins University.

John W. Kendrick is professor of economics at George Washington University and adjunct scholar at the American Enterprise Institute. He was formerly on the senior research staff of the National Bureau of Economic Research, vice president for economic research at The Conference Board, and chief economist of the U.S. Department of Commerce. He has written a dozen books and over 100 articles, about half of them on the subject of productivity and economic growth. His most recent book is *Improving Company Productivity: Handbook with Case Studies* (Johns Hopkins University Press, 1984)

Paul Krugman is professor of economics and management at the Sloan School of Management of the Massachusetts Institute of Technology. In 1983 he served on the President's Council of Economic Advisers. A specialist in international trade, Professor Krugman is the author of several articles and coauthor of *Market Structure and Foreign Trade* (forthcoming).

Donald A. Nichols is professor and chairman of the Department of Economics at the University of Wisconsin-Madison. He is also economic advisor to Governor Earl and executive secretary of the Governor's Council on Economic Affairs, State of Wisconsin. From 1977 to 1979 he was deputy assistant secretary for economic policy and research at the U.S. Department of Labor. He has written on a wide range of topics in theoretical and applied macroeconomics.

William D. Nordhaus is John Musser Professor of Economics at Yale University and a member of the Cowles Foundation for Research in Economics. During the Carter years, he served on the President's Council of Economic

Advisers. He has written on issues of productivity, inflation, and economic growth. Professor Nordhaus's most recent book, of which he is coauthor, is *Reforming Federal Regulation.*

Mancur Olson teaches economics at the University of Maryland. He formerly served as deputy assistant secretary of Health, Education, and Welfare in the Johnson administration where, with others, he wrote *Toward a Social Report.* He is the author of *The Logic of Collective Action, The Rise and Decline of Nations,* and diverse other books and articles.

Isabel V. Sawhill is codirector of The Urban Institute's Changing Domestic Priorities project, of which this volume is part. Dr. Sawhill's areas of research include human resources and economic policy. She has directed several of the Institute's research programs and held a number of government positions, including that of director of the National Commission for Employment Policy. Her publications include *Youth Employment and Public Policy; Time of Transition: The Growth of Families Headed by Women; The Reagan Experiment; The Legacy of Reaganomics: Prospects for Long-term Growth; Economic Policy in the Reagan Years;* and *The Reagan Record.*

Charles L. Schultze is a senior fellow at the Brookings Institution. Mr. Schultze specializes in macroeconomic analysis and budgetary policy. He is the author or coauthor of numerous books and articles on these subjects.

Lawrence H. Summers is professor of economics at Harvard University. He served as domestic policy economist at the President's Council of Economic Advisers in 1983. Dr. Summers specializes in public finance and macroeconomics and is the author of numerous journal articles in these areas. His research interests include the microeconomics of unemployment and the effects of tax policy on investment and asset prices.

CONFERENCE AGENDA

Thursday, September 22, 1983

Welcome and Introductory Remarks—William Gorham, President,
The Urban Institute

Conference Overview—Charles R. Hulten, *The Urban Institute*

"Implications of Growth Accounting Models," John W. Kendrick,
George Washington University

Discussants: Ernest R. Berndt, *Massachusetts Institute of Technology*
Barry Bosworth, *The Brookings Institution*

"Tax Policy," Don Fullerton, *Princeton University*
Yolanda K. Henderson, *Amherst College*

Discussants: Harvey Galper, *The Brookings Institution*
Michael Boskin, *Stanford University*

"International Trade and Industrial Policy," Paul Krugman,
Massachusetts Institute of Technology

Discussants: Robert Baldwin, *University of Wisconsin*
Richard Cooper, *Harvard University*

Friday, September 23, 1983

"Federal Spending Priorities and Economic Growth," Donald A.
Nichols, *University of Wisconsin*

Discussants: Charles L. Schultze, *The Brookings Institution*
John Shoven, *Stanford University*

"The Legacy of Current Macroeconomic Policies," Larry Summers,
Harvard University

Discussants: Benjamin M. Friedman, *Harvard University*

"Institutional Rigidities and Economic Policy," Mancur Olson,
University of Maryland

Discussants: Richard Nelson, *Yale University*
Ned Nadiri, *New York University*

"Economic Model Simulations of Long-Term Growth," Alan S.
Blinder, *Princeton University*

Discussants: Dale W. Jorgenson, *Harvard University*
Frank de Leeuw, *Bureau of Economic Analysis*

Overview and Wrap-Up

Isabel Sawhill, *The Urban Institute* (Moderator)
William D. Nordhaus, *Yale University*

PARTICIPANTS

Alan J. Auerbach
University of Pennsylvania

Martin Baily
The Brookings Institution

Robert Baldwin
University of Wisconsin

J. Gregory Ballentine
*Office of Management and
Budget*

C. Fred Bergsten
*The Institute for International
Economics*

Ernest R. Berndt
*Massachusetts Institute of
Technology*

Alan S. Blinder
Princeton University

Michael J. Boskin
Stanford University

Barry Bosworth
The Brookings Institution

David Bradford
Princeton University

Richard N. Cooper
Harvard University

Frank de Leeuw
Department of Commerce

Ed Denison
The Brookings Institution

Larry Dildine
Department of the Treasury

George C. Eads
University of Maryland

Robert Eisner
Northwestern University

Amitai Etzioni
George Washington University

Benjamin M. Friedman
Harvard University

Don Fullerton
Princeton University

Harvey Galper
The Brookings Institution

William Gorham
The Urban Institute

Edward Gramlich
University of Michigan

Yolanda Henderson
Amherst College

Charles Hulten
The Urban Institute

Dale W. Jorgenson
Harvard University

269

John W. Kendrick
George Washington University

Paul Krugman
Massachusetts Institute of Technology

Jerome Mark
Department of Labor

Gregory B. Mills
The Urban Institute

Mohamed I. Nadiri
New York University

Richard Nelson
Yale University

Donald Nichols
University of Wisconsin

William D. Nordhaus
Yale University

Mancur Olson
University of Maryland

June O'Neill
The Urban Institute

John Palmer
The Urban Institute

George Peterson
The Urban Institute

William Poole
Council of Economic Advisers

Perry Quick
The Urban Institute

Robert Reischauer
The Urban Institute

Isabel V. Sawhill
The Urban Institute

Charles L. Schultze
The Brookings Institution

John B. Shoven
Stanford University

Herbert Stein
American Enterprise Institute

Eugene Steuerle
The Brookings Institution

Chad Stone
The Urban Institute

Lawrence Summers
Harvard University

Emil M. Sunley, Jr.
Deloitte, Haskins and Sells

William Waldorf
Department of Labor